C000130587

PARALLEL LINES

About the author

By the age of 30, Peter Lantos had survived Bergen-Belsen concentration camp, was beaten by the Communist police in Hungary, qualified in medicine, defected to England, sentenced to imprisonment for this "crime" in his absence and had established a career in academic medicine in London. And this was only the beginning.

He is a Fellow of the Academy of Medical Sciences and in his previous life he was an internationally known clinical neuroscientist who has retired from a Chair at the Institute of Psychiatry, King's College London. He is author numerous medical and scientific texts.

After retirement, it was his childhood experiences that gave him the impetus to write *Parallel Lines*, published in 2006 by Arcadia Books London, reprinted in 2007, and translated into Hungarian in 2009. The book has attracted unanimously favourable reviews, and Alan Sillitoe described it as 'something of a genius with the readability of a classic'.

His first novel, *Closed Horizon*, is a vision of the near future in the Republic of Great Britain, where conflicts between individuals and the Surveillance State create complex moral dilemmas. It is a story of loyalty and betrayal, guilt and forgiveness, blackmail and courage. In the words of Baroness Helena Kennedy QC, it is: 'A brilliant and terrifying novel about the fragility of freedom.'

Peter Lantos has recently written two plays, *The Visitor* and *Distorting Mirrors* and is working on a third, alongside his second novel. He lives in London. For more information, visit: www.peter-lantos.com.

PRAISE FOR *PARALLEL LINES*

'Something of a genius ... with the readability of a classic'
Alan Sillitoe

'A remarkable addition to the literature of the Holocaust'
Sunday Times

'Lantos follows clues, detecting and retracing the steps of his past. He finds a woman who slept in the bunk next to him and his mother in the barracks in Bergen-Belsen, as well as a British medical student who came to help after liberation, and one of the US soldiers whom he met in 1945. Reminds us that the end of the war was by no means the end of the hardship, entailing further resilience. I defy anyone to read this account without retrospective anger on behalf of those who suffered' Michelene Wandor, *Jewish Chronicle*

'Anyone who thinks they have read all there is to be said about the Holocaust should read one more book, *Parallel Lines*. A child's clear-eyed journey to hell paralleled by an adult's scientific quest to understand that journey' Anne Sebba, author of *The Exiled Collector*

'I have read few autobiographies more extraordinary ... astonishing' *Observer*

This wonderful memoir ... introduces a narrator with rare gifts'
The Tablet

'*Parallel Lines* is for readers who are interested in history and the Second World War and for those who want that the evil befallen on the Jews of Hungary is not repeated ever again' Veronika R. Hahn, *Népszabadság*, Budapest

'A movingly narrated memoir' Clare Colvin, *Independent*

'Deeply moving' *The Age*, Melbourne

'A classic. I preferred it to Primo Levi's *If This Is a Man*. One of the things I found appealing was his restraint and reserve' Edward Wilson, author of *A River in May* and *The Midnight Swimmer*

A remarkable historical account and autobiography [which] chronicles the odyssey of Hungarian Jews in 1944–45, as they were progressively disenfranchised from the national life of Hungary, culminating in the seizure of their homes, property and livelihoods before sending them on trains to places like Auschwitz for extermination, or, in Peter Lantos's case, to Bergen-Belsen' Michael N. Hart, *Journal of Neuropathology and Experimental Neurology*

'We can now celebrate Peter Lantos's book, which accomplishes something rare: an emotionally moving and, at the same time, clinically precise account' *NU*, Vienna

'A child's perspective on the Holocaust ... a remarkable book. Read it and think about other people elsewhere in the world today who are being persecuted' Professor Philip Hasleton, *Bulletin of The Royal College of Pathologists*

'What sets the book apart, and makes this account so refreshing and, oddly, inspiring, is its simplicity. The horrendous events of the last year of the war are invoked with a child's idiosyncratic susceptibility to detail (Lantos was only five years old at the time) – the noises, the smells, the human proximity – and lack of sentimentality, even when recalling relatives who perished' *Where*, Budapest

'Gripping ... an unembellished account from a child demonstrating youthful resilience. Read this book and be gripped by the drama of Peter Lantos' early life' Roy O. Weller, *Neuropathology and Applied Neurobiology*

PARALLEL LINES

A journey from childhood to Belsen

Peter Lantos

Arcadia Books Ltd
139 Highlever Road
London W10 6PH

www.arcadiabooks.co.uk

First published in Great Britain by Arcadia Books 2006
This B format edition published 2007
Reprinted 2014 (fifth impression)

Copyright © Peter Lantos 2006

Peter Lantos has asserted his moral right to be identified as the author of this work
in accordance with the Copyright, Designs and Patents Act, 1988.

All Rights Reserved. No part of this publication may be reproduced in any form or
by any means without the written permission of the publishers.

A catalogue record for this book is available from the British Library.

ISBN 978-1-905147-57-1

Printed and bound by CPI Group (UK) Ltd, Croydon CR0 4YY

Arcadia Books supports English PEN *www.englishpen.org* and
The Book Trade Charity *http://booktradecharity.wordpress.com*

Arcadia Books distributors are as follows:

in the UK and elsewhere in Europe:
Macmillan Distribution Ltd
Brunel Road
Houndmills
Basingstoke
Hants RG21 6XS

in the USA and Canada:
Dufour Editions
PO Box 7
Chester Springs
PA 19425

in Australia/New Zealand:
NewSouth Books
University of New South Wales
Sydney NSW 2052

Contents

'... *my mind, still lost in flight, once more*
turned back to see the passage that had never
let anyone escape alive before.'

Dante Alighieri: *Inferno*
(translated by Michael Palma)

Foreword

On 19th March 1944, the German Wehrmacht marched into Hungary. Anti-Jewish legislation had been in place since '38, radically restricting Jewish participation in the professions and the civil service, and forbidding mixed marriage. Hungary effectively became a Nazi puppet state and, for five-year-old Peter Lantos and his family, things got much worse.

He didn't understand why his mother was sewing ill-fitting yellow stars on everyone's clothes. It made no sense that they had to leave their comfortable home to crowd into a dirty and inhospitable part of their small town. Why was there never enough food now and less pleasure? His commanding grandmother and aunts had shrunk from their former elegance to sorry states. When the news came that they were soon to get onto a train and leave, he was thrilled.

But the train was not as he imagined, and their first stop in the larger town of Szeged, an operational centre for the collection and deportation of Jews, marked a further point on a descent into the abyss. That abyss came – via Strasshof and five months in an Austrian work camp near Vienna, where the allied bombs fell with deafening regularity – in Bergen-Belsen, the Nazi holding, then concentration camp in northwest Germany, where Anne Frank met her death.

The cold, the stench, the fear, the lice, the epidemic deaths – all these form part of Peter Lantos's extraordinary memoir. Here, a child's singular and vivid recollections are amplified by an ageing man's search for the missing links of his past.

Peter Lantos begins his story with a recurring dream. In it, he is looking for the house in which he was born. He cannot find it. He searches amidst familiar streets, goes back to the station, tries another direction, and gets lost – again and again. Defeated, he gives up. Only then does he discover that he is in the right place. It is the house that has disappeared.

Lantos is one of the lucky ones. His home may have gone, but, unlike several in his family who ended up in Auschwitz, he lived to tell the tale. He and his mother, though not his father, made it through Belsen. Having returned to post-war Hungary, he also made it through 'the dark age of Stalinism', where being a Jew was hardly a social advantage. The family timber yard, first expropriated by the Fascists in 1944, was then expropriated once more by the Communists.

By the time of the 1956 uprising, Lantos was in his penultimate year at senior school. His entry into medical school was at first prevented by the fact that he had been labelled a 'class alien'. But his fearless mother saved the day. Ten years later, he won a research fellowship in London. He didn't return to Hungary for many years, one reason being that he had been tried *in absentia* and sentenced to 16 months imprisonment. Home was now once more lost.

In London, Lantos rose in the medical ranks of neurological research, attaining the prestigious Chair of Neuropathology at the Maudsley Hospital in 1979. His outstanding work contributed to the understanding of Alzheimer's and other neuro-degenerative diseases. Though he had revisited Belsen before during an earlier academic visit to Germany, it was only after 1989 and the end of the Soviet era, that his *Parallel Lines* begin to take shape. Its journey is a riveting one.

When I wrote my novel *The Memory Man*, I had no idea that Peter Lantos existed. Perhaps I dreamt him, since my Austrian hero, like him, is a neuroscientist who works on memory, only to return in older age to those war-time experiences he has long put aside, to confront their dark matter. The novel arose because the story I told in *Losing the Dead* – of my parent's war and its haunting aftermath – held an emotional residue that wouldn't leave me alone.

I read Peter Lantos's *Parallel Lines* some years later. I was struck by the spare quality of a narrative that holds so much remarkable life. I couldn't put it down. We sometimes think there can be nothing left to say about the deadliest moments in the twentieth century's history, but Lantos's story is unique. Each memoir of the holocaust adds the particularity of a lived experience, arresting in its detail and in the ways in which its author metabolises the past.

It is good that Arcadia has brought back this fine book for our attention.

Lisa Appignanesi, OBE

Lisa Appignanesi OBE is a prize-winning novelist and writer. The former President of English PEN and Chair of the Freud Museum London, she is a Visiting Professor in Literature and the Medical Humanities at King's College London. Her novels include *The Memory Man* (winner of Canada's Holocaust Literature Prize) and *Paris Requiem*. Her non-fiction includes the acclaimed *Mad, Bad and Sad: A History of Women and the Mind Doctors* (Virago), *Losing the Dead* and *Trials of Passion: In the Name of Love and Madness*.

Acknowledgments

I wish to thank, in alphabetical order, friends and relatives who shared with me the memory of the events described in this book: Dr Zsuzsa Ágai (Szeged), Mrs Magda Hajdu (Budapest), Mrs Magda Iritz (Nahariya, Israel), Mrs Mária Kiss (Budapest), Mr András Szemere (Budapest) and Mrs Vera Tőzsér (Budapest). The help and encouragement of Judge Jeremy Connor during the preparation of the manuscript is gratefully acknowledged.

I am particularly grateful to Dr Beatrix Bastl of the Institut für Geschichte, Vienna University and Stadtarchiv, Wiener Neustadt; Dr Elisabeth Klamper of the Dokumentationsarchiv des Österreichischen Wiederstandes, Vienna; Dr Elenore Lappin, Institut für Geschichte der Juden in Österreich, St Pölten; Dr Thomas Rahe and Mr Bernd Horstmann, both of Gedenkstätte Bergen-Belsen; Dr Ilona G. Tóth, Director of the County Archives, Szeged Hungary and Dr Stephen Walton of the Department of Documents, Imperial War Museum, London. My thanks are due not only for allowing me access to the libraries or archives under their care but also for stimulating discussions and for practical advice.

The help of the Staff of the Wiener Library, London and of the Town Archives in Makó, as well as Herr M. Schiller of the Landeshauptarchiv Sachsen-Anhalt, in Magdeburg, Dr Eva Drašarová, Director of the National Archives, Prague and Dr Ferenc Tóth of the József Attila Museum in Makó, Hungary is gratefully acknowledged. Two school friends, Dr Ildikó Bencze (Budapest) and Mr János Gábor Farkas (Vác, Hungary) have given me much assistance to rekindle memories of old times. I have greatly appreciated the essay of Mr Attila Stenszky's on the fate of Jews in Makó.

I also wish to thank Dr Szabolcs Szita (Budapest); Professor Karl Flanner (Wiener Neustadt), Dr Werner Eichbauer (St Gallen), and Herbert Schatz (Strasshof an der Nordbahn) for their help in obtaining information about our fate in Austria. Mr Joachim Falta of Wedringen, Germany, was the perfect guide to events in Hillersleben, past and present. I am indebted to Mr László Kovács (Nyiregyháza, Hungary) and to Professor John Hankinson (Newcastle) for the invaluable information they have so generously provided.

The search for family documents led me to a young local historian in Makó, Mr Zsolt Urbancsok, who with strong motivation and enthusiasm embarked on a project to fill a gap single-handedly in the recent history of his town: the fate of the large and prosperous Jewish community during the Holocaust. He has been an enormous help and unfailing source of information during the preparation of this manuscript.

I feel a profound gratitude to Professor George Gross of San Diego, USA who by saving our lives made this book possible. I was also moved by the response of American veterans and their families who replied to my enquiry about our train journey from Belsen.

Gerald Jacobs read the chapter on Bergen-Belsen and gave constructive suggestions.

Finally, I wish to thank Ian Paten (London) who edited the first version of the manuscript, Elspeth Sinclair (London) who made many useful suggestions to the subsequent text, and Richard Bates (Discript Ltd, London) who effectively commissioned the book for Arcadia and gave the book its final shape.

Preface

Recently, I have been dreaming often of my birthplace in Hungary. To be precise it is more of a nightmare than a dream: I am looking for the house in which I was born, but I cannot find it. I remember exactly where it should be: behind my grandfather's large timber yard, in a short, dusty backwater of a narrow street, connecting two wider streets which themselves do not lead anywhere important. I keep retracing my steps with increasing frustration but to no avail: I feel lost in an impossible maze from which I am not going to emerge alive. Desperate, I plan little stratagems: I start at the railway station, a solid point of reference, walk down the wide, straight avenue that runs towards the town centre, with its umbrella of trees, then turn right towards the timber yard, circumnavigate its never-ending fence, pass the two large villas in which my uncles and their families used to live, but end up in a cul-de-sac. Eventually I reach a small deserted square, lined by low houses, their windows darkened by blinds. In the centre there is a tiny carousel for children painted in gaudy colours; two swings move silently up and down, but there is no one around. Frightened by the silence, I change my tactics and start from the opposite direction. I run to the Main Square in the town centre, but soon lose my way again. The place is deserted: there is not a single soul to ask. Defeated and exhausted, I decide to give up the search, to surrender to the inevitable: I will never find the house where I was born.

Suddenly I recognize that I am in the right street after all. But our house is not there any more.

MAKÓ: A SMALL TOWN IN HUNGARY

1

If one is not familiar with the detailed geography of central Europe, finding Makó on the map can be a problem: not surprisingly, since it is only a small provincial town. Searching the Internet for 'Makó' yields a surprising result: 108,204 hits spread over 10,821 pages, depending, of course, on the search engine. But before one can get carried away with chauvinistic pride over the extraordinary popularity of one's home town in the limitless thesaurus of human knowledge, the truth soon hits one: the name is not the sole property of a small town in Hungary. Other contestants vying for attention are not even towns with the same name in different countries. Rather, they are the short-finned shark, Mako *(Isurus oxyrinchus)*; full and semi-rigid inflatable boats and rubber ducks, bearing the trade name Mako, produced in Cape Town, South Africa; and CompAir Mako, a manufacturer of breathing equipment in Texas. Narrowing the search to Makó+Hungary still yields nearly a thousand hits; many are devoted to the town's most famous son, Joseph Pulitzer of Pulitzer Prize fame, who was born there on 10 April 1847.

Potential visitors to Makó should not be discouraged by some of the less helpful Internet sites. One lists three hotels, but none in the town: one is 16 miles to the west, another 37 miles to the north-west, and the third in a different country altogether – in Romania, some 52 miles to the east. However, despite this misinformation there are acceptable local hostelries.

In fact it is not difficult to find Makó: it lies at $46°$ $13'$N, $20°$ $30'$E, in the south-eastern corner of Hungary, close to the border with Serbia and Romania, on the northern bank of the River Maros. At the time of the Austro-Hungarian Empire the town boasted a substantial hinterland of arable land and busy connections with other towns both to the east and the south, but the Trianon peace treaty of 1920 ended all that. Historical Hungary was truncated, losing two-thirds of its territory: all of Transylvania was engulfed by Romania, while the extensive, fertile agricultural land to the south was incorporated into the newly created Yugoslavia. Makó, once the busy commercial centre of a flourishing agricultural county, was thus severed from its surroundings and exposed to two countries with which relations between the two world wars, mainly as a result of Hungary's avowed aim (reinforced by fierce propaganda) of regaining its lost territories, were less than amicable. Although geographically it was not strictly a border town, the sudden loss of all the surrounding land to the south and east weakened its economy and gradual decline followed.

2

The town has been famous for its production of high-quality onions; although cultivation dates back to the beginning of the sixteenth century, only the improved methods introduced from the second half of the nineteenth century, and successful marketing which Jewish merchants were instrumental in initiating, began to provide wealth for the town. As a result, Makó was swiftly urbanized: it was among the first provincial towns in Hungary to build proper roads and to introduce electricity. The debt the town owes to this humble bulb is acknowledged by nothing less than a statue (surely there cannot be many places in the world which have paid such a tribute to the onion) and by an arts centre, which all the locals endearingly call the

House of Onion instead of the more appropriate House of Culture.

With the encouragement of an enlightened bishop, the first Jews arrived in Makó around 1740 and settled in an area not far from the town centre, inhabiting two streets which, although named after Hungarian statesmen, were referred to popularly as Little Jewish Street and Great Jewish Street, the distinguishing epithets relating to the length of the streets rather than to the densities of the Jews living there. Despite this religious segregation, the various denominations lived peacefully together until the 1930s. The first synagogue, a simple unadorned building, was founded towards the end of the eighteenth century and demolished in 1919, but by then the town had two other, more distinguished temples.

Emancipated in 1867, the Jewish community played an increasingly influential role in the mercantile and intellectual life of the town. Their numbers gradually increased, reaching a peak in 1920, when there were some 2,380 Jews in Makó, constituting 6.4 per cent of a population in excess of 37,000. Reflecting this secular advance, two synagogues were erected within twenty years; and the fate of these two places of worship could not have been more different. The Orthodox Jews built their synagogue in the Romantic style in 1895. The synagogue for the Reformed Jews (or Neologues) was altogether a different, grander affair, reflecting the increasing prosperity and confidence of the local community. It opened its gate on 2 September 1914, rather inauspiciously, shortly after the First World War began.

As the elegantly clad worshippers, including my grandparents, were gathering for the inaugural service, no one could foresee that the synagogue would be demolished some fifty years later: the seeds of destruction were sown on that late summer day when Europe bade farewell to peace.

The modest Orthodox synagogue, having fallen into

disrepair after years of neglect, has recently been restored, while the fate of the much grander Reform synagogue has been far less fortunate: it was demolished in the spring of 1965. Lack of proper maintenance weakened the fabric of the building to such an extent that demolition became unavoidable to prevent spontaneous collapse. After protracted negotiations between the town's council and the Jewish community, the decision was finally reached to abandon the building to its fate. Whether the synagogue could have been saved has been disputed ever since, but the fact remains that one of the most attractive and distinguished architectural landmarks of the town was destroyed, first to make way for the headquarters of a local co-operative, bearing the name of Lenin, and later to house the committee of the Hungarian Socialist Workers' Party.

If I were superstitious I could claim that I witnessed an omen of the fate of the synagogue. I was still living in Makó when, during one of the special services to commemorate the anniversary of the deportation of the Jews from the town on 16 June 1944, the large chandelier in the central nave gave way and came crashing down in the middle of a prayer. The sound was as terrifying as it was unexpected. Being at some distance from the site of impact, I remained frozen in place and watched as the chandelier smashed against the wooden pews below, showering splinters of wood and fragments of glass all around. No one in the small congregation was injured, since by then so few Jews remained in the town that large areas of the nave were almost empty, and by good fortune no one was sitting at the epicentre of the impact. In the ensuing panic, I heard one of the women shouting out:

'It is starting all over again.'

3

The centre of the town has evolved around the confluence of several main roads, and for a long time has been devoid of signs of far-sighted town planning. The central square, defying all rules of Euclidean geometry, has grown to become not a square at all, but an oddly shaped triangular space. It bore the name of Széchenyi, the great Hungarian reformer statesman of the nineteenth century, until the Communists changed its name to Lenin Square. After the demise of the Communist regime, of course, it reverted to its original name. But all these changes were in vain, since the local population persistently, and irrespective of the prevailing political system, called it what it has always been known as: the Main Square. The naming game also affected the town's two cinemas: for a long time known as the Park and the Corso, they were officially renamed but hardly ever referred to as the Red Star and Liberty.

At the eastern end of the triangle is the grandest building: the Town Hall, built in 1839 in neo-classical style to replace a much smaller edifice. At the western end of the Main Square, another confluence of roads has created a (yet again somewhat irregular) satellite space, also approximating a triangle. This square boasts another remarkable building: the most amazing edifice in the whole town, arrogantly out of character with everything else around it – a large apartment block of metropolitan pretensions, built in the heady days of 1920s on borrowed money. Undoubtedly at the time it was the smartest address in town, with an elegant pharmacy and a popular patisserie on the ground floor: the former is still there; the latter has, alas, disappeared. The family of one of my cousins lived in this building, and it was from their flat that we witnessed the Russian tanks rolling into Makó after the end of the revolution in November 1956, one gun turret rather menacingly aiming, but fortunately not firing, at the window of the living-room.

In the adjacent square is the imposing local high school, or gymnasium: it was the school in which several of my uncles, my brother and (much later) I were all educated. Built in 1895, it maintained an excellent reputation, even in difficult times. In front of the school was the Russian monument, a white granite column topped with the compulsory red star, here cast in bronze; an obligatory architectural addition to the central squares of every Hungarian town after the Communists' ascension to power.

From the gymnasium a wide street led to a small, rectangular park, a peaceful place until an open-air theatre was built in it. Some of my older friends claimed to have been initiated into the more superficial pleasures of sex among the larger bushes here: there was a sad, mentally handicapped girl who was a willing tutor in exchange for a couple of boiled sweets.

4

Perhaps it is understandable that in my dreams I searched in vain for the house in which I was born. This was a modest building: architectural merit had no place in its conception, only convenience. It was the sort of place children sketch when they first try their hand at drawing: a sloping red roof with chimneys, a monotony of unadorned windows and an equally unembellished door – that was all there was to it. Inside, there was a living-room, a dining-room and two bedrooms: one for my parents, and one for my brother and me. There was a big age difference between us; he was fourteen when I was born, and until then he had sole use of the bedroom. It must have been annoying for a teenager to share a bedroom with a much younger brother, but if my presence, often quite noisy, upset him, he never betrayed it. There was also a small garden with a couple of fruit trees and flower-beds, tended by one of the handymen from the adjoining timber yard, which belonged to my grandfather. This industrial enterprise was the reason for our house being there: on either side of the timber yard a villa was erected for each of the two uncles who ran the family business after my grandfather's death. Our house was a more humble addition at the back.

From the garden we could enter the timber yard through a small wooden gate. This led into a mysterious world of endless surprises waiting to be discovered. The timber yard was vast; its boundaries lay well beyond a small child's horizon. Even much later, as I entered my teens, playing hide-and-seek with friends here proved to be a dangerous exercise: the terrain was varied, with many hiding places.

At the centre of the yard, in a huge raised building (in fact a large shed, open at both ends), stood two towering electric saws. Logs waiting to be cut were piled in alternate layers arranged at right angles. These piles stood on either side of the shed, and gradually disappeared during the day as the logs were transported to the electric saws. These, moving relentlessly up and down, emitted prolonged, high-pitched metallic screams as the logs glided through to emerge as parallel planks at the other end. Only little clouds of sawdust escaped to billow in the air; galaxies of sawdust cascaded down into the space below the raised platform. Digging into the undulating hills of prickly sawdust to hide from impending parental punishment was my ultimate weapon of resistance. The shed was a magical place, soothing and exciting at the same time. Frequently I stood there quite motionless, mesmerized, in the gently swirling clouds, until I was covered by thin layers of wooden snowflakes.

Freshly cut, the wooden planks were loaded on to carts, which ran on narrow-gauge rails towards the far end of the yard, where they were unloaded and piled into neat stacks again, as finished products for the building trade. Since the shed was elevated, there was a slope with an incline of 30 degrees, and each cart travelled under the control of one of the workmen, who applied the brake when the cart was beginning to gather too much speed. In my early teens, before the Communists finally closed down the yard, a journey by cart down the slope was the most exhilarating experience. The sense of danger, of the brake failing at the last moment and the cart hurling us through the solid wooden fence and into the street beyond, mowing down a couple of unsuspecting passers-by, was irresistible.

Not far from the building housing the electric saws was the engine room with its gleaming machines: slowly turning wheels, dignified pistons, protective railings, light bulbs dangling beneath enamel lampshades, white below, dark green above, boxes of alarms, rows of switches, and the rhythmic, repetitive hum of engines going about their allotted task, all in an oily thick fog. The most direct route to the engine room passed the cooling tower. I found its pool of uninviting dark water frightening, and always tried to keep as far away from it as possible. Further away, diagonally opposite our house, facing the main street was the office building, in which, as a child, I did not have the slightest interest. I always excluded it from my perambulations, thus preventing one of my uncles from enquiring about the nature of my business in the yard. But it was from this building that my grandfather and, after his death, two of my uncles – and after their deaths during the war, my mother and her youngest brother – ran the family business.

5

My grandfather made his fortune in the timber industry. With his partner he founded what developed into a successful industrial enterprise. The formula for success was quite simple: large nearby forests, easy transport by rail or river, and the ready market of an expanding county town. By the end of the

First World War the firm's reputation had been established and my grandfather was well enough known and successful enough for his name to be on the list of wanted men drawn up by the commissars of the short-lived Communist terror of 1919. Fearing for his life, he had to go into temporary hiding.

He wanted to run a modern enterprise and purchased the most up-to-date equipment available at the time from Germany in order to keep abreast of any competition. Although by the end of the 1920s there were at least six other similar enterprises, his firm was undoubtedly the largest in the whole county. It also had one of the first telephones in town, immediately after the first exchange became operational in 1900. He built a fair-sized but not ostentatious house for his family in one of the more pleasant streets in town. I do not know whether or not this featured in his choice of location, but the street was outside the Jewish quarter. It was lined by two rows of trees on either side: lime on the side of the houses and horse chestnut by the road. Early summer was heralded by the fragrance of the flowers of the lime trees, which were sometimes collected and dried to be used as infusions in the winter, while the thuds of falling conkers reminded us that autumn was not far off.

It is my grandparents' house which I regard as my own, since when we returned after the war we did not go back to the house in which I was born. I grew up in my grandparents' house, and lived there until I left for university. The building had the graceful air of a provincial patrician town house. Its best features were three pairs of large windows, which were unusually tall for their width, thus enhancing the elegance of the façade. Above them, female heads carved in stone looked down on passers-by, adding a further touch of sophistication. These carvings were not too distant echoes of the Coade heads decorating the doors of the architecturally more venerable Georgian buildings of Bedford Square in London, where I would be living a couple of decades later.

A short flight of steps led up to the hall. All the rooms were large and airy with very high ceilings – as a child I could not look up without feeling dizziness. The floors were made of best-quality wood, naturally hand picked from the timber yard, and covered with Persian carpets. All the furniture was hand-made according to my grandmother's specifications. The kitchen had an oven and a stove, both built into the brickwork. There were four cast-iron hobs. The oven was slightly raised, and its iron door opened to reveal a deep interior: it resembled a small furnace and could accommodate several dishes at the same time. The larder adjoining the kitchen was suitable for a large family with eight children: the floor was covered by specially cut bricks to keep it cool and there were endless marble shelves. Very early on a modern bathroom and a porcelain water closet were installed; these were at the time a novelty and drew admiration from neighbours and visitors. The bathroom may originally have been a pioneering design but it was not modernized after the Second World War, and when we went to live there we had to pump the water manually into a large tank that hung from the ceiling with a marker on its outside, indicating the water level. With no domestic help most of the time, having a bath was also a good biceps-building exercise.

There was a large garden, divided into two. At the entrance and extending round the back of the house there was a flower garden with beds and formal box trees. These were enormous, and a gardener regularly pruned them to maintain their perfect spherical shape. Adjoining the flower garden, further back, there was a much larger garden of fruit trees, including cherry, plum and apricot trees, as well as rows of vines and raspberry bushes. There was a large outhouse with two rooms: one served to store logs for winter, since of course there was no central heating in the house, while the other was used as a garden shed. There was a large loft, to which the only access was by means of a vertiginous ladder: it was here that as schoolchildren after the war we set up our first, and last, secret society. We grandly named it 'The Natural Research and Scientific Society' and took it extremely seriously: we issued membership cards, drew up a constitution and edited newsletters. Regular lectures were given on topics as wide-ranging as the history of the First World War, technological processes used in metallurgy and the life of perennial plants. We organized excursions to the nearby park to collect mushrooms and seeds. To make the loft usable we had removed dust and broken tiles by the sackful; we even managed to furnish the place, albeit sparsely, with a couple of chairs and a small table not needed elsewhere in the house.

The idea of founding the society came from János, a lively little boy who was elected secretary. I served as an organizer, since the headquarters were in our house. We proudly claimed possession of this space, which was entirely our own: adults were not allowed to trespass. I do not remember doing anything there which might have been forbidden or disapproved of by the adults, but this hiding place was our declaration of independence from the outside world, a freedom denied to us everywhere else. We stuck a map on the wall, and planned journeys to faraway countries we did not know and of course could not visit, since travelling to foreign lands by then was all but impossible: the newly-installed Communist regime had closed the country to the outside world. We could not even visit my aunt and uncle, who lived some 30 miles away across the border in neighbouring Romania, a country that was also a member of the Communist block.

6

Our life revolved around my mother's family since we lived in the shadow of their business, and our house, practically attached to the timber yard, was a present from my mother's parents. We regularly visited the large family house, and the most vivid fragments of reminiscence I can evoke involve the domineering figure of Fanny, my grandmother on my mother's side. I never met Samuel, my mother's father: he suffered a massive stroke, became paralysed and dependent on all-day nursing care. His inarticulate cries shattered the peace of the house and he died in November 1933.

My grandfather was by all accounts a gentle man who pursued his prospering business interests with little fuss, and steered a convoluted diplomatic course to avoid any confrontation with his wife, who ruled the house with little inclination to compromise. He fathered ten children; two died in infancy, as was common at that time, while the other eight, five sons and three daughters, all reached adulthood. The sons were well educated to take up professional jobs or continue the family business; the girls were groomed for marriage, and they did indeed marry as soon as they could to escape the suffocating control of my grandmother. My grandfather was a tall, erect man who lost most of his hair early; the remaining tufts on the sides and at the back were drastically trimmed to grey stubble. The photographs and an oil painting portray him as a man with an air of undisputed authority, with narrow, determined lips under a moustache but with a gentle twinkle in his brown eyes. He commanded the respect of his workers, but was also well liked: the firm, although financially lucrative, had never outgrown its original roots as a family enterprise in which personal contacts and genuine concern for individual workers remained the mainstay of successful management.

He led a well-ordered and organized life, which to other people may have seemed monotonous. A carriage arrived every morning to take him to the timber yard, and the same carriage drove him back for more work in the afternoon after his lunch, which he always had at home. He was driven to his house again at the end of the day, in time for dinner. Friday evenings, when his large family gathered together, were the highlight of the week: he sat at the head of the table and blessed the bread and the wine while my grandmother lit the candles. He was not zealously religious, and certainly fell short of his wife's standards. He was a heavy smoker, and on the Sabbath he occasionally disappeared to take refuge in the outside lavatory for a quick illicit smoke. He introduced two of his sons to the affairs of the family business; each lived in a large villa built for them on either side of the timber yard, and after my grandfather's premature death these two uncles continued to run the business without any difficulty. His reputation in the community was acknowledged when he became a member of an exclusive gentlemen's club established in 1857 to provide a forum for the educated classes of society. The club served not only as a casino but also aimed to promote public welfare, art and education: there was a library with its own librarian. In a book published in 1929, just in time to commemorate the tenth anniversary of the Trianon peace treaty, there is an entry on my grandfather, acknowledging that from modest beginnings he had developed the timber yard into the largest and most modern in the county. He played an active part in the public life of the town, and at the time of the book's publication he was vice-president of the Jewish community and a member of the municipal board of the county as well as of the town council.

By all accounts my grandparents' marriage was a happy one: my grandfather's apparently effortless sense of compromise greatly helped this domestic bliss, since my grandmother left little room for doubt as to who was running the household. She was a woman of strong principles and unshakeable opinions. She bullied her husband, remorselessly controlled her children and terrorized the domestics. She was a small woman, but she more than compensated for her lack of stature with a domineering character: she obviously enjoyed running her household with unbridled autocracy. Always simply and immaculately coiffed, she had white hair by the time I was born. She dressed neatly but without any consideration of fashion trends. Her grey-blue eyes projected an ice-cold glaze that commanded immediate attention and brooked no possible contradiction. It was this gaze which instilled fear in the domestics who, during better times, worked in her house. She kept them on a very tight leash, and did not tolerate waste, laziness or lies. Referring to the maids, she was known to say: 'Those who tell lies steal, those who steal also have loose morals,' as if telling fibs inescapably led to prostitution. Ironically, it had escaped her attention (or was she simply reluctant to admit it?) that more than one of her sons had been sexually initiated by the very same maids under her own roof.

No one could doubt her fecundity: she delivered ten children in rapid succession; two died soon after delivery. She was greatly partial to her sons, and this favouritism, which my grandfather, for the sake of peace, did little to redress, continued even when the children had grown up.

My mother endured the particular misfortune of being not only born into the wrong sex but also being the third daughter: she was the fourth child and her birth frustrated my grandmother's wish to deliver a son after two girls and only one boy. This disappointment lingered, and although my mother did not complain, I became aware of her uneasy relationship with her own mother from other members of the family. Even early family photographs betray my mother's Cinderella treatment: in a faded snapshot of the first five children, the two boys and the other two girls and are all elegantly dressed; only my mother stands like a poor relative who happened inconveniently to be there when the photo was taken. The boys are in smart suits and the two other daughters are wearing elegantly tailored dresses with large scalloped collars lined with lace, dainty hats and elegant shoes. In contrast, my mother is clad in a shape-less dress unadorned by lace, her hair is topped by a rather inelegant headdress, which looks like a fully opened fan mis-placed to frame her head, tied with a large clumsy bow under the chin. She is wearing laced-up boots that had clearly seen better days, probably on the feet of her elder sisters.

My grandmother's attitude to her daughter became further aggravated when my mother decided to marry my father: my grandmother was infuriated by my mother's decision and was firmly convinced that her least-favoured daughter had made the wrong choice. On this occasion she would be vindicated: my mother had indeed made the wrong decision, but not for the reason that gave rise to my grandmother's disapproval.

7

I know shamefully little of my grandparents on my father's side: they were practically unknown to me, and I do not have any childhood memory of them. They did not live in Makó: my father was born in a small place that could hardly claim to be a town in south-eastern Hungary. I cannot recall any visits to his parents; perhaps I was too small to remember. I cannot sum-mon up the sounds, smells, colours or noise of their house; the faces I remember are those of uncles and aunts from pho-tographs, now lost, taken at the time. Obviously there was a heavy but understandable imbalance in family ties: I spent my childhood in the shadow and under the influence of my moth-er's family. Even after the war, as an adolescent, when I spent many of my summer vacations with one of my father's sisters, who, being childless, regarded me as her son, I made little effort to find out anything beyond her amusing vignettes of a large family.

In the archives I learned that my grandfather, Samuel (he had the same name as my other grandfather), was born in

1861, and at the time of my father's birth in 1893 he was a shopkeeper. Thanks to the meticulous records of the Jewish community, I even know when and by whom was he circumcised, but not much else. My grandmother, Eugenie, was eight years his junior, and judging by the number of their children it must have been a happy marriage. There were, as in my mother's family, eight children: four boys and four girls.

My father received a standard education, and trained as an accountant. He met my mother at one of the society balls, and after a formal introduction he became a regular visitor to my grandparents' house. My grandmother disapproved of his courtship. She regarded him an unsuitable future son-in-law, and was opposed to one of her daughters marrying below her status: she did not hold the profession of accountancy in very high esteem. But eventually my mother's persistence and my father's considerable charm, which worked wonders on women, as my mother found out all too late, won my grandmother over, and they married in 1923. My mother was twenty-three, and my father seven years her senior.

My father was at least an inch shorter than my mother, who, to make this difference less noticeable, chose to forgo the wearing of high-heeled shoes when they were together. He lost most of his hair while still quite young, and what remained at the sides and back was regularly cut very short. He dressed well and took great care to appear well groomed. He was not attractive but had features women might find engaging: deeply set, dark, demanding eyes, diverting attention from an unremarkable nose and severe but sensuous lips. He had delicate pale skin which, as it appeared to be one size smaller than the skull it covered, was stretched over his face to emphasize finely chiselled features. A formal photograph, taken soon after my birth, shows him in an unsmiling, stiff pose, wearing a dinner-jacket: the picture, although faded, has a strange quality of reflected light – the shine of his satin lapel, the gloss of his black tie, the lustre of his skin and gaze.

Originally he worked for a private bank and was apparently competent at his job, but during the great meltdown of the world economy and finance in the late 1920s he lost his position. He was then employed by one of my uncles, who at the time ran a small bus company: in my mother's passport application in 1934 his occupation was described as controller of a bus company. When the anti-Jewish laws were introduced he could not obtain any employment, and worked for the family firm until this was expropriated in 1944.

My mother, Ilona (or as everyone knew her, Ili) was a tall woman with an erect posture and an elegant walk. She could not be described as beautiful even by an admiring son, but she was undoubtedly handsome in the way English women are often described: unremarkable individual features adding up to a pleasing effect. It was the animation of her face I recall most: slight changes could be employed with devastating effect. Her laughs were never throaty but reined in. She had dark brown, wavy hair; when it turned grey and then white she never made any attempt to dye it. Her hairstyle did not change much over the years after the war: swept back at the front and sides and rolled up at the back. She had deeply-set green-brown eyes, and well-drawn lips. A foundation cream, powder and lipstick were all she used for make-up; these she could apply in seconds without even resorting to a mirror. She always dressed simply but elegantly, although in the immediate post-war years what women wore in Hungary was dictated by the availability of materials and accessories rather than by current fashion trends. All her dresses were made for her by a dressmaker who usually came to our house to take measurements and organize fittings. This was necessity rather than luxury: good-quality ready-to-wear dresses hardly existed at the time, and when they gradually appeared in the shops they were more expensive than bespoke tailoring. Her wardrobe was limited: in the summer she preferred light cotton dresses, silk for the odd special occasion. For my graduation she wore a two-piece black costume, edged in black and white, a sort of provincial mutation of the Chanel classic, and black court shoes; the photograph of her on this occasion is one of the few I still have of her. Only in the 1960s did more fashionable accessories become available: although these cost a fortune, they quickly disappeared from the shops, and were subsequently carefully looked after. A smart Italian dove-grey merino wool cardigan I bought for her sixtieth birthday was found tidily folded in her wardrobe eight years later, after her death. She wore sensible shoes and avoided high heels: even after my father's death she maintained this habit.

Recently two photographs of her came to light courtesy of my former history of art teacher, who unearthed them in the archives of the local museum in Makó. I had never seen these before, and it was a shock to open the file containing the electronically scanned pictures on my computer and see my mother's face on the screen. The first was a passport photograph, to accompany an application made in 1927 to visit her sister in Romania, and it captured a woman with deeply set eyes, her hair set in the latest fashion of the period. To the clerk in the passport office she was a woman of medium height, with dark hair, green eyes, regular mouth and nose. In the other picture, taken in 1934, she is posed with my brother, who was nine years old at the time: the formality of the composition is broken more by their intimacy than the carefully retouched individual features.

My parents' marriage was not an entirely happy one. The problems started quite early. My mother did not realize that during the period of his courtship my father stayed in touch with an informal circle of young men, all bachelors at the time, who met regularly to enjoy each other's company, play cards (usually for money) and drink. They also devoted a considerable amount of their time to seducing women, and in this activity they were not particularly selective. My father, as my mother admitted rather reluctantly later, was a moderate drinker, an addicted gambler and a ferocious womanizer. Unfortunately his successes came not in playing cards but with women; in this respect he was both predatory and opportunistic. I know from one of my uncles, who was also a member of this circle, that my father was successful on more than one occasion in wagers made among friends as to whether he could seduce a particular woman. My mother soon found out about these infidelities, but their marriage survived and later settled into a mutual understanding. Preserving their union required generous tolerance on the part of my mother; occasional solitary visits to her sister in Romania served as a temporary escape from the brutality of disappointment and betrayal. When, as an adult, I asked her whether she had considered divorce, her reply was that she had never seriously entertained the idea. My father needed her, and her sons needed a father, was her explanation.

The initial difficulties in their marriage were not helped by the sudden death of their first child, a boy, who died of a respiratory infection before his first birthday. One year later my mother delivered another son, who, as he grew up, served not only as a bond between my parents but also as someone on whom my mother could focus, until my birth, much of her unspent love. I was born fourteen years later: my mother was by then nearly forty, and at the time delivering a child at such an advanced aged bordered on impropriety, if not indecency – it was not behaviour in which ladies of a certain social status should indulge. Clearly, my birth did not have my grandmother's official approval.

8

It is difficult to summon up more than fragmentary impressions of my brother, since the age difference between us was
too great. I must have been a nuisance to him, since from the
age of two, by the time I learned to articulate my bodily needs
to the outside world, I shared a bedroom with him, and there
could hardly be anything more inconvenient for an adolescent
boy than having a rumbustious toddler as a room-mate. Yet he
never showed any sign of impatience, and after one of my occasional tantrums, usually caused by the withdrawal of my favourite food as punishment, he acted as a calming influence.
He even found time to play with me. The most exciting game
involved him picking me up from the floor or my bed and
lifting me high in the air, well above his head; not relaxing his
grip on my waist, he would suddenly lower me, giving me the
sensation of free-fall. He would then shift his grip and, holding
me under my arms, whirl around with increasing speed until I
was flying horizontally through the air and the chandelier
blurred into a circle of light above my head.

György, or Gyuri, as everybody called him, was a gangly
youth whose high forehead was framed by dark brown hair. He
wore glasses from an early age to remedy the short-sightedness
of his enquiring dark brown eyes. By all accounts he was bright
and at school easily achieved excellent marks without difficulty:
the most persistent image I have of him is sitting at his desk,
reading. There were books everywhere, and I soon learned that
these should not be interfered with in any way: the only time
he raised his voice was if he could not find a book I had care-
lessly picked up and placed elsewhere. He was very shy, and
although girls found him attractive he lost his virginity quite
late, as related by a worldly-wise elder cousin, who often came
to visit us, and who persuaded him to overcome his inhibitions
and visit a brothel with him in Budapest. After the event, as

they were leaving, the cousin was keen to hear about the newly-acquired experience, and eagerly enquired: 'Gyuri, what was it like?'

To which my brother's response was: 'I did not like the smell.'

I could never verify a further embellishment to this story – according to this cousin, my mother apparently financed this little excursion to ease my brother's passage into manhood.

As a teenager, I was determined to find out more about my brother. I knew my mother would be naturally biased, so I talked to relatives and friends who had known him. I found it disconcerting (and it also made me somewhat jealous) that no one had a single unkind word to say about him. I even managed to get a copy of his Certificate of Final Examination, a type of baccalaureate, taken in 1943 in his secondary school. He scored the highest marks in all six subjects: literature, history, Latin, German, mathematics and physics. In the same year he also excelled in other subjects that did not form part of the baccalaureate: religion and ethics, philosophy, art history, English and a subject topical at the time, civil defence. And his results were not any different in economic and social knowledge, geology and ethnography, natural history and chemistry – other subjects taught in lower classes. He finished his studies with distinction.

As a teenager, following in his footsteps in the same school, I passed the photographs of my brother's class in the corridor many times a day, reminding me of his success. I was frustrated by the feeling that I would never be able to live up to his reputation. But this was a rather immature sentiment that temporarily gripped me during the emotional turbulence of adolescence. And it was also immensely futile, since by then he was not alive.

BEGINNING OF THE JOURNEY

1

The changes that uprooted our lives were progressive: hardly noticeable tremors at first, but gradually they developed into an earthquake that irreversibly shattered our existence. It was the spring of 1944: I was in my fifth year, and my birthday at the end of October seemed far away. During that season of changes I could not know – even my parents did not realize – that at the end of October, instead of celebrating my birthday, we were going to be struggling for survival in a foreign country. Even when the adult world had been turned upside down during the early years of the war, my life had remained firmly anchored in daily routine, protected from unforeseen upheavals by my parents. That spring the secure, constant existence I had known gradually disappeared.

The subtle erosion of daily routine was the first sign. Every weekday, after breakfast, my mother took my hand and walked with me to the villa belonging to Sándor, one of her brothers. I always enjoyed these short walks, since we could reach the villa without entering the street: the back door from our house led to the timber yard, and we could reach their garden through a small door from the yard. The walk gave me a sense of security: all this was ours, with no intrusion from the outside world. As we passed, the workers often paused in their tasks, taking off their hats to greet my mother.

My uncle Sándor was one year younger than my mother, and had become head of the family business in his early thirties after my grandfather's death. When we arrived at the villa my aunt, Anna, a petite woman, always immaculately dressed as if going to a reception, came to open the door; my uncle had already left for the timber yard. Their daughter, Zsuzsi, was exactly my age, and we were great friends. She was beautiful, with bone-china skin, long black hair and black eyes. Only rarely did the occasional disagreement between us develop into open warfare, and our harmonious coexistence enabled our parents to engage a trainee Montessori teacher to look after us. She was a young woman who was always kind; patiently answering our endless questions although, being reasonably well behaved, we never really tested the limits of her tolerance. One day the teacher was not there any more, and we never saw her again. The daily walk to the villa became less regular.

The pattern of our visits to my grandparents' house also changed. It had become customary for us to set out to join the family for dinner on Friday evenings after the service in the synagogue. These meals, heralding the Sabbath, were set pieces of family occasions, orchestrated and presided over by my grandmother. On these evenings she ran an open house, and surprisingly she showed an element of flexibility: no family member was turned away, even if they arrived unannounced. An extra place setting was laid, the maid brought in whatever food was to be found in the kitchen, and the evening proceeded without interruption. More often than not there were several grandchildren around: we had to sit at a separate table, although we ate the same dishes as the adults. My mother also visited my grandmother during the week, and occasionally she took me with her. I liked these visits: while my mother was busy talking to my grandmother, I was free to explore the house and could venture out into the large garden where, in the summer and early autumn, I could sample some of the ripening fruit. I also noticed that there were fewer adults at the Friday evening gatherings. At my questioning, my mother explained that one uncle or another had been called to the front to help fight the war. This was the first time I had heard that a war was going on.

The atmosphere in our house had become tense, although I could find no reason for the change. My parents frequently interrupted their conversation or changed the subject when the maid entered the room. Or they issued warnings to each other, my mother telling my father in German: '*Nicht vor dem Kind*', not in front of the child. I hated this because I knew I had been excluded from a secret, or at least from something important I could not share with my parents.

2

Suddenly something occurred that, in a way, explained everything that had happened hitherto and everything that was going to happen. One day I noticed my mother busily sewing a large yellow Star of David on one of my father's jackets. Although she was good with her hands, the six-pointed yellow patch sat rather clumsily below the lapel, covering most of the outside pocket. It was my father's favourite navy blue double-breasted jacket with thin white stripes, and the large six-pointed yellow patch looked all wrong: it was too large, out of all proportion to the size of the jacket, and sewn on with im-provised stitches as if it were a temporary sartorial embellish-ment. It did not escape my attention that several other yellow stars had already been prepared to be stitched to other gar-ments, including her costume and overcoats. I did not under-stand why we should wear the Star of David. My mother explained: 'There is a new law. All Jews have to wear it. It should be seen by everybody. It must be worn on outside gar-ments. So there is no mistake. Jews should be clearly identi-fied.' Her sentences were uncharacteristically concise; they sounded like single shots in the stillness of silence.

'So I also have to wear it?' I enquired.

'No, you don't,' she answered. 'Children less than six years of age don't have to wear it.'

Having already made up my mind, I stated firmly: 'I will also wear it.' I felt excluded and wanted to be part of this new venture. And to strengthen my case I asked whether my brother would wear it, although I knew the answer.

'Yes, of course,' she said. 'This is his jacket and overcoat, they are next.'

'And Zsuzsi?' This was my last hope: if Zsuzsi was to wear it, I certainly should not be left out.

'No, she will not. She is your age, not yet six.' From her intonation I sensed that further questioning was not going to lead anywhere. My mother, visibly upset, was not in a compromising mood. 'I will wear it, your father will wear it, your brother will wear it, but you and Zsuzsi are not going to wear it.'

I was not to be easily pacified, however. 'But why do we have to wear it?'

'I have explained to you. Because we are Jews, and every Jew must wear it. Unless they are small children under the age of six.'

'But I know we are Jews; we go to the synagogue, we light the candle on Friday nights; so why do we have to wear the Star of David on our jackets?'

'For other people to know that we are Jews,' was her reply.

'But why should other people know that we are Jews?'

I felt I was rapidly moving beyond my mother's limit of tolerance to the uncharted territory of confrontation. This, I knew, I should avoid at all costs. But she repeated her previous explanation in a full, final sentence that brooked no appeal or contradiction: 'There is a new law now; an order everybody has to obey: all the Jews must wear the Star of David, not only in Makó, but everywhere in Hungary.'

And from that day on my parents and my brother wore the Star of David. At first I was conscious of being visibly marked out everywhere we went: I thought that everyone was gaping at us. The first time we ventured out in the street, I feared that only my family was marked by the star, but I soon saw that other people were also wearing it, and this gave me a little more confidence. Soon it became part of our life: we had to accept that we should be marked to warn other people who we were so they could avoid us, if they wished, as if we were carrying some terrible, untreatable infectious disease. We obeyed the order without protest or even question, since there was no choice: we were labelled for easy separation from other people.

And there were other signs of change. The most obvious was the maid's disappearance. My mother, who from that time on had to run the house all by herself, explained that she had had to go back to her family to look after her parents. But I observed on my visits to Zsuzsi's villa that their maid had also gone, as had their part-time handyman, who looked after their garden and occasionally also came to our house to help with odd jobs.

As a child, I was accustomed to having nice meals three times a day, the long intervals between main meals bridged by little snacks mid-morning and in the afternoon. Even when we had a maid my mother did most of the cooking herself, and although I was a fussy eater, I never had any reason to complain. But despite all my mother's efforts our meals had become more monotonous, and my previously unbridled expectations concerning lunch and dinner had gradually diminished. Meat of all kinds, previously in abundance and so often on the menu, became rare, and when my mother's frequent excursions to the market yielded a much-coveted chicken, nothing was wasted. Dishes were reheated the next day, and we had to learn quickly to be satisfied with smaller portions.

To compensate for the lack of meat, my mother embarked

on baking more cakes and sweet biscuits; these latter I adored and became addicted to. Even now I can easily summon up their crumbly, vanilla-scented taste and their light golden colours. They became a culinary symbol of permanence and continuity: at a time when the whole world was being turned upside down, they reminded us of life's little everyday rituals, which were fast disappearing. In later years they became part of our lives again: small rewards for jobs well done. When I left home at the age of eighteen to study medicine, my mother walked with me to the station and on the platform produced a brown paper bag full of these biscuits.

3

By the spring of 1944 the war was beginning to encroach even on our everyday routine, despite my parents' valiant attempts to maintain a semblance of normality. Mainly from snippets of conversations and from overheard fragments of news on the wireless, I became aware that things had become much more serious. My mother explained that the Germans had occupied Hungary, and this was not good for us, since they did not like the Jews. It was their order that we should wear the yellow star. Until then the disappearance of uncles to the front had been the only indication that a war was going on. Since the conflict had started before my birth, it was an established fact, a part of life: it had little effect upon us; it was a distant war, acted out in a different universe. I had not connected the changes in our life with the war.

But now a new ritual my parents developed did not escape my attention. The focus of this was the wireless: all other activity seemed to cease in the house as they rushed to listen to the set. Sometimes they left the dining-table without even finishing their meal, as if summoned by a secret call, to take seats on either side of the small table on which the wireless was placed. Occasionally they behaved rather oddly while listening to the news: instead of sitting comfortably back in the large armchairs, they sat stiffly on the edge of their seats, turning their heads towards the wireless, my mother's hair nearly brushing the loudspeaker, to catch the barely audible sound. I could not understand why they should be listening to the news in such an unnatural position, as if they were eavesdropping: why did they not turn up the volume so that everybody could hear the news, as they used to do at other times, while relaxing in their chairs? On these occasions my father, normally inseparable from his cigarette case and lighter, even forgot to light his cigarette: usually, in spite of my mother's protests, the familiar click of his lighter could be heard before he left the dining-table. From their faces I could see that the news was not what they wanted to hear, and they would switch off the wireless with a gloomy expression on their faces. I heard a sentence repeated again and again, with which they seemed to console each other: 'The war will end before anything can happen.'

Of course, I did not know it then, and it dawned on me only many years later when, as an adolescent, I did the same: my parents were listening to the World Service of the BBC, a sombre, covert little ritual, sanctified by shared secrecy in the pursuit of truth. Then one day the wireless disappeared. My mother explained that Jews had been ordered to hand over their wireless sets to the authorities; they were thus prevented from listening to the news.

4

Suddenly an event occurred which broke up our family. It was the day when my mother's despair became palpable, as if months of suppressed frustration and humiliation had breached her defences of self-control finally to erupt to the surface. Even my father, who must have for a long time studiously cultivated detachment to delude himself into believing that somehow he stood outside events, was now confronted with a fact that could not be explained away. I can recall even now the day my brother left home.

I was playing with my favourite toy at the time: a velvety grey mouse, which when wound up with a key could run around on the floor with effortless speed. But it also performed an amazing trick: when whizzing around on the oval dining-table it never fell off the edge. I was completely absorbed in placing little obstacles in its way to see whether it would crash suicidally into the crystal ashtray when a hand unexpectedly and abruptly descended from nowhere and lifted the mouse up: I was suddenly robbed of the pleasure of watching the impending collision. It was my brother. This intervention would normally have led to a declaration of war, but even before I could scream, let alone kick, I detected that he was in a solemn mood. Looking up, I could see my parents behind him, as if they had come to make an important announcement. But only Gyuri spoke: 'Doggy, I am going away.' (Originally he called me Puppy, since I was so much younger, and gambolled around the house, quite often on all fours, and until the age of two I did not always observe the rules of domestic hygiene. Later, I protested that I was not a puppy, but a dog. And this name, which I liked, had stuck.)

'When are you coming back?' I enquired.

His answer was chilling. 'I do not know,' he said.

My father intervened, trying to reassure me. 'Gyuri has to go away to help in the war. He will come back, but we do not know when. It won't be too long.'

'Is he going where Zsuzsi's father has gone?' I asked.

My father looked at my mother, and they both said at the same time: 'Yes.'

'And the other uncles went to the same place?'

My parents' answer was again the same: 'Yes.'
'And will they all come back?'
My parents just nodded.
'That's all right, then.'

With this optimistic statement, the conversation came to an end. Gyuri picked me up, as he had done so many times before, holding me under my arms, and twirled me around in the air. My parents stood there watching silently: two members of the chorus of a Greek tragedy who had forgotten their lines. Then, as carefully as he had lifted me up, he lowered me to the floor and leaned over to kiss me, first on the top of my head, then on both eyes and on both cheeks. And then he was gone.

We never saw him again.

5

Unexplained activity in the house was a sign that something was afoot. My mother was carrying out what appeared to me to be a second spring cleaning, systematically going over the rooms, turning out wardrobes and rummaging through drawers. The whole exercise was unnatural since the annual spring cleaning had been completed only a few weeks earlier, and I expected some explanation, but none was forthcoming. I found my father's involvement even more ominous, since he never showed the slightest interest in any domestic work: now he stood by my mother's side and, although he was doing very little, I could hear him saying: 'Take this coat' or 'No, I do not want this jacket'.

After a while, I realized that this was not spring cleaning but a careful process of selecting clothing. My mother pulled out each drawer, emptied its contents and, lifting each item, paused for a moment, as if assessing each garment for its quality. A few items were collected in a small pile ready to be packed, while the rest were hastily replaced in the drawers or wardrobes. My first thought was that we must be going away for a summer vacation, although summer had not yet arrived. My hopes were shattered and replaced by suspicion, however, when I noticed a couple of the items earmarked for packing: they were heavy winter overcoats rather than flimsy shorts and cotton shirts for a summer holiday. I plucked up my courage and asked: 'Are we going on a holiday?'

'Yes,' said my mother, 'we are going away, but not for a holiday, and we are not going very far either.' She looked at my father and asked me to sit next to her. She explained that the following day we would have to leave the house and that we were going to live, for a short time, in another house with some other people, also Jews, but we would not have to leave the town. Other people, many we knew, including Zsuzsi and her mother, my grandmother and other cousins and relatives, would also be leaving their houses.

She consoled me with the promise that the three of us would remain together, and that I would be able to play with other children. But I would not have any of it: I was adamant that I was going to stay and would never leave our house. I wanted to play with other children in our garden, not in some other place I did not know. Nor did I want to share a house with other people, even if I knew them. And to give weight to my objection I started to howl – my ultimate act of disobedience, but used this time to no effect.

My father put his hand on my head and said: 'We do not want to go, but we have to.'

I did not understand why we had to leave the house where we had always lived. I did not understand who had ordered us to do so, and I did not understand what wrong we had committed to be punished in this way. But I knew that further protests would be in vain. My mother finished selecting the belongings we were allowed to take, and prepared everything for the next day.

My whole world seemed to come to an end. The comfort of

everyday routine and the security of our lives, all of which had been taken for granted and never questioned, had gradually been undermined by forces I neither knew nor understood. The increasing tension at home, the secret sessions of listening to the radio, the deterioration in our food, the wearing of the yellow star, the departure of my uncles and my brother – all had increased my suspicion, which gradually turned into fear that despite the protection of my parents something terrible would happen. And now this fear grew into terror, prompted by this latest catastrophic event: we were leaving our house, the final anchor of certainty that tied us to the world we knew.

And in the morning we left: a short bald man of fifty-one, an elegant woman of forty-four, and a boy not quite five years old. This is how our journey started.

6

What I could not understand had been clear to my parents for some time, and the forced departure from our house was merely the culmination of a sequence of anti-Jewish legislation promulgated by increasingly right-wing governments. Anti-Semitic legislation was already making its presence felt in Hungary in the wake of the First World War. As early as 1920, the proportion of Jewish students who could study at universities was curbed, first by reducing their numbers in accordance with the percentage of Jews in the overall population. This legislation, subsequently referred to as *numerus clausus*, must have had the dubious distinction of being Europe's first anti-Semitic law. The fact that in later years Jewish students were completely barred from higher education was but a logical development in a carefully planned process.

The invasion of Hungary by the Wehrmacht on 19 March 1944 precipitated the execution of the Final Solution: for all practical purposes Hungary became a vassal state of the Third

Reich. The puppet government of Sztójay, with the full support of the Hungarian Fascists, the Arrow Cross Party, readily agreed to collaborate fully with the Germans. And thus the large Hungarian Jewish community, having hitherto escaped deportation to the concentration camps, had to face its own extermination. The soil had already been prepared for the Final Solution: in rapid succession several new anti-Jewish laws had already been passed from 1938 onward; these drastically restricted Jewish participation in the economic, political, intellectual and cultural life of Hungary, a contribution that had been both substantial and persistent. Three laws passed between 1938 and 1941, popularly known as the Jewish Laws, formed the core of the disenfranchisement of the Jews from the national life of Hungary. The first, in 1938, without defining a Jew, restricted to 20 per cent Jewish participation in the legal and medical professions, in engineering, arts and journalism, as well as in key administrative positions. The second law, passed in 1939 and this time giving a definition of Jewishness, further reduced the quota in the professions to 6 per cent to reflect the proportion of Jews in the overall population of Hungary. Jews were excluded from state and local government service, from public bodies and institutions, and were ordered to declare all the land and housing in their possession. If these two laws served only to assuage the anti-Semitic sentiments of the middle and lower middle classes, the third law, passed in 1941, was blatantly racist. The ninth paragraph defined a Jew as someone who has at least two grandparents born into the Jewish faith. Moreover, all those who were members of the Jewish (or, in official parlance, of the Israelite) religious community, irrespective of their ancestry, were defined as Jews. Non-Jews were forbidden to marry Jews.

A 1941 decree dealing with the defence of the country forbade Jews of conscription age to serve actively in the army: they could join only as labourers in ancillary units. As fodder for forced labour, all ranks, however modest, were denied to them, even if they had previously served as officers in the Hungarian army. One year later Jews were prevented from buying agricultural land and property either by contract or in auctions.

And the pace of anti-Jewish legislation gathered further momentum after the German invasion of March 1944. This invasion destroyed even the illusion of Hungarian independence: Admiral Miklós Horthy, Regent of Hungary, appointed the Hungarian ambassador to Berlin as prime minister and foreign secretary. There was an element of tragicomedy about Horthy. Constitutionally Hungary was still a kingdom, but without a king; Horthy was head of state with the title of Regent, representing a defunct royal house. He was also an admiral in a landlocked country that possessed neither a navy nor a merchant fleet. Horthy had tried, too late and only half-heartedly, to extricate Hungary from the clutch of Nazi Germany, and he failed abysmally; the Führer lost patience and ordered German troops into Hungary to prevent the country negotiating a separate peace with the enemy. The Hungarian press reported the arrival of the German troops as an event in accordance with a joint agreement to strengthen the fight against the common enemy. But a communiqué from the German foreign ministry was more blatant, stating that a special envoy had been dispatched from Berlin who, in addition to his duties as an ambassador, had special rights to further German–Hungarian co-operation in the interests of the common war effort. The goal was, the communiqué declared, the quick and smooth removal of a certain clique organized by those individuals who intended to reduce Hungary's participation to a minimum. To replace Kállay (the previous right-wing prime minister) and his Jewish protectors, a new government of righteous, self-sacrificing and patriotic men had been formed, determined to continue fully the common fight with all the force of patriotic fervour.

Barely ten days after the invasion Jewish telephone

subscribers had to report, within three days after the order became effective, their name, religion, occupation and address. Those who worked in war industries were instructed also to provide the name of their employer, the nature of their employment and the site of the telephone connection. Failing to report a telephone connection or providing false information could incur a prison sentence of up to six months. Thus the telephone had become a potential weapon of betrayal. At the same time, invoking legislation passed in 1921, in the interests of public order and safety, all individuals of the Jewish race were ordered to hand in their wireless within forty-eight hours. Those who benefited from confiscated wirelesses included the local fire station, the administrative offices and the army. Those who disobeyed this order were threatened not only with prosecution for breaking the law, but also with internment. The last day of March 1944 saw the publication of a clutch of anti-Jewish decrees under the umbrella title 'Decrees for the regulations of the Jewish question', regulating such issues as the wearing of a distinguishing mark, membership of the Law Society, the employment of domestics, and the ownership of motor vehicles.

All individuals of the Jewish race older than six years of age, irrespective of sex, were ordered to wear above their left breast, with immediate effect, a clearly visible canary-yellow Star of David measuring 10 × 10 centimetres, made of wool, silk or velvet. There is a touching sense of liberalism here in the wide choice of material permitted, but the mode of attachment was strictly defined: the distinguishing mark had to be firmly fastened by sewing it to the over-garment to prevent easy removal. To underline the importance of singling out the Jew from the rest of the population, the Ministry for Internal Affairs had decreed on 12 April 1944 that those who failed to wear the distinguishing sign should be interned. Police raids soon followed to find and punish those not wearing the star.

A decree issued on 21 April 1944 ordered the sequestration

of the contents of all Jewish shops, together with their furniture and fittings. By this time the names of Jewish lawyers had been struck off the Law Society's lists, and a similar fate awaited Jewish journalists and actors.

My home town did not lag behind the national trend for implementing discriminatory anti-Jewish laws. As early as September 1939 all individuals, firms and banks with a trade permit or licence were obliged to register with the appropriate financial or industrial authority. Since about 20 per cent of those with such licences were Jewish, Bertalan Bécsy, the mayor, decided not to grant any such licences from January 1940 until the proportion of Jewish licence-holders was reduced to 6 per cent, in line with the percentage of Jews in the town's population. In the same year the local council, at the instigation of the mayor, passed a by-law forbidding the participation of Jewish merchants, craftsmen and tradesmen in national, monthly or weekly fairs, in daily markets and pilgrimages: they were prevented from using public spaces to sell their merchandise and thus their livelihoods were threatened. Despite the gradual exclusion of Jews from the public, economic and social life of the town during the early years of the 1940s, their lives themselves were not threatened until the German invasion in March 1944.

From then on the discriminative measures took a more serious turn, in accordance with the impeccable logic of the Final Solution: first, remove the Jew from public life; then take away his livelihood; finally, destroy his life. The mayor of Makó had in fact ordered the sequestration of twenty-five Jewish businesses early in April 1944, before the relevant decree was issued, and the closure of a further sixty Jewish shops completed the process of excluding Jews from the mercantile life of the town. Concerned that Jews might try to remove some of their own goods from their shops under the cloak of night, at the end of April a curfew was ordered, forbidding Jews to leave their homes between 7 o'clock in the evening and 7 in the morning. A decree issued on 16 April 1944 ordered Jews to declare all their property and belongings: ownership of houses, land and enterprises, furnishings, bonds and shares, precious metals and stones, jewellery, contents, fixtures and fittings of shops and other ventures. All legal transactions completed after 22 March 1944 were declared null and void.

The local newspaper encouraged its readers to report to the financial directorate those who helped their Jewish friends and neighbours to hide some of their valuables or to deposit them with Christian friends who were willing to help. To denounce these people was a patriotic act, the paper announced. In May 1944 typewriters and bicycles belonging to Jews were confiscated and handed over to the representative of the local administration. Books by Jewish authors were removed from public libraries, and by the beginning of July four hundred volumes had been destroyed in Makó. The public was exhorted to remove books by Jewish writers from their private collections, and a local bookbinder was instructed to pay a nominal sum for every hundred books handed in.

Beyond all the official decrees and restrictive measures there was also spontaneous hate: on 25 April 1944 the mayor published his house rules, in which he prescribed the relationship between municipal workers and their Jewish clients:

> In order to encourage a positive public spirit in our town and to promote and to strengthen the energy, the readiness to fight, the working ability and the belief in the final victory of our civil servants in my office, I order the following. Official affairs of the Jew should be conducted without any superfluous word, without any conversation. The official affairs of the Jew should not have a priority over that of a Hungarian. To shake hands with the Jew is forbidden. It is forbidden to help the Jew with submitting an application. A municipal employee should not be seen, anywhere, in the company of the Jew. To sell tickets to the Jew to the open air bath and to allow the Jew to enter the local park are forbidden.

As part of a national plan for the Final Solution, a decree aimed at concentrating Jews in ghettos was published on 28 April 1944, in direct consequence of an earlier top-secret document, which had declared that the aim of the Hungarian Royal Government was, within a short time, to get rid of the Jews. This cleansing process would take place by region according to a nationwide plan: all the Jews, irrespective of sex and age, should be transported to specifically assigned areas or camps. From now on Jews could live only in ghettos, and no time was wasted in implementing this law. On 2 May a high-powered delegation, including László Endre, the Secretary of State responsible for Jewish affairs, and Imre Finta, a captain of the gendarmerie, in the company of two Gestapo officers, arrived in Makó to ascertain that immediate plans had been put into motion. On 6 May 1944 the deputy leader of Csanád County, in charge of the implementation of the law, officially declared the establishment of a ghetto, and for this purpose he specified one of the least prosperous parts of town, a low-lying area in which the houses were plagued by damp. The inhabitants of this area were reluctant to leave their homes, however, even for the promised better accommodation in the houses vacated by Jews, and they began a campaign in the town hall for their right to remain in their homes.

The local paper enthusiastically welcomed the opportunity to cleanse a Hungarian town of Jews: Jewish boys with their wavy ear locks, old Jews with their kaftans and bored Jewish girls who were so spoilt by their wealth that they could do nothing but mount fashion shows would be replaced by clean, hardworking Hungarian families. The detailed planning and execution of the transfer of the Jews to the ghetto locally became the responsibility of the mayor. Only three days were allowed for completion of the move, with a deadline of 20 May. All the Jews of the town, some 1,800 souls, and a further 120 who had been transferred from neighbouring villages, were requested to abandon their homes to live in a specified area. The mayor ordered that this move should take place in three phases: in the first, the Jews would move, as a temporary measure, into a roughly triangular area in the centre of town where a large percentage of Jews already lived and where both synagogues were located. In the second phase, non-Jews would leave the area earmarked as the permanent ghetto to be resettled elsewhere. Finally the Jews would move into this area vacated by the Christians. The leaders of both the Orthodox and Reform Jewish communities assured the authorities of their full collaboration, and requested only that the existing small Jewish quarter with its two synagogues should be the site of the ghetto. They invoked the total loyalty of the Jews to Hungary, their sacrifices during the First World War, and their contributions in difficult times. They declared that these patriotic manifestations were clear evidence of their willingness to become fully assimilated into Hungarian society. If they expected more lenient treatment or a friendly gesture, however tentative, their anticipation was frustrated: their letter was never answered. On 17 May, the mayor instructed the chairman of both Jewish communities to implement the decree immediately and in full, and to complete the evacuation of Jews from their homes and their resettling in the temporary ghetto by 20 May.

To quicken the pace of herding the Jews into the ghetto, the police temporarily relieved restrictions on movement and agreed that the transfer should be carried out between 6 a.m. and 9 p.m. None the less, the plan was over-ambitious, and despite the full collaboration of the Jews the original deadline had to be extended to 23 May. There was very little attempt to hide the fact that the Jews would be completely dispossessed: they were allowed to keep and carry to the ghetto only a fraction of their belongings, and what they could keep was strictly regulated – one bed, one chair, one mattress, one blanket, two coats, two changes of clothing, two pairs of shoes and four changes of underwear. It was forbidden to keep gold and silver objects, even if they were religious items, or precious stones; nor could they take valuable carpets or bone china with them. Valuables left behind were catalogued and stored. Their value was set against the cost of resettling the non-Jews who had to vacate their houses in the area designated as the permanent ghetto. The Jews were obliged to clean and, if necessary, paint their rooms before they finally departed.

The mayor did not waste time in issuing a proscriptive decree on 24 May, the day after the move to the temporary ghetto was completed. Jews were not allowed to leave the area of the ghetto without permission. Jews could go to the market only between the hours of 9.30 and 11 in the morning. Jews were not allowed to seek medical help outside the ghetto, since there were adequate numbers of Jewish doctors within. In case of a serious illness requiring hospital admission, Jews could be admitted only by permission of a public health officer. Jews could purchase medicines only in the single pharmacy specified in the decree. Jewish craftsmen who had a trade licence and whose craft had not been proscribed or limited were allowed to continue to attend their workplace. Jews who breached or evaded this decree would be severely punished. Public notices were posted reminding the population of their obligation to report any Jews or anybody else suspected of being Jewish who had remained outside the ghetto. Clubs, societies or associations with even the remotest Jewish connection had been summarily dissolved. Jewish men who had not been called up for labour service were ordered to present themselves, as and when required, for 'defence' work, usually involving hard physical labour. Despite the efficient execution of the initial part of the process, phases two and three of the plan were never implemented since events moved too fast and overtook the meticulously produced plans.

7

As we walked away from our house towards the ghetto in the warm air of late May, my parents must have realized that their lives were going to change irreversibly: nothing would ever be the same, even if we could return. At this stage our loss was only material, but so total that it changed not only individual aspects of our lives but also the entire landscape of existence. Being expelled from our house so brutally put an end to the carefully cultivated self-deception which, in the light of increasingly blatant discriminatory measures, could no longer be maintained. The best apologists for crimes against Jews were the Jews. They believed that the unthinkable could not happen, a fool's escape from the obvious: the unthinkable is always upon us. Narcotized by a poisonous cocktail of self-delusion and arrogance, a belief in the security of permanence, they suddenly found that they were guests who had over-stayed their welcome and were now going to be unceremonially evicted.

When the war was over I asked the most obvious of all questions: why did the family not try to escape while it was possible? The answer I received was evasive. Apparently discussions had been held about emigrating, since the family had the means to buy, if necessary by bribery, its exit, yet all the arguments had ended in doing nothing. We continued to wait, to hope that the anti-Jewish laws were temporary, to doubt the stories of refugees, to believe that the war would soon end, since the Allies were preparing to open the second front, to reinterpret the news from foreign broadcasts, and to accept only what it was convenient to accept. Even if reports of the mass murder of Jews were true, it was happening elsewhere: it was a tragedy befalling others. Such horrors could never happen in Hungary, and even if they did, somehow our family would be spared. Mesmerized by fear and paralysed by incredulity, we placidly waited for the unthinkable to happen. And when it did happen, it still remained unthinkable.

In the summer of 2003 a document came to light in the Makó archives, a form filled in by my father in his regular, flowing hand. It is a declaration, according to decree 1600/1944, concerning the property of the Jew. His occupation is specified as day-labourer, since by the spring of 1944 he had lost his job. My mother, brother and I are listed as members of the same household. And there was very little to declare. No property. The house in which we lived was a gesture of 'grace and favour' from my grandparents. We did not own land. A pathetic list contained fixtures and fittings and domestic appliances, a couple of carpets, and under a particular subheading for silverware a single silver pencil. No bonds, no shares. Under precious metals and jewellery: a pair of gold earrings and a gold ring. Only one ring. This must have been my mother's wedding ring. But where was my father's? Had it found its way to the pawnshop? Had it been buried together with other valuables in the garden? Or had it been given for safe-keeping to kind neighbours? At the end of the form, under the last heading, debts, there are two entries. One for 11,199.02 pengő, the other for the more modest sum of 543.13 pengő, borrowed from the family firm: no doubt through the good offices of my mother, who must have mollified my grandmother into bailing my father out. The document was signed by my father in Makó and dated 30 April 1944.

My parents decided not to surrender everything at this stage and tried, as so many other people did, to keep some personal mementoes, jewellery and money. On the day of the liquidation of the ghetto, when we left our town, at a body search carried out in the courtyard of the synagogue, the gendarmes took away a wristwatch, a pocket watch and some cash, 1,679 pengő, from my mother. This was recorded in another file recovered from the archives: it is an inventory of valuables, jewellery and money, confiscated from the Jews on 16 June 1944.

While we lost nearly all our possession, the timber yard did not close: the mayor had different plans. On 26 May 1944 he appointed a caretaker to run the enterprise. It was an odd choice since the new director did not have sufficient previous experience to manage what was, by local standards, a substantial industrial complex. He justified his appointment by stating that the two uncles, who were the directors after my grandfather's death, had been conscripted to hard labour and my eldest uncle, who had recently been looking after the day-to-day affairs of the firm, was by then in the ghetto. Apparently no better qualified Christian employee was available, the mayor asserted, to take on the responsibility.

The local newspaper triumphantly reported the takeover on 4 June 1944. The expropriation by the so-called Public Welfare Co-operative, the article said, was of major importance, not only for the man in the street but also for the enterprise's workers. A new spirit would permeate the previously Jewish-owned factory: the collective spirit of the people. The main aim of this new force, the newspaper concluded, was above all not profiteering but the welfare and protection of the public. After a hiatus, production restarted two weeks later in the presence of the mayor, who expressed the hope that the now Hungarian-run enterprise would be more successful and more productive than it had been in Jewish hands – the reinauguration of the factory was the beginning of a better future. Behind these publicly avowed noble intentions, however, more mundane interests were at work, motivated by personal greed. And problems must have started soon, since less than five weeks after the appointment of the new director a controller was appointed to oversee the enterprise at the request of a high ministerial official. And at the mayor's post-war trial, the real reason behind this appointment was laid patently bare.

8

We must have been a pitiful sight. A couple of neighbours came to say goodbye – our departure was an event in the small street – but soon we were gone and the house, deserted, stood lifeless behind us.

The ghetto was in a state of pandemonium. In a small area about 2,000 people were forced to establish their homes, albeit temporary ones, within a couple of days. Those who already lived within the ghetto were reluctant, not surprisingly, to surrender their privacy to intruders they hardly knew or who were complete strangers. There were arguments and shouting, shoving and jostling, while enforced boundaries between families were negotiated and uneasy compromises made. Furniture and personal possessions, transferred to a new alien environment, were often piled up in disarray, and even if carefully stacked presented an unnatural still-life, like fragments of a broken picture or jigsaw pieces that do not fit: chairs on the bed; blankets and pillows on the table; foodstuffs in the washbasin; pots and pans in the bathroom; clothing piled up everywhere, waiting to be stashed in drawers – life suspended and waiting to be reassembled.

Given the overcrowding, privacy was the first luxury to go. We had our own room, and being only a small family of three we were fortunate to have a reasonable space. Other, large families fared much worse, seven or eight squeezed into a single room. We shared, as everybody else did, the kitchen and bathroom: I did not much care about the kitchen, but I hated the room called the bathroom. It was alien and intimidating, without the facilities I had been accustomed to; I loathed the foul smell, and detested the bare bulb dangling ominously from the ceiling.

Despite the reassuring presence of my parents, suddenly I was lost in a world that was not new, since it had all the components of a previous life, but which had been reconstructed in a

confusing way. I had lost all the certainties of my daily existence, the signals that divided the days into convenient little
packages of meals, playtimes and moments set aside for story-
telling before the light was switched off. Gone were the great
occasions outside the daily routine, or rarer treats worth waiting and preparing for: visits to my grandparents' house, secret
wanderings in the timber yard, invitations to one of my uncle's
houses, the noisy assembly of my cousins. These were all
events of the past, suddenly taken away, never to be returned.

We still had our meals, but these were not the occasions I
enjoyed and looked forward to at home; there were no flavours
worth cherishing until the next meal. For the first time in my
life I remained hungry and craved food most of the day. Lunch
and dinner became little more than snacks without any sense
of occasion. Between the permitted hours of 9.30 and 11 in the
morning, my mother paid her regular visit to the market with
diminishing returns: food was becoming scarce. May was too
early for seasonal fruit: no baskets of strawberries, mounds of
apricots, plums and peaches, no pyramids of melons and
watermelons, only miserable offerings of apples stored during
the winter. There was no niche for me in which to play inside
the house; only the open street offered opportunity, but playing
in the street was discouraged. We could visit my grandmother,
my uncles and aunts and cousins, since they were also in the
ghetto, but these were very different from the visits I remembered. During those first chaotic days it was not even easy to
find them, and when, after searching, we finally saw them in
an unfamiliar house the visit brought little joy: even I could
sense the pervasive gloom. My feeling of being lost was increased by meeting my relatives in such an alien environment,
wrenched from their previous existence. The adult conversation
must have been about subjects they did not want us children to
hear, since silence fell or the subject was changed as I entered
the room.

My grandmother, perhaps because she was so old, tolerated this change worse than anybody else: robbed of all the paraphernalia of power, she became a small, sad woman who looked painfully out of place in a strange and shabby room. Here she ceased to preside, larger than life, over her household, commanding respect and fear in equal measure from whoever entered her domain. I hardly recognized my aunts, who had lost their usual elegance: they were worn and worried, their hair neglected and their dresses creased.

9

May turned into June, and the days became longer and the weather warmer. We had been told that we had to leave the ghetto: we were going to be transported to another town. Hearing this news, I could not say I was sorry; in fact I was elated, since I thought that wherever we were going, it could only be better. But the first signs of the next stage of the journey did not augur well. We were told that we had to leave most of our remaining belongings behind: only parcels and suitcases not exceeding 50 kilograms were allowed. This made it difficult for my mother to select the items of clothing she deemed essential. Only some bed linen, blankets, cleaning materials, toiletries, one suit or dress, one change of underwear and one pair of shoes were allowed. Non-perishable food could also be taken, but no tea, coffee beans, rice or alcoholic beverages. Personal belongings could not include any jewellery or other valuable objects. Writing materials were also strictly forbidden. I had to surrender the couple of toys I had saved from my large collection, with the exception of my favourite: the mechanical mouse, which I quietly secreted in my pocket.

I was anxious to know where we were going. My parents answered my persistent questioning by saying that we were not going very far: we would be travelling by train to Szeged, a much bigger town than Makó, and much nicer. The idea of a train journey cheered me up, and I looked forward to the trip, fortified by the knowledge that I had secured my favourite mouse as a travelling companion.

On the morning of our departure we had to get up very early: it was still dark when the officials came for us with gendarmes in tow. We were directed towards the synagogue. Here men and women were separated. But before we were taken to the station something else happened, an event I did not understand until much later. All the women, including my mother, were herded into the synagogue. When my mother eventually returned to us she was visibly distressed and dishevelled. Her dress was rumpled and her hair tousled. A quick glance at her face was sufficient to confirm that she had been crying. In a hushed voice, and in staccato sentences, she recounted what had happened inside the synagogue to my father, who, in a rare gesture of tenderness in front of me, drew her into his arms and kissed her. I could not hear a single word: she was deliberately trying to save me from the horror she was describing.

Many years later, as a teenager, I was attending one of the high holiday services; it must have been Rosh Hashanah, the New Year. It was a late September day; the synagogue was full of light. I was sitting on my own: it was not difficult to find an empty row; the community had been decimated by the war, and the remaining congregation could fill only a small proportion of the seats.

I always preferred to sit alone: I enjoyed the freedom of space around me. In this way I could also avoid being drawn into the smalltalk in which my fellow worshippers frequently engaged, and which as a teenager I disliked. There was perhaps another, less noble reason for my preference for solitude: to hide the fact that my mastery of Hebrew was poor and I had to use one of the prayer books with Hebrew on one side and Hungarian on the other. The service had reached a stage where the monotonous murmur of prayer had died down, followed by a deep, protracted silence before the cantor, a short man with a velvety voice, was due to embark on the next incantation. Suddenly, in the suspended air of expectation, I spotted the corner of a piece of folded paper, jammed between the side and the lid of the drawer of the pew to secure the lid in its precarious vertical position. Out of curiosity, I tried to ease the paper out, and as it yielded to my pull the success of my endeavour echoed throughout the synagogue. Instead of stopping in a horizontal position, the lid completed a full 180-degree trajectory and came to rest, unhinged, against the wooden legs of the pew. The noise was short and sharp. Everybody turned towards me and inquisitional faces looked at me accusingly: even the women in the gallery bent over to peer down to identify the culprit. Worst of all, the cantor abandoned his fixed gaze at the altar and turned towards the congregation. His fully opened mouth clapped shut again as he emitted, instead of the expected tremulous incantation, an irritated little cough. After weathering this public embarrassment, I audaciously decided, as the service resumed, to finish my exploration. The paper did not yield any secrets: it was yellowed and apparently blank. But as I gingerly lifted the lid to reposition it, I noticed a couple of words scribbled on it. The handwriting was in soft pencil, but only slightly smudged, written by an uncertain, shaking hand. A very short sentence, and a date. 'We have all been humiliated. 16 June 1944.'

The date, of course, was familiar, but the sentence did not convey any particular emotional charge. On the way home, I questioned my mother, who had also been in the synagogue and was no doubt embarrassed by my earlier interruption of the service, about the meaning of the inscription I had found. She fell silent as if she could not talk in the street. She answered only as we arrived home and had closed the gate behind us. On that day, 16 June 1944, all Jewish women from the ghetto had been herded into the synagogue with their luggage. At the entrance they were searched, and anything in excess of the permitted clothing was confiscated: all remaining valuables, including wristwatches and even wedding rings, were taken away. They were then shepherded up the few steps to the altar, and in front of the Ark of the Covenant their bodies were searched for hidden jewellery. Their private parts were not exempt.

Official records prepared after the war stated that the examination was carried out by midwives under the supervision of doctors. To facilitate the examination there was a water container with five litres for each midwife: about 500 women were examined using this single container, with no change of water. One of the supervising doctors demanded that the women should be stripped naked for the examination, but the mayor refused the request.

10

The journey to Szeged started badly. It was an early summer day, but instead of wearing only a light summer suit I was dressed as if we were preparing for a winter outing. I wore a shirt, a sweater, a suit and an overcoat; my mother wanted to keep as much of our clothing as possible without exceeding the weight limit. I protested about wearing all these warm clothes in summer, but gave up when she promised that it would be only a short trip. I had been eager to exchange the ghetto for something better in this large city nearby, and had imagined travelling in comfort, sitting on a cushioned seat, facing the direction of travel, listening to the whistle of the locomotive and seeing clouds of steam floating by the window. But it all turned out rather differently. We were brusquely ushered onto trucks: these were so crowded that there was no space to sit down. Mercifully, the journey to the station was short.

When we arrived I could not help noticing that the train

waiting for us could not be more different from the train I had expected: the carriages did not have large glass windows, only narrow rectangular openings, each barred with iron rods; these were wagons for transporting animals and goods. As we climbed the steps from the platform, I had to be lifted up by my father. Inside there was no compartment, nor any seats: the wagon was an empty space, which quickly filled up as people climbed in. They behaved not like passengers on a normal train, but more like frightened animals, fighting for a little space, clutching their luggage, as more and more people were squeezed in. I could hear the gendarmes shouting outside, exhorting people to be quicker, and screaming as more and more people were shoved into the wagon. Blows rained down on those who were too slow to mount the steep steps of the wagons with their heavy luggage. I clung to my mother, but later there was no point, since I was pressed against her by the weight of bodies. I was terrified that a sudden current of movement might separate me from her. Standing between my parents, I could hear the clink of heavy metal as the doors were bolted from the outside. Then the whistle blew, and the train slowly pulled out of the station.

The mayor of Makó had charged each 'passenger' one pengő to cover the expense of the transport from Makó to Szeged. The next day, 17 June, the local newspaper failed to report that some 1,600 members of the Jewish community that had been established in the town for centuries were herded like animals to the railway station, forced into wagons built for transporting animals, and deported to an unknown destination. Other events made the headlines, however. The county assembly celebrated the seventy-sixth birthday of Admiral Horthy. An air raid created havoc at the livestock market. And on that day the sun rose at 3.46 in the morning and set at 7.43 in the evening.

SZEGED: DESTINATION UNKNOWN

1

The journey to Szeged was terrifying and seemed never-ending. In the crowded wagon the air, depleted of oxygen and polluted by sweating bodies, soon became stifling; there was no space in which to move, or even to stretch a leg or an arm. I could not see anything since adults were towering above me. When I looked up only the ceiling of the wagon met my eyes through the narrow gaps between closely packed bodies. Although Szeged was only 20 miles away, a journey that normally would take little more than an hour, it was evening by the time the train reached its destination and the doors of the wagons were unbolted. We arrived not at the main station, our usual terminus in happier times, but at a much smaller station in a leafy suburb.

For me Szeged remains the town where I studied medicine and spent the first few years of my professional life, until my departure to London in 1968: the memories of our transit through the city have been erased by subsequent events. Only recently have I tried to recover a missing piece of the jigsaw puzzle of our journey: the few weeks we spent in Szeged. Our short stay there was nothing but the continuation of life in the ghetto in Makó, only much worse. Szeged is none the less an important milestone in the journey: it was the last place we stayed in Hungary before we crossed the border to Austria. It was in this town that our fate was finally sealed and the time-table for our transport decided.

2

At a specially convened meeting in Szeged, on 10 June 1944, the mayor of Makó was instructed, by two secretaries of state responsible for Jewish affairs, László Baky and László Endre, the Hungarian Eichmanns, to arrange the transport of Jews from his own town within a week; in any case no later than 16 June. In the overall plan for Hungary's part in the Final Solution, Szeged played an important role: it was the centre for the south-eastern sector of the country, one of six operational zones for the collection and deportation of Jews. Even before our arrival three to four families were crowded in a single flat, and a request by the leaders of the Jewish community for a living space of 8 square metres was turned down. Here the Jews were separated from the rest of the town as much as possible, and the over-zealous officials did their best to achieve this aim: the ghetto was surrounded by a fence 2 metres high, through which there was only one exit, constantly guarded. The windows of houses on the edge of the ghetto were painted white: even the sight of Jews might pollute innocent non-Jews. Buildings outside its boundaries earmarked for housing Jews or converted Jews had large yellow stars painted on them.

The ghetto was policed all the time, and no one could leave without permission and without a police guard: any contact with the outside world was prohibited. Those entering or leaving were searched. It was decreed that food supplies should be organized internally by a committee nominated by the Jewish Council; medical assistance consisted of what could be provided within the ghetto – even serious diseases could be treated only in a hospital within its boundaries (but no such hospital existed, since a request to transform a school into a hospital had been refused earlier). Even the daily rhythm of life was strictly regulated: the wake-up call was at 6 in the morning, and lights were switched off at 9 in the evening. It was decreed that silence should prevail at all times.

The ghetto was liquidated on 16 and 17 June, and the Jews transferred to a brick yard: this became the collection centre from which all the Jews from south-eastern Hungary were transported to various concentration camps.

3

On arrival from Makó we were taken to the grounds of a football club in Új-Szeged: this was a temporary holding area, from which Jews were transferred to the brick yard. We stayed in the football stadium only for a couple days – as soon as a transport of Jews had left the brick yard, freeing up some space, we were transferred there. Those who had arrived at the football ground first were fortunate, since they were able to occupy the changing-rooms and the storage spaces, while the rest had to make do with makeshift accommodation on the terraces. Small temporary tents had been erected, and we managed to get one of these. This provided a precarious shelter for the three of us, until one day a heavy downpour soaked everything we had.

For the first time I became aware of how the rules of polite behaviour had been abandoned under previously unknown pressure. The thin veneer of civilization, observed in everyday life, polished by compromise, had cracked, even at this early stage of the journey, when the fight was not for survival, only for small privileges. Arguments over a better place in the queue for water or a couple of extra inches of space to sleep were common. The gendarmes were everywhere, and they did not hesitate to use their truncheons to punish the slightest trespass. Many trespasses they simply invented, using them as an excuse to confiscate objects they coveted, or just to demonstrate their power. They were the masters: they could do anything they wanted. I quickly learned not to go anywhere without my mother. It was here in our rain-soaked tent that my parents finally abandoned the attempt to hide the fact that our journey was not going to end here: we were going to travel further from our home, to a foreign country.

We remained in the brick yard for a week, waiting for the train that was to deliver us to an unknown destination. I recall very little of this week: only memories of squalor and the stench of the latrine remain. By now it was difficult to keep clean, and with every passing day our personal hygiene and appearance deteriorated. Although we still had a bar of soap, it was hard to get hold of water. My mother used a wet towel in an attempt to keep me as clean as the circumstances allowed, but her daily effort was rewarded with diminishing returns. My hair was combed, as usual, but I missed the daily changes of fresh clothes and was bored with the monotonous choice available to me: I recalled with fondness my wardrobe at home, full of smart suits, trousers and jackets, sweaters and shirts. I kept wondering what had happened to them, and who might be wearing them. I hated to go to the latrine, and tried to postpone these visits as long as I could: I urinated surreptitiously anywhere in the yard when I thought no one was watching, but of course, in such a crowded place, many inmates noticed what I was doing. But by then they could not be bothered to reproach me.

For a while more than 8,000 men, women and children were crammed together in a place originally deemed suitable to serve as temporary accommodation for 2,000 – trains from other provincial towns continued to disgorge more and more weary passengers. The only landmark in the brick yard I remember was an enormous chimney: a solitary exclamation mark against the sky. We were often summoned to a large empty space around this chimney and kept waiting until a couple of officers arrived to harangue the crowd into surrendering any valuables they might still have, threatening that if they later found anything hidden, those in possession of jewellery or money would be shot.

One day I heard my mother and father arguing. I kept hearing the same word, 'lists', again and again, and I could not understand why my parents were so agitated. After the war my mother explained that the German officer in charge of the deportation had demanded from the leaders of the Jewish community a list of names of those under twelve and over fifty years of age. The implication was that the young and the old would go on separate transports, and my mother wanted to ensure that the three of us would be on the same train. Rumours started to circulate that we would be taken either to Poland or to Germany, and that our departure was imminent.

In the mean time our transport had been meticulously organized. The Secretary of State responsible for Jewish affairs, learning from the extensive experience of Eichmann in such matters, had specified every detail. Each train would be made up of forty-seven wagons. The twenty-third and the last wagons would be reserved for the guards. The unit of twenty guards would consist of a commandant and nineteen gendarmes. Each wagon would carry seventy to eighty people. Each would be equipped with two buckets: one for water, the other for urine and excrement.

4

Hungarian Jews deported this late in the war served as ideal negotiating cards. And the cards were soon to be played. With defeats followed by withdrawals on the eastern front, the source of cheap labour, the *Ostarbeiter* – workers from the east, who arrived more or less voluntarily to fill the gaps in the workforce – had dried up. This impending crisis forced Eichmann, who had previously been impervious to requests to release Jews for money, to agree on 14 June 1944, two days before we were deported from Makó, to negotiate with the Hungarian representatives of the Zionist Aid and Rescue Committee the transport of 30,000 Jews to Austria. According to the original agreement, this stay of execution would benefit 15,000 Jews from Budapest, while the rest of the quota would be made up from the provinces. When the figures were broken down for each provincial centre, the leaders of the Szeged ghetto were asked to select their share of 3,000 Jews. A committee of five had the unenviable task of drawing up this list, but once it had been completed the order was unexpectedly changed to reduce the number of selected to 2,400. Apart from distinguished Jews only children under twelve and adults older than fifty should be included. Such a list was prepared and read out in the brick factory at Szeged on the afternoon of 22 June 1944, to an uncomprehending and increasingly agitated crowd. No one knew for certain what would happen to those who were selected and what would be the fate of those who had not been included on the list, but there was no doubt that families would be broken up. My mother, being in her forty-fourth year, had not been selected, but my father, just entering his fifty-first year, a borderline case, probably was on the list. I was just approaching my fifth birthday, and so in principle I should have been included.

After the announcement of the names of those selected, panic broke out. Seeing the terror of the crowd, the commanding SS officer withdrew the list with immediate effect. He issued a new order two days later, on 24 June: 3,000 of those not included on the list of 2,400 should volunteer for the first transport. According to rumours, which immediately started to circulate, those on this first transport would remain in Hungary: it was not surprising that there was no shortage of volunteers.

Between 25 and 28 June 1944 three trains carrying 8,617

men, women and children left Szeged. The first train was marshalled to Auschwitz, while the other two were directed to Strasshof in Austria, outside Vienna. Although this has been disputed, apparently one of these two transports was originally also destined for Auschwitz, but was redirected to Strasshof to compensate for an earlier mistake. A train-load of Jews from another provincial town was erroneously sent to Auschwitz instead of Strasshof, and the Germans allowed one of the Auschwitz-bound trains from Szeged to be diverted to Strasshof instead. My parents and I were on one of the two trains travelling to Strasshof. My aunt Anna and my cousin Zsuzsi were on the train to Auschwitz. The gendarmes in charge of the trains could report with pride that all the transports were running on time and without any problems.

The arithmetic of fate is straightforward. Had we been on the train to Auschwitz, as a child of five I would have been sent immediately to a gas chamber – so my original chance of survival was one in three. The mistaken dispatch of a train-load of Jews to Auschwitz increased my chances of survival to two in three. In effect, I survived at the expense of other children.

Whether they were travelling to Auschwitz or Strasshof, the passengers on the trains did not know their destination. Those directed to Auschwitz were more likely to perish. Auschwitz was a place dedicated to destroying human beings, an aim it fulfilled with remarkable success. Yet many people survived. Strasshof was not destined to play such a prominent role in the Final Solution; it had only a small supporting role to play in the drama of Hungarian Jewry. Called in at the last moment as an extra, it offered a chance of survival.

STRASSHOF: IN A FOREIGN COUNTRY

1

The journey was interminable. The train progressed slowly and jerkily, now regaining speed, now slowing to a standstill, as if the exhausted engine had lost its momentum in the summer heat. The grinding and screeching of the brakes heralded only the false promise of arrival. When the train was stationary the conditions within the wagons deteriorated: movement at least brought in some fresh air, but in the immobile wagons, deprived of oxygen, the atmosphere soon became suffocating. The most coveted position was the area next to the tiny windows, and scuffles broke out between those competing to get closer to the source of fresh air. The containers for excrement and urine were overflowing, and passengers fought to get away from this foul-smelling area, but with about eighty people in each wagon there was not much room for manoeuvre. Without food or water, we were hungry and thirsty. The stench of sweat, urine and excrement was inescapable. But worst of all was the boredom, the monotony, the soul-destroying nothingness of waiting. No explanation was forthcoming from my parents: nobody knew where the train was carrying us.

Day gave way to night and then the sun rose again, and on the fourth or fifth day – or was it even longer? – the train came to a halt. We thought we had arrived, but we did not know where: the doors were not opened to release us to our mystery destination. It was rumoured that we were somewhere near Vienna, since the train had passed through the Austrian capital. After an age, we started to move again, and shortly thereafter the train braked again to a final stop. The doors were opened: we had arrived in Strasshof.

2

The first feeling was relief after the increasingly claustrophobic confinement of the previous days. From the railway sidings we were herded to an open field, where we had to form a line to pass in front of soldiers who were preparing a list of names. The suitcases and small packages we had been allowed to carry from Hungary were taken away, and we had to undress to be disinfected against lice: the smell of the disinfectant was nauseating and lingered for a long time. After days on the train, deprived even of elementary sanitation and unable to wash ourselves, we had become increasingly filthy and foul smelling: now we had the opportunity to shower, a luxury that recalled a seemingly distant past. After showering we retrieved our belongings, and for the first time after several days of hunger and thirst we were given some hot food and water. The food tasted revolting, like nothing I had tasted before, but we ate it ravenously, and arguments broke out among those who tried to get second helpings.

My parents found out after a while where we were, but they did not know how long we would be staying here or what we would be required to do. I did not understand the language the soldiers were speaking, and my mother explained that it was German, a language both my parents spoke. The soldiers were either German or Austrian, she said, and we were no longer in Hungary. This was a confusing discovery, since I could not understand why the enemy was kinder than our own people. Here we were treated better than at home: we were given food and drink, and they did not beat us. At least, not until we encountered our first Ukrainian guards. They were not prisoners like us – they had voluntarily joined the Germans in their retreat from Russia – but their privileged status did nothing to diminish their appetite for cruelty. They carried thick, long sticks, and these they wielded to devastating effect. Their savagery was unprovoked and indiscriminate: it was not necessary to commit what they could have perceived as a crime, or even a minor trespass against regulations; our very existence was enough to trigger their brutality. Incomprehensible as it was, they apparently enjoyed beatings us: they found sadistic delight in crushed bones and bloody faces.

Although I did not realize this until much later, it was in Strasshof that, for the first time I witnessed the practical implications of the concept of punishment without crime or cause: you are guilty simply because you exist. It was also here that I made my first anthropological observation, to be confirmed later elsewhere: the women guards were the more vicious of the species; in their brutality they easily outperformed the men. It was a shock to see women beating up defenceless prisoners who could have been their mothers or their children.

Strasshof was immeasurably large to a child. The first night after our arrival we slept in the open air, under a tree, and it was a great luxury, after wakeful nights on the train, to sleep under the warm summer sky. We rediscovered the use of our limbs: we could stretch our legs and flex our arms. We folded some of our spare clothing to improvise pillows. Later we moved into one of the barracks: this was regarded as promotion to a better, more comfortable place, but I would have preferred to stay in a tent, or even better to sleep in the open air. Occasional torrential downpours convinced me, however, that we were safer under a roof. But the barracks, made of wood, were filthy and crowded, and during the night bedbugs feasted on our bodies. The makeshift wooden beds had two or three tiers; there were no bedclothes and we slept on the wooden planks. These we tried to make more comfortable by lying on some of our clothes.

There were other members of my family in Strasshof, including three cousins and at least one aunt, but the place was large and I do not remember ever seeing them. As we were selected by different employers to work in different places, our paths separated.

One day my grandmother died. I cannot recall how: my mother later said she had suffered a heart attack. I do not remember any burial ceremony: my parents said a prayer, and that was all. My mother cried, but I was standing by her side without shedding a tear, numb and motionless, paralysed by fear. But death did not become my grandmother: it was strange to see her, the commanding matriarch suddenly diminished to a small, silent corpse, lying motionless under a foreign sky. Her silence was anomalous and ominous: there was no longer anyone to order around or quarrel with. She timed her death well, the last act of a resourceful woman with a long and full life: by dying suddenly in Strasshof, she avoided the later, harder stages of the journey, and saved herself further suffering and humiliation.

The days passed with monotonous regularity: roll-calls in the morning and the evening, a long wait for morning coffee, a longer wait for lunch and then for the evening meal. The food consisted usually of a vegetable soup, the infamous dietary staple of the concentration camp, the *Dörrgemüse*, in which, in most cases, no known vegetables could be identified. Occasionally I would fish out bits of leaf, bulb or the stem of an unknown plant: these my mother could sometimes identify as nettle or dried onion stems, usually discarded or used to feed animals. It tasted revolting, but I learned to eat it without protest: my mother explained that there was not going to be anything else, and we would die if we did not eat whatever we were given, however horrid it tasted. And since I was always hungry, further convincing was not necessary. This encounter with the unpalatable soup was the basis of a discipline to which I voluntarily subscribed throughout my later life and adhered to without the threat of starvation: I never leave food on my plate.

We did not stay long in Strasshof. The camp served as a marketplace for slave labour, and my mother and father, being relatively young and able, were soon selected by an employer to work in Wiener Neustadt.

WIENER NEUSTADT:

NOT FAR FROM VIENNA

1

The choice of freshly arrived manpower from Hungary on offer
in Strasshof was limited, and its quality far from ideal. Most
able young men had already been drafted in Hungary to serve
in ancillary corps as fodder in the German war effort. Jews, ill-
treated and malnourished, died by the thousands on the eastern
front. The Jews deported to Strasshof were thus mainly the
elderly, women and children. As we stood at roll-calls waiting to
be inspected, potential future employers, sometimes dressed in
military uniform but often in civilian clothes, passed along our
lines and picked those who seemed most promising and physically fit. Every day selected inmates left Strasshof, and since no
further transports were arriving, the overcrowding eased and
those who remained in the camp benefited from better accommodation. Latecomers, who on arrival had been sleeping in the
open air, could move into the barracks. Still, those who remained behind after each selection undoubtedly felt dejected,
and my parents were in high spirits when a silent nod signalled
that they should leave the line and follow their new master.

The journey in a truck from Strasshof did not last long. We
did not know the name of the place where we were going, but
my parents had been told that we would be staying near
Vienna. They were relieved at the news that at least the three
of us could remain together. There was also hope that the next
place would be better than the one we had just left. In this
assumption we were not disappointed.

2

In more peaceful times Wiener Neustadt, a small, picturesque town 30 miles south of Vienna in Lower Austria, could have been marketed as a holiday destination. With good transport to the cultural attractions of Vienna, and not far from the tranquillity of Vienna Woods, it could have been an ideal low-budget holiday location for those who could not afford the more elegant spa town of Baden near by. But our stay in Wiener Neustadt was not a holiday, nor was the town a holiday destination.

Wiener Neustadt became a militarily important industrial complex: from 1940 onwards its aircraft factory, the Wiener Neustädter Flugzeugwerke, manufactured one-quarter of all the Messerschmitt 109 fighter aircraft. In a factory that used to produce steam engines for the railways the assembly of A4 rockets began in earnest from 1943. All these developments rendered the place an important strategic target for the Allies, who, by the second half of 1944, were virtually unchallenged masters of the sky. During twenty-nine major air raids they dropped some 50,000 bombs, reducing the town to rubble and ashes by the end of the war. Of course, these bombing raids, which took place with increasing frequency and intensity as time passed, had a profound effect on our life.

3

On a scale of deprivation, life in Wiener Neustadt was considerably better than in Strasshof. We were not surrounded by barbed wire and families could stay together, although working conditions were strictly controlled. An order on the employment of Jews issued by the President of the Labour Office of the Lower Danube District (Gau Niederdonau) on 27 June 1944, in time for our arrival a few days later, painstakingly defines in seventeen points the work regulations. Jews are aliens and as such not members of the German business community (*Betriebsgemeinschaft*). Consequently, German labour laws cannot be applied to Jews. They are to receive free food and accommodation, and their work is to be remunerated on a scale according to age, sex and type of work: men are to earn more than women, the old more than the young, and industrial work is to be better remunerated than agricultural labour. The bank account into which salaries are to be paid is clearly specified and is controlled by the SS.

This was followed by the publication on 9 August 1944 of a further, even more detailed document, guidelines on the treatment of Hungarian Jews, by the Sondereinsatzkommando in Vienna. In thirty-two detailed points this edict spells out the 'dos and don'ts' of everyday life. No one could leave the camp without supervision. Children over the age of ten should be as productive as adults. Free time should be spent within the camp. Contact with other work groups or other nationalities was forbidden. Accepting food, presents or money was forbidden. Smoking was forbidden. Children over the age of two had to wear a distinguishing mark on their outer-garments. During air raids the Jews could not use the shelters.

Despite all the restrictions, it was a relief to be free of the wanton violence of the Ukrainian guards: even if their cruelty was not directed at us, we often had to witness their brutality in silent acquiescence. Leaving overcrowded Strasshof behind us, we had regained some of our lost privacy, and a semblance of normal family life had been restored, although our daily routine remained far from normal. We lived in a small room in one of the houses in the camp, which, as far as I recall, we did not have to share with anybody. The interminable waiting at roll-calls in the morning and in the evening was soon forgotten, and the days developed a certain rhythm, the monotony of which was interrupted only by air raids. Shortly after the morning wake-up call we cleaned ourselves: here there was no shortage of water, at least, so we were never thirsty and were able to maintain a reasonable standard of personal hygiene. For breakfast we drank some unidentifiable hot, thin brown liquid – it could have been coffee, tea or even soup – occasionally with a thin slice of bread, but mostly we had to do without bread. A truck then arrived to transport us to an open field, where the adults started work repairing roads damaged by bombing. I passed the days by inventing little games in my mind, watching the clouds or playing with other children within the radius prescribed, and closely supervised by my mother. Our repertoire of games was restricted, since we did not have any toys – not even a ball to throw around. But we were resourceful, as children are when left to their own devices: we played hide-and-seek in the nearby copse, organized running competitions on the freshly repaired stretch of road, collected wild flowers and offered them to unsuspecting women, chased butterflies and tried, in vain, to catch them, and identified shapes in the amorphous formations of clouds.

The greatest game of all was the air raids: these created mounting excitement and a sense of real danger. Everybody was terrified by the sound of the sirens, but nobody bothered to hide their satisfaction at such obvious evidence that the Nazis were losing the war. And as the months passed the raids became more frequent and more frightening. Hearing the first wail of the sirens indicated that the game was on. Everyone ran away from the road: we were not the target, but the road on which the adults were working was. Sometimes the planes passed overhead without releasing their bombs. Occasionally we could see them drop their bombs, like dead birds falling out of the sky, over the town. Usually the bombs fell on factories, and we could see the white plumes of the explosions, and columns of grey-black smoke rising on the horizon. When the sirens started up a truck was dispatched to collect and return us to the camp. As the truck appeared on the horizon we began to sprint towards it, and climbed on board as soon as it stopped. The moment the last person had been helped on to the truck, the driver revved his engine and sped away from the open field, leaving a trail of dust behind him. Sometimes, if the truck was late or the sirens did not give sufficient warning, we could see the aircraft formation in the distance: as they got nearer the roar of their engines became more menacing. After a while we became experts in assessing the degree of danger: from the sound of the explosions we knew how far away the target was. We were never hit, but the damage in town was all too obvious after the raids.

I do not know how it happened, but I remember that on one occasion we became stranded in the fields. We must have wandered away from the road, and when we heard the sound of sirens we hurried to the usual pick-up point. By the time we got there, however, we could not see the truck. We remained under the open sky as the first formation of bombers emerged from its camouflage of white cloud. We started to run away from the road and, after a short distance, in the middle of the field, we found a couple of trees: this was the best shelter available, although it was unlikely to provide much protection against exploding bombs. I obeyed my mother's order to lie face down in the long grass, and she lay next to me, wrapping one of her arms around my shoulders and partly covering my body with hers. Lying there listlessly, we waited for the by now familiar sequence of aerial fireworks and their attendant terrifying sound effects: the barely audible hum growing as the planes approached, reaching a climax of ear-splitting roar as they passed overhead, and the detonation of the bombs hitting their targets. Usually these were only distant thuds, but occasionally the bombs exploded nearer, the blasts making the air vibrate and shaking the earth. The most exhilarating part was waiting for the sound of the explosions: the longer the silence, the further away the hit. As we silently counted, holding our breath, my mother suddenly said: 'If we are going to die, at least we should see what happens,' and without any further explanation she turned over to face the sky. I quickly followed her example.

It was a warm sunny day, the blue sky dotted with only a few clouds. The roar of the bombers intensified as they passed overhead. They discharged their load over the town: we could hear the distant thuds of the explosions after the sound of the engines had faded. But suddenly the sky burst into a million suns, as if the Creator were sending an army of his messengers cloned in his own image to reward us for daring to look into the face of death. Or was this blinding light the harbinger of a spacecraft that was going to land at any minute in the field? Or a miniature milky way of stars descending to earth from another universe? Or nothing more than the Allies' new secret weapon to stun the enemy? Shimmering strips of light were still descending in billowing waves, floating and dancing, swirling in the breeze. We could hardly bear the intensity of the light and had to close our eyes from time to time. But as the strips of light fell nearer to earth we discovered what they were. The magic evaporated: billions of strips of aluminium foil cascased down from the planes to interfere with enemy communications. And they formed a loosely-woven metal carpet on the long grass. I gathered several handfuls and squeezed them into a ball: it became a new toy to enliven the tedium of the days for a while.

4

We had no wireless and any contact with people in the town was discouraged. News of the war did not reach us: only whispered rumours circulated, never confirmed. Then we unexpectedly acquired, albeit for a short time, an Austrian friend and a reliable source of news. Franz suddenly appeared in the house where we lived one day. He must have been my father's age, but to me he seemed ancient. His suntan betrayed the fact that he must have been working in the open air for a long time; his long light brown hair had also been bleached by the sun. An unkempt beard framed his face. He pushed a battered bicycle plagued by rust: it was surprising that the wheels, which had long ago lost their proper shape, were still able to turn. Before the war he had been an engineer, he said, but had recently become a farmhand. He clearly felt at ease and confided in us without prompting. He hated the Nazis. He also disapproved of what they had done to the Jews. But he was a messenger with good news, and confirmed the rumours that the war was going badly for the Nazis: the Allies were making progress on the second front, Paris had been liberated, and the Germans were withdrawing on the eastern front. It was only a question of time before the Red Army reached Hungary and Austria. The war would soon end and we would be free. This was the news my parents were waiting for.

Our mysterious visitor then cycled away, and we did not know whether we would see him again. But he came back a couple of days later. Again, he appeared unexpectedly, stayed for a short time and left abruptly. I did not know then that these were clandestine visits; little acts of defiance, solidarity and courage. One day he brought me a set of coloured pencils in a tattered cardboard box. It was an old set – the ends of a couple of pencils bore the visible teeth marks of someone desperately searching for inspiration – but they were all freshly sharpened. He explained to my mother that these had been his son's when he was a child, and this son was presently at the front. Overwhelmed by such generosity, my mother, after thanking him profusely, said: '*Aber wir haben kein Papier.* But we do not have any paper.'

The next time he turned up with a small dog-eared notebook

of lined sheets, not ideal for drawing but probably the best he could lay his hands on. He came again a couple of times, and then he disappeared all of a sudden. We never knew what had happened to him. Was he warned by our employer that his visits were disapproved of? Was he imprisoned for another act of defiance? Was he called up for military service despite his age? Or was he killed in one of those air raids, which he, like us, both dreaded and welcomed at the same time? We will never know. But we sorely missed his visits, the news he brought and the bridge he formed between us and the outside world.

5

Hunger was a constant companion. As time passed there was less and less food. The brown fluid masquerading as coffee and the hot liquid with its few slimy floating islands of vegetable, served as soup, still made their unwelcome appearance on the daily menu, but the slices of bread became even thinner, and the occasional treats of jam or grisly meat or salami rarer. Help sometimes came from unexpected quarters, however. We would be walking in the street when suddenly a door would open, a hand would appear as in a puppet show, the rest of the body remaining hidden behind the door, and a piece of bread or an apple would be hurriedly pressed into our hands by our invisible supporters. Before we could say thank you the hand would be withdrawn and the door shut. Sometimes these little acts of kindness were more courageous and defiant. A door would open and we would be asked in a hushed voice to enter. The invitation would be reinforced with a quick tug on the arm while our anonymous benefactor, after carefully scanning the street, produced a glass of milk. '*Bitte, schnell. Für das Kind. Please, quickly, for the child.*'

During the summer and early autumn, when the weather

was still warm, we left the window of our room open and, returning to the house in the evening or late afternoon, we occasionally found a couple of apples, a slice of bread or a small portion of cheese wrapped in paper on the floor.

We also became more enterprising in acquiring sustenance. Not very far from where we worked there was a farm with a large pigsty. My mother discovered that the pigswill contained boiled potatoes: some still in one piece in their skins. We would attempt to fish out these treasures, but timing was crucial: we had to get there before the pigs had a chance to bury their greedy snouts in the trough. In this daily race our luck ebbed and flowed; usually we were too late and the troughs were already empty by the time we got there.

6

We spent five months in Austria, yet the information at my disposal, and the recollections I can summon up, remain the sketchiest of the whole journey. While impressions of events have been indelibly imprinted on my memory, the names of streets and villages and towns we passed through or worked in have been lost. The names I do recall are Wiener Neustadt, Leitha and Wiener Neudorf. I have a fragmentary recollection of being transported from Wiener Neustadt across the River Leitha to Neudorf to work in the fields or to repair roads, but my parents, my travelling companions, are not alive to say: 'Oh yes, this is where we were.'

I am frustrated that I cannot account for the place where I spent five months of my life, ashamed of not remembering, angry at not being able to find the missing pieces of the jigsaw. Dates I know, but the precise locations where our everyday drama unfolded have been buried beyond recall. I need some-where to anchor the flotsam and jetsam of my memories of that distant summer and autumn somewhere in Austria. A witness who could say: 'Yes, we remember you; you were with us in that village. We remember your parents. Your father was a quiet man, did not say much, could not do much, however hard he tried. He was very weak by then and did not have much will to go on. But your mother was different, a strong woman and a good worker; no doubt the employers liked her.' But there are no such witnesses. Not even a list, compiled by a conscientious bureaucrat, with our names on it.

A book published over a decade ago, in 1991, provided me with a lead, however. Written in Hungarian but with a summary in both English and German, *Roads from Hell* by the Hungarian historian Szabolcs Szita is an excellent document on the fate of Hungarian Jews in Austria in 1944 and 1945, a scholarly analysis of the historical background to one of the least well-documented chapters in the Final Solution of Hungarian Jewry. The book lists all the places where Hungarian Jews deported to Strasshof were later engaged in slave labour, chiefly in Vienna and Lower Austria but sometimes further afield in Czechoslovakia. And in this list was a place that sounded vaguely familiar: Richterstrasse, in Wiener Neustadt. And Wiener Neudorf is just across the River Leitha. Could it be that I had recovered the name and address of our employer in Wiener Neustadt? The submerged memory of that distant summer and autumn of long ago chimed with the information provided by the book to point to a more precise place on the map. Yes, there had been children there. And yes, we had repaired roads. But how could I be certain that this was the place we had been?

As I researched I had a sudden compulsion to recover yet another lost fragment of my life and to find out more about the death of my grandmother in Strasshof. I cannot pretend that in thinking of my grandmother I am assailed by angelic images of a kindly, silver-haired old lady, liberally dispensing chocolates to her numerous grandchildren. She was not like that at all. She was a strict woman with firm favourites, and I was not one of them. I was five when she died, and shamefully I cannot summon up any fragment of those golden moments children so easily conjure up when they think of their grandmother. As in life, she remained in death the faded image of a distant woman. Yet after so many years I wanted to know the details of her death. But where should I start? Where could I find a lead?

Being so meticulous in the business of death, the Nazis must have left some records – a directory or a register, a list of names containing all the relevant information about those who arrived in Strasshof. Did not I recall that we had to line up on arrival and have our particulars taken? Others have confirmed this. Szita also states in his book that the directory of new arrivals prepared in Strasshof was later stored in Vienna, and handled by several Hungarian women. Vienna was a suitable place to start my search.

7

The Documentation Centre of Austrian Resistance (Dokumentationsarchiv des Österreichischen Widerstandes) is in the Old Town Hall (Altes Rathaus) in Wipplingerstrasse, in the very centre of Vienna. The Documentation Centre was established by ex-resistance fighters and anti-Fascist historians in 1963, and twenty years later became a foundation with government support.

The Centre's offices are on the far side of a quadrangle. I was ushered into the office of the Director, Dr Elisabeth Klamper. We had already exchanged a couple of e-mails, and fortunately I was saved the chore of explaining further about the purpose of my visit. By way of introduction she explained that the fate of Hungarian Jews in Austria was not the primary thrust of research at the Centre, but if there was any relevant document to which I wished to have access she would be happy to help. In the mean time one of her assistants undertook a computer search and downloaded some references available in the archives. Among these I found one of the documents I had been seeking: Werner Eichbauer's 'Die "Judenlager" von Wiener Neustadt, Felixdorf und Lichtenwörth' (Jewish camps of Wiener Neustadt, Felixdorf and Lichtenwörth). This is a doctoral thesis, resulting from a research project at the Institute of Contemporary History of Vienna University, published in March 1987. On page 17 I found my first lead: about one-third of the inmates in Wiener Neustadt were from Makó. There is an analysis of the camp in Gymelsdorfer Gasse, but nothing about Richtergasse. In Gymelsdorfer Gasse, in the middle of August 1944, there were 234 Hungarian Jews: fifty men, eighty-eight women over twelve years of age, sixteen unsuitable for work, and eighty children.

There are two attached lists with names, birthplaces, birth dates and identification numbers: one for adults, another for children. I could not find our names: neither my parents' nor mine. But I recognized many other names from Makó, and on the list of children I come across the M brothers: I knew all three, and the youngest, who at the time was under four years of age, became a good friend of mine at secondary school.

But more interestingly, Eichbauer states that the number of inmates did not change until January 1945, and decreased for the first time, to 227, in February. Since we left Austria at the end of November, and on 7 December we arrived at the next staging post on our journey, we could not have shared the fate of the Jews in Gymelsdorfer Gasse. Most of the inmates were assigned to Rudolf Babka, undertaking heavy clearance work in the severely bomb-damaged town.

If there was a camp in Richtergasse, why is it not mentioned in this thesis? Was there a separate list for Richtergasse? Or were we omitted from this list? Is it possible that we were not in Wiener Neustadt but in another work camp altogether? I managed to trace Eichbauer: I telephoned him and later we exchanged letters. He was helpful, but his research for a Ph.D. degree had been undertaken some fifteen years previously. He confirmed from his notes that the lists published in his thesis were based on material in the archives in Wiener Neustadt, and at the time these lists were the only ones available.

I also met Dr Eleonore Lappin, who works in St Pölten, outside Vienna, at the Institute for the History of Jews in Austria. She is a tall woman with straight brown hair going grey at the roots and large, expressive brown eyes. I told her about our journey, about our stay in Austria. She smiled. 'You know,' she said, 'they did not mean to kill you.' She was referring to the deal between the Nazis and Jewish organizations.

I asked about the death of my grandmother, providing her with some of the basic information, including her maiden and married names. In a death register she found someone with the same surname but the wrong first name who had been born in 1874 and died on 7 July 1944 in Strasshof. The first name of the deceased was that of my mother: is it possible that they had confused the name of my mother, who had reported the death, with that of my grandmother? The date of death was plausible: my grandmother died soon after our arrival at the beginning of July. But my grandmother's birth certificate, which I received a few weeks later from Hungary, dispelled any lingering doubt: she had been born in 1866, eight years prior to the birth of her namesake.

Dr Lappin was full of sensible advice, and encouraged me to contact a couple of people who might be able to help. The name of Dr Karl Flanner, a local historian who chronicled the fateful years between 1938 and 1945 and was imprisoned by the Nazis during the war, came up again, and I decided to contact him the next day.

He decided to put a notice in a couple of local papers and in the official town gazette, requesting information about our family's stay in Wiener Neustadt in the summer and autumn of 1944. But not surprisingly, nobody had any recollections concerning us.

8

The train took thirty-five minutes to reach Wiener Neustadt from the Südbahnhof in Vienna. Wiener Neustadt is now an affluent place: it is difficult to envisage the town flattened by Allied bombing towards the end of the war. Prosperity is everywhere: new houses, many painted in subdued pastels, enticing shops and lovingly restored old monuments. Two halves of a department store straddling a busy street are connected by a bridge: the aspiration of a larger town. Even the old railway station is being rebuilt in stainless steel, plate glass and polished granite.

The town's archives are housed in a venerable building. This is one of the oldest archives in Lower Austria, with an extensive collection dating back to the Middle Ages. As I pressed the bell, an elegant woman with blond hair and grey-blue eyes, wearing a stylishly cut white linen dress, answered the door. By a strange coincidence she was Dr Beatrix Bastl, senior lecturer at the Institute of History of Vienna University, the archivist of Wiener Neustadt I came to see. She spoke fluent English, and this made my task of explaining the nature of my visit much easier. I told her that I came to see whether there was any evidence of our stay in the archives. I wrote down our names, my father's, my mother's and mine, with dates and places of birth. Disappointingly, she could not find our names in the register. I told her that we probably had worked for the building firm of Rudolf Babka in the Richtergasse camp. She produced a book, *Addressenbuch der Stadt Wiener Neustadt 1937*, the address book of the town published by the community of

Wiener Neustadt in the year preceding the Anschluss. In this we found Marie Babka, shopkeeper (*Gemischtwarenhändlerin*), and Rudolf Babka, dam builder (*Deichgräbermeister*), both who were living at that time at Wetzsteingasse 14. Among the advertisements at the end of the book, there was one devoted to Rudolf Babka's firm, the Enterprise for Civil Engineering and Road Building.

Richtergasse is a short street towards the edge of town. It is a quiet, leafy, cleanly-swept street with chestnut trees on either side. One side of the street is fully built up, lined by well-maintained private houses with small front gardens. But on the other side of the street, among the houses with uneven numbers, there is a long gap after number 5: a space with a few overgrown bushes, tall thistles, unkempt grass and wild flowers adjoined by a car park on the corner with Gymelsdorfer Gasse. Was this empty place the site of the camp where we lived and from where we were transported to work for nearly five months from July to November 1944? Or is it a bomb site bypassed by town planning? And was Rudolf Babka our employer? I needed to find answers to these questions.

From Richtergasse I turned the corner into Gymelsdorfer Gasse, a street leading to the centre of town. There was another, much larger camp on this street, but the prosperous present has masked all remnants of the past: it is an immaculate street with no guilty signs of forced labour. From an open-air pool the happy cries of children were the only noise to disturb the torpor of the late summer afternoon. The most distinguished building in the street is the Bösendorfer house at number 42, the site of manufacture of some of the most venerated musical instruments in the world. The labour camp was just a few yards away at number 52, where the open-air baths are at present.

9

Wiener Neudorf is a small village across the River Leitha, a long but pleasant walk from the town centre of Wiener Neustadt. As a last resort I tried the archives there. The archivist confirmed that there were two work camps associated with the Ostmark aircraft engine factory: to these slave labourers from various countries and of different religions were assigned. But while there was general information on the camps, no individual lists of workers have survived.

In the end I had to accept defeat: I will never know for certain in which places we stayed and for how long between the beginning of July and the end of November 1944. But one thing is certain. At the end of November we continued our journey from Strasshof.

Bergen-Belsen

1

The routines of everyday life accustomed us to life in Austria: the wake-up call in the morning, a rushed attempt to wash ourselves, the breakfast of warm coffee, accompanied on good days with a little bread and jam, the arrival of the pick-up truck to take us to the fields, the little diversions and games I indulged in while my parents were working in the field or repairing roads, the excitement of air raids, the ride back from the fields, the occasional encounter with people from the town, the evening meal. This last was far from enjoyable, but none the less we looked forward to it, hoping that something more palatable than the customary vegetable soup would arrive, even if only in the form of a piece of gristly, sinewy meat.

During late autumn the weather suddenly turned cold: freezing winds swept in from the mountains. Despite my mother's foresight in packing some warmer clothes for the journey, we soon realized how insufficiently we were protected against the plunging temperatures. Feeling cold combined with hunger produced a sensation of permanent weakness and malaise.

One day – it must by then have been late November – our life in Wiener Neustadt came to an abrupt end, without warning. We were not prepared for the next stage of the journey, and for a while no one knew for certain where we were going. First we were transported back to Strasshof. Being herded back to the camp here was a shock – the sight of the railway tracks fanning out towards unknown destinations posed a new threat

rather than offering any expectation of escape or hope of returning home. But the camp had changed dramatically. The
barracks were still there, as was the forest, but the place itself
had become quieter. There were not many people around: it
was all so different from the crowds we had encountered on
our arrival in early July. Where had all the inmates gone? What
happened to the noisy, argumentative, displaced people milling
around?

Soon we knew the reason. We stayed in Strasshof for a few
days only, when we were ordered to collect our belongings and
were marched to the railway station for yet another journey.
We were packed into wagons without food or drink, the guards
shouting and shoving those who did not climb inside quickly
enough, making liberal use of their truncheons to underline
their orders and to ensure that no space was wasted in the
wagons. The abrupt departure, the brutality of guards and the
overcrowding were ominous signs. Most disturbingly, we still
did not know our destination. Rumours circulated, some
freshly minted, others reprocessed: we were going to be transported to concentration camps in the German-occupied territories in the east, or to camps within the Reich. The more
optimistic insisted that we would be exchanged for German
prisoners of war and would soon be heading home.

We feared the worst, but the reality turned out to be more
terrible than nightmares.

2

Bergen-Belsen concentration camp lies on the Lüneburg
Heath, in Lower Saxony, northern Germany, some 40 miles
north-east of Hanover. The nearest town of any size is Celle, a
picturesque place which now merits two stars in the Green
Michelin guide, indicating a tourist attraction worth a detour.
But as its double name suggests, Bergen-Belsen was located

between the small town of Bergen, some four miles away, and one mile from the tiny village of Belsen. Of the two places only Bergen had a railway station, and it was there that the transports disgorged the future inmates of the camp after an excruciating journey.

The name Bergen-Belsen first appeared on 27 April 1943 in a list of addresses in a circular issued by the SS Main Office of Economic Administration, an organization responsible for the overall administration of the concentration camps. On 10 May 1943 the same organization officially declared the establishment of the 'Bergen-Belsen civilian internment camp'. But this was soon changed to Bergen-Belsen 'detention camp', for the simple reason that a civilian internment camp could be more easily subjected to the scrutiny of international bodies, including the Red Cross.

Bergen-Belsen occupied a special position in the intricate system of German concentration camps: it was not conceived as an extermination camp. Indeed, it did not fit conveniently into any of the categories of camp – extermination, labour, experimental, sick, training, or a combination of these functions. It was purely accidental that people, destined to become bargaining cards in negotiations with the Allies, were dying there by the thousands; a mere hitch in the brilliant scheme to obliterate the lives of millions. If Auschwitz, Buchenwald and Mauthausen were the pinnacles of achievement of the Final Solution, where mass extermination was carried out with clockwork precision, Bergen-Belsen was clearly a failure. Human beings died there not because they were systematically murdered according to some plan: they died of starvation, infection and deprivation. The end result may have been the same, but the original intention was quite different. In Bergen-Belsen events did not follow the master plan: it was the dissonant chord in the perfect harmony of a masterly orchestrated *Götterdämmerung*. Its transformation from a military camp for the

German army to a prisoner-of-war camp, and its later trans-
mutation into a concentration camp, was gradual, and evolved
through various phases.

Its origins date back to 1936, when it opened as a labour
camp: some thirty barracks were erected to house German and
Polish workers who were building further accommodation for
the military at a time when German rearmament was steaming
ahead. In the next phase of its existence Bergen-Belsen was a
prisoner-of-war camp: some of the workers were evacuated to
make space for the first French and Belgian prisoners of war,
who arrived there in 1940 after France's demise.

Following the invasion of the Soviet Union on 22 June 1941,
plans were drawn up to extend the camp in anticipation of a
much larger population of prisoners. In place of the workers'
camp a vast central space was created, and further barracks
were built, while the whole camp was surrounded by fences
with barbed wire and watchtowers. The remaining workers left
and Bergen-Belsen was officially designated Stalag XI C/311, its
purpose now to accommodate captured Soviet soldiers.

By November 1941 around 21,000 prisoners of war had arrived, but the camp itself was not ready: the construction of
the barracks had been delayed, and the prisoners were housed
in temporary accommodation, many in hastily erected tents.

The transformation of Bergen-Belsen from a prisoner-of-war
camp into a concentration camp, the next phase in its evolution, began as late as 1943. Stalag XI C/311 gradually emptied
towards the end of 1942, and was finally disbanded in 1943.
Although it continued to house a hospital for Soviet prisoners
of war, the vacated space seemed ideal to accommodate Jewish
hostages. It was part of the overall administrative machinery of
concentration camps, yet the special (if not exactly privileged)
position of Bergen-Belsen was acknowledged by its name: it
was an *Aufenthaltslager*, or detention camp. At the beginning of
1943, the plan to hold Jews for future exchange with those

Germans who had been interned by the Allies was approved by von Ribbentrop, the Nazi foreign minister. In the spring of the same year Himmler ordered the establishment of a special *Lager*, and Bergen-Belsen was chosen. The first group of so-called exchange Jews arrived there in July 1943.

Nothing was left to chance in the plans. Jews to be selected for this special treatment and saved from extermination camps were meticulously defined at the outset. They included those with connections with influential people in enemy countries, those who could be used as hostages to apply political or economic pressure, and prominent Jewish leaders. Not all the Jews who arrived in Bergen-Belsen fulfilled these criteria, however. Soon the camp's administration realized that most of the so-called exchange Jews were remaining in the camp far longer than planned, and that the exchange programmes were not progressing as smoothly as originally envisaged. At this stage the SS Main Office of Economic Administration became reluctant to maintain Bergen-Belsen's status as a place of detention solely for exchange Jews, and in March 1944 the camp was assigned a new function: it became a reception camp for those prisoners who were too exhausted or sick to be able to contribute anything further to the German war effort. The Nazis cynically called it a recuperation camp, although no measures were taken to provide medical help for those invalid people who arrived there from the end of March 1944. Thus, gradually during the course of 1944, Bergen-Belsen was transformed into a concentration camp.

The event that clinched this transformation was a change in the immediate management of the camp: on 2 December 1944 the commandant, SS Major Haas, not entirely trusted among the highest circles of the SS, was replaced by SS Captain Josef Kramer, who had previously served in the Auschwitz-Birkenau extermination camp, an excellent training ground for the atrocities that would later take place in Bergen-Belsen. Kramer was ideally suited to be commandant during this closing chapter of the camp's history: he was known to be mercilessly brutal and at the same time unquestionably subservient to his superiors. He brought several of his closest collaborators with him from Auschwitz, and they proceeded to transform Bergen-Belsen into a hell on earth. As more and more transports arrived, carrying inmates who had been evacuated from other concentration camps, the overcrowding, appalling sanitary conditions, epidemics and starvation, and the cruelty of the SS guards, resulted in the images of death and deprivation that shook the world after the camp was liberated. Some of those inmates who had the misfortune to be guests of both concentration camps compared Bergen-Belsen unfavourably with Auschwitz. It was only a few days after Kramer's appointment that we arrived in Bergen-Belsen from Strasshof.

3

The map of Bergen-Belsen lies in front of me. To be strictly accurate I am looking at several maps: there are three schematic drawings at the end of Eberhard Kolbe's book about the camp, published in German in 1962. These clearly show three stages of evolution: the layout of the camp until the autumn of 1944, between November 1944 and the end of January 1945, and from February until April 1945. The expansion of the camp was impressive. New barracks were built, latrines dug and additional fences erected to provide reception areas for the new transports. One of the maps shows a sketch from 1942/43 of Stalag XI C/311: the layout of the prisoner-of-war camp. Although Bergen-Belsen became a single administrative entity, there were different camps, sometimes separated by an internal fence through which all communication was forbidden. The origin and the destination of the inhabitants of these separate camps were different. The Star Camp originally accommodated some 4,000 Jews destined for exchange, mostly but not exclusively from the Netherlands and Greece. The name of the camp referred to the Star of David, the symbol its inhabitants had to wear, although as a special dispensation they were allowed to remain in civilian clothes. The much smaller Neutrals' Camp housed citizens of neutral countries, while the Special Camp housed several thousand Polish Jews who had arrived in mid-1943 holding so-called *promesas*, temporary passports, which were never honoured, to South American countries. The Prisoners' Camp was the first to be established and its inmates, the *Häftlinge*, had to wear the striped uniform: they were obliged to work, and in general their treatment was worse than that meted out to the inmates of other camps. A Large Women's Camp and a Small Women's Camp were established later to accommodate those transported from other concentration camps which, being in the east, were in immediate danger of falling into Russian hands. The Hungarians' Camp was established in July 1944 for 1,670 Hungarian Jews who were to be exchanged for money and goods. The inmates here were also allowed to wear civilian clothes without the Star of David emblem, and they were exempt from work. This original group left Bergen-Belsen in two phases: in August and on 4 December 1944. We arrived the next day and, although it is impossible to be certain, we must have occupied the barracks freshly vacated by our compatriots, who by then were travelling towards freedom. Our fate, however, was going to be quite different from theirs.

4

The journey to Bergen-Belsen was unlike any we had undertaken before. The hunger, the thirst, the physical discomfort in the overcrowded wagon, the stench of excrement and urine overflowing from the bucket were all familiar from previous transports, but it was the cold which made all the difference. Even the initial warmth generated by closely pressed human bodies soon dissipated as the outside temperature sank well below zero at night. It was early December, and snow had already fallen in some of the places we passed through. This time there were no desperate fights for fresh air in the vicinity of the tiny window: blasts of wind occasionally swept in clouds of snow. All sense of time disappeared. It was a journey into oblivion, as if time would erase all our faculties, demolish the very physical existence of our bodies, and the wagons would arrive empty.

This arrival was very different from our arrival in Strasshof in July: Strasshof had felt temporary from the moment we disembarked from the train, but as we drew into the station at Bergen we knew we had reached our final destination.

As the door of the wagon was unbolted we saw that the SS were waiting: we were expected. The cold was so penetrating that some people were reluctant to leave the safety of the wagons, but the guards' exhortations were unambiguous. 'Raus! Raus! Out! Out!' they shouted, and they did not hesitate to beat those who were slow to disembark. But not everybody got out: as they emptied, a couple of people remained, lying on the floor; they had died unnoticed during the journey. The wagons had been so packed that they could only fall, to be trampled underfoot, as people disembarked.

We were lined up and ordered to march, and we did so without a word of protest: how we had the strength I do not know. I remember that my mother was alternately pulling and pushing me: she was too weak to lift me up and carry me. We were on a wide road, lined by fir trees, silent and overbearing witnesses of our march. I do not know for how long we walked, but it seemed for ever. Although we were exhausted no one dared to stop for more than a second, since those who did so were immediately set upon by the guards and beaten. The wind was also our enemy: from time to time it unleashed with such ferocious gusts that it was as if it intended to sweep the road clean of us, blots on the landscape of an inclement winter. It was a walk to the end of the world, yet it was only four miles to the camp from Bergen station. Suddenly a group of low buildings appeared on the horizon, set back from the road: we had arrived.

5

I recall little of the chaos that attended our arrival, but two events I will not forget. First, we were separated: my father was ordered to go one way with other men, while my mother and I had to join a large group of women, some of whom were also with children. This was an ominous sign: a further proof that life in Bergen-Belsen was not going to follow the pattern of the months we had spent in Austria. And suddenly we deeply regretted that we had been forced to leave our temporary home there. We had plumbed the depths of self-deception to convince ourselves that the summer and autumn we had spent in Austria were somehow only a mild aberration of normal life: after all, we had been able to live there as a family and had not been separated. We could even claim that we had enjoyed an element of freedom, since we could talk, even if only furtively, to the Austrians, who also helped us whenever they could. Even the brutality of the Ukrainian guards in Strasshof had been forgotten: it had been haphazard and opportunistic. But Bergen-Belsen was something else again.

As my father disappeared with the other men, the guards herded us to a barrack in which we were ordered to deposit our last remaining belongings before we were subjected to a disinfection procedure.

Like everybody else, my mother had surrendered the luggage we had carried from Strasshof, but she was still clutching close to her body a small dirty canvas bag, apparently reluctant to relinquish it. One of the guards started to shout at her, demanding that she deposit the bag with the rest of her luggage at once. And to encourage her, the guard, a well-built blond woman in SS uniform, wearing polished black boots, drew closer to her. What happened next was over in seconds, yet I mentally recorded it in slow motion, and replayed it many times subsequently. My mother said, first in Hungarian, then in German: 'Nein. Dieses ist mein Schmuck. No, these are my jewels,' and she drew the canvas sack even nearer to her body.

Such a display of disobedience was unexpected, and silence suddenly chilled the air around us even more. The guard stepped back and hit my mother so hard that she fell over backwards. But even in falling she did not let the bag go; only as she lay on the floor did she release it. A couple of shrivelled apples and a single onion slowly rolled out. The silence remained unbroken. No one laughed. Poor woman, they must have thought, she has lost her mind. Nobody had any jewels by then: everything, including wedding rings and religious objects made of gold or silver, had been taken away in Hungary. It was unimaginable that anybody could have retained items of jewellery.

My mother was ordered to stand up. She obeyed, and looked at me with a vacant stare I had never seen before. She did not see me. I called to her; she did not respond. She did not recognize me. Suddenly I was terrified.

The guard left the barrack, and came back with a man wearing a soiled white coat. We were ordered to go with him. My mother started to move, falteringly, as if she were uncertain of the next step, as if she were walking in her sleep. I automatically followed her: the moment of terror, when I had thought I would be separated from her, had passed.

We walked along several barracks and entered another low building. We were in a large room crowded with beds, each one occupied, some by two people. There were a couple more people wearing white coats. I realized that we were in the camp infirmary. We waited until they found an empty bed for my mother. She must be very ill, I thought, because she still does not recognize me. When I talked to her, she looked straight through me without answering. I did not know where my father was: he must have been in one of the men's barracks, but I could not simply walk out and try to find him. Where would I go? Whom could I ask?

My mother remained silent, and continued to ignore me, as if I were not there. I was alone. I did not know what to do. One of the men in white came, and gave my mother an injection. Soon she fell asleep. Suddenly a woman appeared and asked in my own language: 'Are you Hungarian?'

I nodded.

Then she said: 'Do not worry; your mother will be all right. She is just exhausted, she needs some sleep.'

I did not believe her, thinking she probably wanted to console me. But she was right. The next morning my mother woke up and began to talk to me as if nothing had happened. That same day we were discharged from the infirmary.

6

We were assigned to one of the barracks for women within the *Ungarnlager*, a collection of barracks for Hungarians. Ours, number II, was a low stone building with rows and rows of three-tiered bunks. Since we had arrived late we could claim only what at the time were regarded as the least coveted places, on one of the top tiers. Although even this third level was not very high, it required some acrobatics to reach it, and I needed my mother's help to get into my bunk. In reality it was not my bunk, it was a space I shared with my mother. Illusionary boundaries were created by our remaining personal belongings,

returned to us after disinfection, and there were frequent trespasses on the part of those claiming the adjacent territory.
There was a thin mattress filled with straw, so hard that it was
not much of an improvement on the wooden boards of the
bunk, and a flimsy blanket, insufficient to keep out the cold.
But there were no sheets or pillows, and we made our bed with
our own remaining clothes. Despite all our efforts to make a
warm nest, the bunk remained a hard and uncomfortable place
to sleep.

Later we realized that we were fortunate to have top bunks:
no emaciated legs ever dangled in front of us, nor were we ever
the unfortunate victims of the incontinence of those lying
above. The weak and the exhausted could not always reach the
latrines in time and soiled their own bunks and those below
them, events which became increasingly common during the
outbreaks of dysentery and other gastrointestinal infections.
Being on top, we also benefited from the parsimonious light,
when there was electricity, by the bulb dangling above our
heads. We also had a little more space: the distance between
the tiers of bunks was small, creating a claustrophobic space
for those sleeping on the first and second levels, but although
we on the top were less protected from the cold we had only
the ceiling above us. By the evening we were exhausted and
weak but the cold kept us awake long after we climbed up to
our bunks.

In the centre of the concrete floor of the barrack stood a
couple of makeshift wooden tables and benches: some of the
inmates had their meals there, while others withdrew to their
bunks to eat their food. A single latrine often overflowed. It
was difficult to obtain water: sometimes there was not enough
for drinking, and using water to wash ourselves or our underwear became a luxury. A large, bitterly cold space was our
'bathroom'. Several taps dispensed freezing water over a long
trough, which ran the entire length of a wall. It took great

determination to undress in the cold air and wash ourselves in the icy water, but my mother mercilessly subjected herself and me to this daily cleansing.

Arguments, sometimes quite violent, erupted unexpectedly over the smallest offence against perceived personal rights. Nerves had become frayed and tempers easily flared up. There was a code of behaviour according to which no one had an iota more privilege than the next inmate: not a gram more bread, not a spoonful more of the dreadful soup, not an extra inch of space on the bunk. This code was rigorously observed, and the transgressors had only themselves to blame for the ensuing fury and retribution. Yet unspoken allowances were made: those who closely watched the ladling out of the soup to make sure that some of the unspecified floating objects were evenly distributed never protested if the person serving the soup tried to fish out some solid material from the liquid if a child was next in the line. There were, of course, tactical considerations in terms of getting the best out of the vegetable soup: the exercise of patience, controlling one's instinct to rush to be served first and waiting for the end of the line, was thought to be rewarded by a liquid enriched in vegetables. But such tricks were easily seen through, and the server was told to stir the broth at regular intervals. And she was carefully supervised by the other inmates to make sure she did so.

Bergen-Belsen was created neither for forced labour nor for extermination. We were allowed to live, but we passed the days in gruelling monotony. From our new perspective the months we had spent in Austria seemed like a vacation. Here there was simply nothing to do. Those, usually men, who were marched off to work outside the camp were privileged to be released even for a short time. Women with small children were exempt from work. Playing with children my own age was out of the question: my mother would not let me out of her sight even for a couple of minutes, and we had nowhere to play.

As winter progressed we rapidly lost weight and were too tired to play or do anything. The little strength we preserved, which we needed to survive from day to day, was drained by endless waiting at roll-calls. In Wiener Neustadt these had been speedy affairs to confirm that we were all present; here in Belsen they became a form of torture, devoid of their *raison d'être* of counting heads.

The day started with such a roll-call, or *Appell*. We were ordered to proceed without delay to a large space, the *Appellplatz*. We had to line up and wait to be counted. The head counts usually did not add up. There were those who were too weak or sick to leave their barracks, those who had been admitted the previous day to the infirmary, and, most often, people who had simply died unaccounted for. So the weak and the sick were ordered from the barracks to join those already freezing on the *Appellplatz* and we were recounted, sometimes several times. Before and between the head counts we were kept waiting, standing to attention, sometimes for hours, sometimes all morning.

From where we stood we could survey the parts of the camp immediately surrounding us: the low-built barracks of the *Ungarnlager*, the paths leading to the other, more distant group of barracks, and the barbed-wire fence surrounding the camp – so flimsy yet impenetrable, charged with high-voltage electricity and surmounted by watchtowers from which guards surveyed the ground, offering no hope of escape, only of death. Those who were brave or desperate enough chose this route, escaping from life under the cloak of darkness. Their bodies would be found in the morning, sometimes at the bottom of the fence, where they fell after being electrocuted, sometimes crucified on the fence, their hands grasping the barbed wire. On such occasions we were not allowed out of our barracks, but during the spring, as an epidemic began to take hold and the corpses lying around had grown to be part of the internal landscape of the camp, no one bothered any more about these suicides. By then death had lost its power to shock, and suicide was no longer a heroic gesture. Death came naturally, easily and abundantly.

During roll-calls nobody could leave the lines. Not alive, anyway. The guards shouted and beat people. Maybe our numbers did not add up; maybe they did not like a particular face; maybe they were having a bad day. Meanwhile we froze. Cold rain fell and often it snowed. But the wind was the worst: the razor-sharp gusts that blew off Lüneberg Heath, lashing every inch of uncovered body and penetrating the flimsy defences of our clothing, even through an overcoat. We tried to stamp our feet and rub our hands to generate a little warmth, but any movement was discouraged and disobedience punished.

Before the morning roll-call we were sometimes given some coffee: a disgusting brown liquid which did not taste of coffee but at least, being hot, warmed us up. Later, when we became overrun by lice, we used this coffee to wash our hair, in the vain hope that this would rid us of some of the head lice. Lunch was *Dörrgemüse*, a vegetable soup, most often prepared from turnips, used for animal feed. It looked revolting and tasted worse. On good days there was potato soup, but this contained only peelings; the potatoes must have ended up on the guards' plates. After lunch there was another endless roll-call, or sometimes nothing to do until dinner. For dinner we received a ration of bread, occasionally supplemented by a little butter, a slice of sausage or cheese. On a couple of occasions we enjoyed a veritable feast. Real delicacies were distributed through the good offices of the Red Cross: a little sugar, marmalade, biscuits and meat. The arrival of these food parcels was also a sign that the world had not completely forgotten us.

Bread was the currency of the camp: it was literally life. The distribution of bread, in the hands of the guards, became a cruel game. Originally the allotted portion was two slices, but towards the end of winter the ration was reduced to one slice, and was regularly replaced by a watery soup. Instead of daily portions, sometimes two or three days' rations were distributed in one go. The temptation to eat it all in one act of uncontrolled gluttony was too great, and many people could not resist. My mother made sure that we did not do anything foolish, and a piece of bread that represented three days' rations was cut into three equal parts, and no amount of pleading, begging or crying would persuade her to allow me to eat the next day's ration.

The cardinal sin in the camp was stealing someone else's bread. Bread rations, if not consumed immediately, were kept constantly within sight. Rations that had been stashed away sometimes disappeared, and if anybody was caught stealing bread they faced the contempt of the whole barrack. The cruellest punishment the guards could mete out was complete withdrawal of the bread ration: this they frequently did in response to the smallest transgression or the slightest sign of disobedience. At the end of each day we climbed into our bunks exhausted, cold and hungry.

7

It was at one of the never-ending roll-calls that my informal education got under way. On that day the weather was even more inclement than usual, and the wind particularly pitiless. We had been standing on the *Appellplatz* waiting to be counted since the beginning of the morning, and although the cold was stupefying, the boredom was even worse. Since we did not have gloves, our hands were frozen. Gaining temporary relief by secreting my frozen fingers in the warmth of my pockets was not approved of by the guards.

'Move your fingers,' my mother said, and then suddenly raised one of her own. 'What is this?' she asked.

'A finger,' I said.

'No,' she said to my surprise, 'it is one finger.' And then she stuck out another finger and said: 'Two fingers.' She raised yet another finger. 'Three fingers.'

And this is how my education started in Bergen-Belsen. By the end of the roll-call we had counted to ten. This was easy, since I already knew the numbers up to ten, but in the following days, during many hours of waiting, I progressed to simple adding up, subtraction, dividing and multiplying. I repeated everything many times, since there was neither paper nor pencil with which to write anything down. The lessons frequently continued in the barrack. Had we stayed longer in Bergen-Belsen I might have ended up as precocious as one of those child prodigies who, by the age of ten, are studying mathematics at a prestigious university. In any event, these furtive lessons helped not only to alleviate the boredom but also to preserve our sanity.

Many years later, at school, I did very well in mathematics. Our maths teacher, who advised me to become a mathematician and was disappointed when I decided to study medicine instead, gave us various mathematical theorems during his class. Whoever solved the problem first was rewarded with the top mark for the day. I achieved this quite regularly, and attributed this success to my early lessons in mathematics in the camp.

8

To vary this informal tuition in elementary mathematics, my mother extended my education to German. She taught me only simple words, and no grammar: I could not construct a sentence, and my rudimentary vocabulary was limited to the commonest nouns and a few verbs. Some of the words were already familiar: *der Tod*, death; *der Hunger*, hunger; *die Kalte*, the cold; *der Durste*, thirst; *der Schnee*, the snow; *der Regen*, the rain; *der Wind*, the wind. These were the words I heard most regularly, and I learned them first. But of course I memorized many other words, more suited to everyday life. I was taught to ask politely and to say thank you politely: *Bitte sehr* and *Danke sehr*. I do not recall using these expressions of good manners: in Bergen-Belsen they were totally superfluous to any social intercourse, since nobody asked, and nobody said thank you.

Death played the leading role in our lives as the freezing winter took its toll. We would wake up in the morning to go to roll-call and notice that some people were not moving. They had died during the night without anybody noticing. Their corpses were removed after daybreak, but in some cases left in their bunks until their neighbours complained to the barrack leader. Even during the interminable hours of the roll-call people would silently fall: some of exhaustion, too weak to stand. They were revived, but others did not move, and their bodies were dragged away by other inmates.

As spring arrived, life got much worse. Although winter had eased its grip, and temperatures had become more tolerable, our food ration was further reduced. Bread became rarer and the portions smaller, and days passed without any solid food. By then our diet consisted chiefly of the hot brown liquid masquerading as coffee and the muddy liquid pretending to be soup. Our calorie intake must have been negligible.

We were all infested with head and body lice, and once they became established the fight against them was lost. But my mother did not give up that easily, and hunting for parasites became part of our daily recreation. Lice brought typhus, and an uncontrollable epidemic broke out. Death from starvation and exhaustion was an individual, polite form of death, but dying from dysentery or typhus was a public event. The bodies were disposed of in the crematorium, a building just visible on the horizon. We had become accustomed to the billowing smoke emanating from the chimney, but even the wind could not dispel the smell of burning flesh.

As the epidemic took hold, demand for cremation outstripped capacity, and new ways were devised to dispose of the dead. Mass graves were dug, into which the bodies were thrown by the inmates. Or a bonfire would be constructed of alternating layers of corpses and logs, a practice eventually stopped to spare wood. As spring arrived and the weather became milder, the smell of burning flesh was replaced by something far more obnoxious and penetrating: the stench of decomposing corpses. Bodies were lying everywhere: unburied, unburnt, abandoned. Corpses ceased to be a taboo, a reminder of the sanctity of human life: they became undisposed litter in an alien landscape.

9

I remember the day my father died. It was before roll-call early one March morning, when winter had still not completely surrendered to spring. Someone came looking for my mother. She said nothing. She took my hand and we walked together to the infirmary, the same barrack where she had been taken after her breakdown immediately on our arrival. And there he lay: a small, emaciated corpse on a hastily made-up hospital bed. My mother stood by his bedside, motionless. She did not cry; not there, not then. I did not cry either, nor did I feel any emotion. Surrounded as we were by so many corpses, this was just another death. It was only natural that everybody should die. Even my father.

He should not have died; there was no need for him to die, at least not then. In a way he had chosen to do so. He gambled on his life and he lost. Had he been wiser or more disciplined he might have survived. It was his addiction to nicotine, a habit stronger than the will to live, which precipitated his death. He had been a heavy smoker throughout his life, and in Bergen-Belsen he traded his bread ration for cigarettes. In a limited black market, prized items occasionally surfaced, secreted away from parcels sent by the International Red Cross. The commonest transaction, however, was the exchange of bread for cigarettes. Bread was also exchanged for services such as washing soiled and dirty underwear.

Although my father lived in a different barrack, we had been able to meet him after the roll-calls. It had not taken my mother very long to find out that he had been bartering away his bread for cigarettes. She had earlier made a business arrangement: she volunteered to wash other inmates' dirty underwear for a scrap of bread or a little jam. Some of this she passed to my father. The craving for cigarettes was stronger than hunger, however, and he continued to barter away his life.

I do not know what happened to his body later. Was he cremated? Was he burnt on a pyre? Buried in a mass grave? Or left unburied, as so many corpses were during the final days of Bergen-Belsen, to be found by the British? I do have his death certificate, however, issued in my home town, Makó, after the war. It says: 'Leipniker Sándor, born on 21 July 1893 in Kevermes. Died on 13 March 1945 in Bergen-Belsen.' Nothing more, nothing less. It is an official document, bearing the crest of the town, duly stamped and signed, issued in some dusty office at a comfortable distance from the place where he died.

But I also have another death certificate, unofficial but more authentic, not stamped and not signed, written in a regular hand in German. I received this document by courtesy of Dr Thomas Rahe, director of the Bergen-Belsen Memorial. Towards the end deaths were not recorded officially: too many people were dying for the camp administration to keep up. Or perhaps death was simply too common, too cheap to be worth recording for posterity. But one of the inmates, a Hungarian

Jewish doctor, meticulously catalogued the deaths in secret. My father's was given the number 257. His name, birth date, birthplace, occupation, his address in Hungary (only the name of the town), his wife's name (both married and maiden names) are followed by the names of his mother and father with the places and dates of their deaths. He died at eight o'clock in the morning on 13 March 1945. Cause of death: enteritis, myocardial degeneration, cachexia. Cachexia, as defined by medical dictionaries, is an extreme state of general ill-health characterized by malnutrion, wasting, anaemia, and circulatory and muscular weakness: the face of death on the living. In the bottom right-hand corner of his entry, which occupies the upper third of a page in a small notebook, there are also four digits: 8432. Was this his prisoner's number, the sole means by which he was to be identified in the camp?

As a last act, Bergen-Belsen has delivered a final surprise. Although the Nazis destroyed most documents, a secretly obtained copy of the original list of the Hungarian transport of 7 December 1944 has survived. Soon after the train arrived, one of the SS officers ordered the compilation of a complete register of the new arrivals. The appointed senior prisoner who undertook the task secretly prepared three copies instead of the requested two: one for the SS and one for the administration in charge of provision of supplies. The third remained with him. Each numbered entry had the name, sex, birth date and birthplace of the prisoners, and their new identity: their prisoner number. During the coming months, on this carefully hidden copy, he recorded those who had died, but from March so many inmates had perished that he was unable to follow the events.

After the liberation of the camp this copy travelled to Hungary. Upon his death many years later, his daughter who had also been imprisoned in Bergen-Belsen, found the register among other family documents. Married to a German, she had taken the register with her to Germany where it had been collecting dust until her death. It was her husband who realized the importance of the list and who approached the Bergen-Belsen Memorial. And thus after sixty years the list was delivered to where it belongs.

On this list we became numbers. My father was prisoner number 8432. My mother was 8517. And I was 8431.

10

As the weather turned milder in early spring, the sorties of Allied aircraft overflying the camp became more frequent. This gave the commandant an excuse to order a blackout, and after six o'clock in the evening all lights were extinguished – not to spare our lives, but to save electricity.

Those in the know had suddenly started to circulate rumours that the British army was approaching and the camp might be evacuated. The hope that one day we might be exchanged for German prisoners of war still flickered. And this was more than wishful thinking or self-deception to keep up morale: fulfilling Bergen-Belsen's original function there had been exchanges of prisoners and some inmates had been released from the camp: one transport of 222 Jews, who had entry visas for Palestine, was evacuated in June 1944 and reached its destination. The second exchange took place in January 1945, one month after we had arrived in Belsen: more than 100 American Jews with South American visas were handed over to the International Red Cross, and these fortunate few were put on a train heading for Switzerland. These departures rekindled our hopes, and when the camp authorities announced in April that a number of trains would be organized to transport people from Bergen-Belsen, the camp was stirred up with excitement and uncertainty.

My mother decided that we must leave the camp, and that if

we had the remotest chance we should get on one of the trains. Her wish was granted, since we were selected to be on one of the transports. We were told to pack our belongings and prepare for the journey. This did not take long. There were a couple of false starts, however: we were told to leave the barracks, but kept waiting outside and then ordered back again. There were rumours that the transport would be cancelled and we feared the worst: we were going to stay in Bergen-Belsen. We did not know then that the camp's days were numbered: the British army was going to liberate it a few days later.

Eventually the final obstacle preventing our departure must have been cleared, since we were ordered to march to Bergen train station. The same painful march on the same road along which we had marched some four months before at the beginning of December, but in the opposite direction. We walked slowly, often stopping to regain our strength, but this time our guards were more patient and did not harass anybody. When we arrived at the station, the train was already waiting for us. As usual, we did not know our destination, but the assumption was that we would be heading east, since the British were approaching from the west. According to rumours, our destination was Theresienstadt, another camp not far from Prague. But our apprehension was outweighed by the feeling that wherever we were going it could only be better than Bergen-Belsen. This was our conviction as the train pulled out of the station and headed east.

11

We embarked on our train at Bergen station on 6 April 1945. On 12 April two German messengers, carrying a white flag, crossed the front line to notify the British 2nd Army of the existence of a concentration camp at Belsen containing some 60,000 people, many of whom were sick with typhus, typhoid fever and other diseases. This information must have been available to British intelligence for some time, since the RAF had taken well-defined aerial reconnaissance photographs during the course of 1944. Interestingly, one of these photographs is used today in an information leaflet for the Bergen-Belsen Memorial: numbers and letters mark various components of the concentration-camp complex, superimposed on an aerial photograph taken on 13 September 1944.

An agreement was reached to establish a neutral zone measuring 8 × 5 kilometres around the camp, and warning signs declaring DANGER – TYPHUS with white flags were erected along the access roads. On 13 April Lieutenant-Colonel Taylor, commander of the 63rd Anti-Tank Regiment, Royal Artillery, was instructed to take charge of the area around Belsen. Heavy fighting in the region had delayed the liberation of the camp by forty-eight hours. Although there have been claims that smaller units entered the camp earlier, the regiment officially liberated Belsen on the afternoon of 15 April 1945. Despite their previous knowledge of the camp, the British were not prepared for what they were going see when they arrived at the gates of Belsen.

What they found in the camp has been exhaustively documented, described by thousands, including eyewitnesses, surviving inmates, liberators and guards. The transcript of the so-called Bergen-Belsen trials conducted by the British in nearby Lüneburg in December 1945, before the Nuremberg trials got under way, fills several volumes. The liberation and its immediate aftermath were also captured on film. These images, once seen, are indelibly burnt on the retina: the mass graves filled with skeletal corpses; other corpses littering the ground singly, in small groups or in their hundreds, sometimes in several layers stacked one on top of the other, in an infinite variety of macabre death tableaux; corpses lying on floors and bunks in the barracks, sometimes side by side with the living, those who could not move and were soon to die themselves; Nazi guards carrying corpses on their shoulders and tossing them into the mass graves; bulldozers driven by British soldiers shoving mounds of corpses ahead of them; the emaciated bodies of the survivors, some too weak to acknowledge those who have saved them, others standing with vacant, uncomprehending expressions in their eyes, not believing that the horror has ended; the woman kissing the hand of the first British soldier to enter the camp; the commandant, Josef Kramer, being arrested by British soldiers and led away in shackles; the frightened group of female guards, some still in jackboots, most turning away from the camera but a couple defiantly facing the lens; and the solemn line of elegantly dressed German civil dignitaries, rounded up by the liberators and brought to the camp to bear witness.

In the main camp of the complex, Camp 1, referred to as the 'Horror Camp' by the British, there were some 22,000 to 28,000 women, 18,000 men and 500 children. Camp 2 consisted of brick buildings and originally served as the Panzer Training School and accommodation for the Wehrmacht and the SS: by April 1945 it housed an estimated 15,000 male prisoners. Nobody could arrive at a precise number of the dead, but there were approximately 10,000 corpses. Every day they died in their hundreds: 800 died on the day of liberation. Apparently no food and hardly any water were provided for four to five days before the British army arrived. After his visit to the camp, Dr W. R. F. Collis reported in the 9 June 1945 issue of the *British Medical Journal* on 'naked walls of bodies around the huts, many of which were filled with the dead and dying. Next to nothing had been done for these people for months. For a week they had almost no water. There they lay either three persons to a bunk designed to hold one, or on the floor in foul rags drenched in excreta, covered with lice. Death came chiefly through starvation, typhus, tuberculosis and dysentery: 500 a day dying of disease'. Sanitation he found non-existent; the latrines were totally inadequate and as a result of starvation, weakness and apathy the inmates defecated or urinated where they lay or sat, even inside the huts. There was no running water or electricity.

The British did not waste time. The 11th Armoured Division entered the camp at midday on 15 April and four hours later the Divisional Field Section began an unparalleled operation of medical relief. At the order of Brigadier H. L. Glyn Hughes, Deputy Director of Medical Services of the 2nd Army, who visited Bergen-Belsen personally, five medical units arrived two days after liberation, followed by a reinforcement of three further units. Lieutenant Colonel J. A. D. Johnston, the Senior Medical Officer, drew up an operational plan to transform a cesspit of infection and death into a hospital and place of recuperation.

The measures to be taken included burying the dead, the evacuation of patients from Camp 1 to suitably clean buildings in Camp 2, after delousing and cleaning, the transfer of fit inmates from Camp 1 to Camp 2, the treatment of all inmates with DDT, providing suitable nourishment for patients, and ridding the camp of rubbish, rags and excreta. On 18 April the SS guards were forced, at gunpoint, to bury the dead in mass graves. But there were too many for individual attention: in addition to the estimated 10,000 found at liberation, a further 13,000 perished soon afterwards.

The evacuation of Camp 1 progressed according to plans: inmates were called out of their huts, registered, bathed and disinfected and then transported to Camp 2. A 'human laundry' operated to clean and delouse the inmates: on a conveyor belt batches of twenty were scrubbed clean of caked dirt and faeces and sprayed with DDT to get rid of lice. By 30 April all the inmates had been cleaned and deloused; by 18 May the evacuation of Camp 1 was complete, and 13,834 patients were admitted to the hospital in Camp 2. Captain Winterbottom, the

1a My mother (on the right of the picture) with two of her brothers and sisters.
Three more siblings (all boys) were to arrive later.

1b My mother's parents with two of my
cousins and my brother (on the
right). István on the left died in
Auschwitz. The photograph was
taken after my grandfather had
suffered a stroke. (Magda in the
background died in 2005 in Israel.)

1c My mother and brother: a passport
photograph of 1937 (Courtesy of Dr
Ilona G Tóth, Csongrád-County
Archives, Szeged, Hungary.)

2a Architectural details of the family house in Makó.

2b The old timber yard is hardly recognisable today: only the run-down engine house has survived (not pictured here).

3a Welcome to Strasshof: the railway station today.

3b Bergen-Belsen today, with scattered graves, a memorial stone and the obelisk with the wall of remembrance in the background. (Courtesy of Bernd Horstmann, Bergen-Belsen Memorial.)

4 The aerial photograph of Bergen-Belsen taken by the Royal Air Force on 13 September 1944. My mother and I stayed in the barracks arrowed. Superimposed is the current layout of the Memorial.

```
 1134.F. Leipnik Ede       -Donat Erneszti      25.III.1878.Nemetsztpeter 8430
 1135.Kn. Leipniker Peter                        22.XI 1939.Mako            8431 D
 1136.M. Leipniker Sandor                         20.VI. 1892.Kevermes      8432 D
 1137.Kn.Leitner Sandor                           14.X.  1928.Hajdunanas    8433 D
```

5a Part of the list of the Hungarian transport which arrived on 7 December 1944.
(Courtesy of Bergen-Belsen Memorial.) My father's and my name are arrowed.
We were prisoners 8432 and 8431, respectively. My father's entry is crossed out
with an undulating line with the additional comment in Hungarian: died 13/III.
(My name was changed by deed poll from Leipniker to Lantos in 1961.)

```
 1219.F. Lukacs Gyula                                   1966.Debrecen   8516
 1220.F. Leipniker Sandor  -Schwarc Helen      8.V.  1900.Mako          8517 D
 1221.   Lustein       Jeszo                  25.XII.1896.Kavasarhely   8518 B
 1222.F. Lusteiner Dezso  -Kahan Helen        28.XII.1895.Kurosliget    8519 B
                                              11.VIII.1922.            8520 B
```

5b My mother's entry (arrowed). She was prisoner 8517.

5c My father's unofficial death certificate, recorded secretly by a Hungarian Jewish
doctor in German. The cause of death is given as enteritis, degeneration of the
heart and cachexia (an extreme state of general ill-health caused mainly by
malnutrition) (Courtesy of the Jewish Museum, Belgrade.)

6a The liberation of Bergen-Belsen. Josef Kramer, the Commandant being arrested by the British. He was later hanged with ten of his accomplices. (Courtesy of the Imperial War Museum, London; BU 3749.)

6b One of the mass graves is filled in with bodies in front of the barracks. (Courtesy of the Imperial War Museum, London; BU 4245.)

7a A survivor de-lousing his clothes. (Courtesy of the Imperial War Museum, London; BU 3765.)

7b On 21 May 1945 the destruction of the last barracks by flamethrowers to erase remnants of Bergen-Belsen was watched by a large crowd. (Courtesy of the Imperial War Museum, London; BU 6676.)

8a In April 1945 a contingent of British medical students arrived in Bergen-Belsen
to help with the rehabilitation of the liberated prisoners. A group of medical
students from St Mary's Hospital Medical School: John Hankinson is first on
the left, standing. (Courtesy of the Imperial War Museum, London.)

8b The watch from Bergen-Belsen, a gift of Professor John Hankinson, on my desk.

9a Our train liberated by the Americans outside Farsleben, near Magdeburg. (Courtesy of Professor George Gross, San Diego, USA.)

9b The last remaining Nazi guard surrenders to the Americans. (Courtesy of George Gross.)

10a The survivors leave the train to greet their liberators. (Picture by Major Clarence L. Benjamin and provided by George Gross.)

10b A group of survivors pose for a photograph in front of the train. (Courtesy of George Gross.)

11a George Gross, the commander of one of the two tanks which liberated our train in 1945.

11b George Gross with the author in San Diego, in 2003. (Courtesy of John Gross, San Diego, USA.)

12a The railway line near Farsleben today where our train was liberated sixty years ago.

12b The tombstone in Farsleben cemetery commemorating some of those who died during the journey from Bergen-Belsen.

13a The cemetery of Hillersleben. The Americans accommodated us in the housing estate in which German officers and administrators of the Wehrmacht had lived.

ДОБРО ПОЖАЛОВАТЬ

13b A decaying building in Hillersleben with Cyrillic script, a reminder of the Russian presence.

14a My brother at the age of nineteen before he was taken to forced labour.

14b With my mother soon after our return from Bergen-Belsen.

14c Uncle Jenő with two Russian friends in October 1946.

15a The high school (Gymnasium) in Makó with the Russian monument in the foreground. Demolished during the heady days of 1956, rebuilt after the demise of the Revolution and finally removed after Communism collapsed.

15b The Jewish cemetery in Makó. The overgrown tombstones witness the decline of the Jewish population in the town.

16a With my mother (on the right), Aunt Márta and Uncle Lajos in 1954.

16b Graduating from high school in 1958, celebrated by visiting and serenading the teachers, a custom which has survived to the present day. In the background is the Reform Synagogue, demolished in 1965.

physician in charge of the stores, performed miracles: he equipped 7,000 beds in one week, requisitioned and distributed clothing and footwear for the inmates from a temporary depot jokingly called 'Harrods', organized a team of plumbers and carpenters for the hospital buildings, and even initiated a nightclub, the Coconut Grove, to assist in the rehabilitation of the patients. The British effort was enormous in scope: an estimated 3,000 troops were directly involved in the relief operation. Moreover, in response to an appeal from the military, six detachments of British Red Cross volunteers arrived on 23 April. They were followed a week later by a large group of medical students from London: they provided not only medical help but also wrote some of the most harrowing eyewitness testimony.

As soon as the evacuation of Camp 1 was complete, the last huts were ceremonially destroyed by fire. At the time the immolation must have been conceived as a logical act of cleansing and decontamination, to destroy the last vestiges of filth, infection and death. It was also an act of purification, to erase Bergen-Belsen from the face of the earth and with it the evil that had created it. Yet it also destroyed the evidence, since now there is emptiness where Bergen-Belsen concentration camp once stood: the memorial is the only reminder standing on the windswept ground.

12

The final act in the tragedy of Bergen-Belsen was played out in the autumn of 1945 in the law courts of Lüneburg, a town not far from the concentration camp. Josef Kramer, the camp commandant, together with forty-four other people, was charged with war crimes by a British military court under a royal warrant issued on 14 June 1945. There were two counts of indictment: the first for crimes committed in Bergen-Belsen, and the second for crimes committed previously in Auschwitz-Birkenau. Eleven defendants were charged with both counts. The indictment was not only for war crimes in general, the accused being 'together concerned as parties to' various crimes; specific charges were also brought for the murder of named individuals as well as other, unnamed persons. The issues the court had to consider fell into two categories: acts of personal killing or brutality, and responsibility for the death, suffering and conditions of the victims in general.

The trial opened on 17 September 1945 and finished exactly two months later, on 17 November. The court was a military one, and consisted of five British officers. One of the accused fell ill, and did not appear at the trial. All were represented by defence counsel. The proceedings occupied fifty-four working days: a relatively short time for the prosecution and defence to present their case, for witnesses to be heard and for the judge to sum up. On 17 November 1945 the sentences were announced. Of the forty-four defendants, thirty were found guilty while fourteen were acquitted of all charges. Six defendants were found guilty on both counts; five, including Kramer, Dr Fritz Klein, the camp doctor, and Irma Grese, the youngest and most sadistic of the female guards, were sentenced to death. Of the twenty-four defendants found guilty only on one count, six were sentenced to death. The sentences were reviewed by Field Marshal Montgomery, who by then was in charge of the British zone of occupation. Clemency was denied to all those who had been found guilty. There was no appeal.

After the trial the eleven defendants sentenced to death, eight men and three women, were transported to a jail in Hameln, a small town on the Weser river in Lower Saxony. An execution chamber was hurriedly constructed by the Royal Engineers of the British army. Albert Pierrepoint, the official executioner, was flown in from Britain. On 12 December he made the necessary arrangements for the executions by carrying out a number of test drops before declaring the gallows satisfactory. In the afternoon the prisoners were weighed and measured to allow individual adjustments to be made. On 13 December 1945 all the eleven condemned were hanged and officially declared dead. After the three women were executed individually, Pierrepont paused to have a short tea break. The eight men were hanged in pairs, and the whole procedure was over by one o'clock, just in time for lunch.

For several years after the executions in Hameln, Pierrepont's memoirs revealed that he received a plain envelope at Christmas containing a five-pound note. On the first occasion there was a small piece of paper enclosed with the single word 'Belsen' written on it. In subsequent letters there was no message, and after a few years the gifts ceased to arrive altogether.

13

From early adolescence I knew that one day I would go back to Bergen-Belsen. Not as part of a formal act of pilgrimage, since this did not appeal to me, but as an incidental visitor, remaining as detached as possible from the emotional burden of past experience. I had been waiting for an occasion when I could visit the camp without too much prior planning, and such an opportunity unexpectedly presented itself a couple of years after I had settled in England.

In the summer of 1973 I was invited to spend a couple of weeks in Cologne at the Max-Planck Institute for Brain Research. Having submitted my Ph.D. thesis to London University earlier in the summer, I had a few free weeks before my examination in September.

I looked forward to a brief stay in Cologne. Even the request to give a seminar on my newly acquired results did not dampen my enthusiasm; on the contrary, I regarded this presentation as a dress rehearsal for my Ph.D. viva. The institute in

Cologne had an excellent reputation in brain research, and its director, the late Klaus Zülch, was internationally recognized as a leading authority on brain tumours. Zülch was the proto-typical old-fashioned Prussian professor, a tall, erect man, with neat white hair and glasses; his face complete with duelling scars. He gave the impression that contradicting him might not be the best way of promoting one's career, but he wore his authority naturally and with grace. When he first attended a meeting of neuropathologists in London after the war, several of his British colleagues responded to him with measured cold-ness. Although as a doctor he served in the Wehrmacht, whis-pers that he swam with the tide during the war were unfounded. While I was in Cologne, Zülch decided to attend a meeting in Göttingen, and offered a lift to one of his assistants, who was then to continue to the town of Celle, further to the north. When they asked me whether I would like to join them I was happy to do so. This was how I conceived of the idea of revisiting Bergen-Belsen, a few miles from Celle.

The journey from Cologne to Göttingen was speedy: we stopped only once to have a light meal of plump herrings and beer. By late evening I had arrived in Celle and checked into a hotel with a feeling of mounting gloom. I was alone, and sud-denly the visit to Bergen-Belsen did not seem such a good idea. I regretted having set out on this journey unprepared, and wished I had remained in Cologne. I had a fretful night; sleep did not come easily and did not linger long. I awoke early and dishevelled. The sunshine of the previous day had gone; it was a cold, grey autumnal day.

At the advice of the hotel's receptionist I took a local bus to Bergen, where I asked about further transport to Belsen. The answer was not encouraging: '*Nein, es gibt kein Transport nach Belsen.* No, there is no transport to Belsen.' My enquiry as to how to get to the memorial in Belsen was treated with caution, if not reluctance, as if I had been asking about an obscure and remote place at the end of the world, not about the next village immediately down the road. Bergen was reluctant to share the shame of its name being associated with such a notorious concentration camp. And who could blame the law-abiding decent citizens of this perfect little town for wanting to distance themselves from the events of so many years ago? They had every right to do so. But what did they know? Had they seen what was going on four miles away behind the trees? Did the wind carry the smell of burning flesh from the crematorium? Or the stench of rotting corpses? What did the woman I asked about transport do during the war? Did she live in Bergen? Did she know? Was she one of the guards? Did she approve of the camp? But these were impolite questions in such a well-manicured, peaceful and prosperous little town.

I walked beyond the end of the town and continued towards the camp. The last time I had marched on this road, in the opposite direction towards Bergen station on 6 April 1945, the journey seemed interminable. I could cover the distance of four miles in an hour and a half, but on impulse I decided to hitch-hike. The road was not very wide, allowing only one lane in each direction: traffic was light, and cars passed at great speed. No one stopped. Both sides of the road were guarded by fir trees, tall, dense and regimented. I remembered these trees, which had witnessed our march from the station to the camp, and four months later our march in the opposite direction to embark on a train headed for yet another unknown destination. Or were these different trees, planted after the war, innocent of their predecessors' secrets?

As I walked slowly along the side of the road, occasionally stopping to wave a thumb at the passing cars, an unexpected wave of uneasiness overcame me: the pretence of being a casual visitor to Bergen-Belsen cracked open to reveal a deep fear of going back. The phalanx of fir trees engulfed me, and I hated their disciplined regularity. I thought about turning back and hiring a taxi when suddenly a car braked and pulled up. As I turned around a voice asked me in immaculate English: 'Are you going to the memorial?'

'Yes, I am. Would you give me a lift?'

'Of course. We're nearly there.'

The driver was, I discovered during the brief ride, an officer in the British army, a man in his late thirties with the drilled elegance of his rank: freshly pressed uniform, highly polished shoes.

'Have you been here before?' he asked as he stopped in front of the gate. 'A sad place,' he added.

'Yes, I have been here before,' I confided, 'in 1944 and '45.' I could not help thinking that he already knew the answer. 'Thank you for bringing me here.'

He sped off, waving goodbye. As I walked through the gate of the memorial, my apprehension evaporated and I felt a sense of elation. The British had liberated the camp, and now a British officer had delivered me to the memorial: an auspicious start to my visit. But my light-headedness was soon replaced by anxiety: among the array of memorials and graves there were no reference points to the past. Although I knew that the British had burnt down the barracks, only now did I appreciate fully that nothing remained of the original camp. All the evidence had been obliterated. As I wandered around aimlessly I made the decision to return again in the future.

*

I revisited Bergen-Belsen for the second time thirty years later, in the autumn of 2003. This was a very different visit from the first, planned and with time to spare. I made an appointment with the director of the memorial. I wanted to look at some of the documents in the archives.

Celle is an appropriate place from which to visit Bergen-Belsen: a picturesque medieval town with 700 years of history. The centre is a warren of tidily laid-out streets lined by old, and some not so old, timber houses. As in so many other immaculately restored German towns, it is difficult to decipher just how much of the original architecture survived and how much had to be rebuilt after the war. But whatever destruction the war visited upon Celle, the town of today breathes quiet self-confidence and affluence.

The day I set out from my hotel in Celle on my second visit was as grey as thirty years earlier and subject to sudden changes of weather: quick downpours and fierce gusts of wind alternated with sunshine. I arrived early at the bus terminus, a modern glass and stainless-steel complex next to the mainline railway station. The place was deserted, save for a small, boisterous gang of teenagers. Several were listening to their portable CD players; they nearly all smoked, and an overweight girl flirted with a tall, under-nourished boy. The bus pulled in on time. The journey lasted one hour as the bus slowly wound its way through prosperous little villages and suburbs. This was Lüneburg Heath, an area now accommodating one of NATO's largest European firing ranges and exercise grounds. War games are played out over the ground scarred by tank manoeuvres and scorched by heavy artillery. Its proximity to the border with the German Democratic Republic endowed this region with strategic importance: one Third World War scenario envisaged the tanks of the Red Army rolling through this plain to capture the Ruhr and Paris beyond. I was the only passenger to disembark at the Bergen-Belsen Memorial. It was the last stop. By then the sun had finally given up; the sky had been invaded by charcoal-grey clouds, whipped along by icy winds.

Several monuments have been built on the scarred landscape: a central obelisk with inscriptions commemorating those who perished here, a Jewish memorial topped with the Star of David, a large wooden cross for the Christians, a separate Soviet memorial, and a German commemorative stone.

The grounds are vast and fortunately have escaped aggressive landscaping; mercifully there are no formal flower-beds. Everywhere there are graves – mass graves claiming to be the resting place of 5,000 dead, 3,000 dead, 500 dead. Who knows how many bodies are buried here? A few individual graves show the identity of the dead. Who were they? Paths meander through the grounds. There is an abundance of heather: humble and ubiquitous, the appropriate floral tribute, in all shades of white and pink and mauve and lilac. I wandered aimlessly, devoid of thoughts and feelings. Where was my father buried?

The place was desolate. I was on my own. The rain came down with renewed vigour, whipped by the cold gusts of wind. I escaped into the shelter of the House of Silence: a modern building preserved for prayer and thought. Its solid walls of slabs of black granite lean outward, as if trying to escape the burden of silence inside. Massive stools made of blond wood are scattered around for the weary to rest on. The rain drummed on the glass roof.

I hurried back to reception in time for my appointment with Dr Thomas Rahe, director of the Bergen-Belsen memorial site. He is probably in his forties, slim, agile, with enquiring eyes behind rimless glasses, informally dressed in chinos, an open-necked shirt and sweater. He is the current guardian of a piece of German history, and I felt an impulse to ask why he was doing this particular job, but of course I did not dare. He confirmed that all personal documents had been destroyed by the Nazis: most of the material presently in the archives was amassed later from individuals, Jewish organizations and the British military. He also verified that we had arrived from Strasshof on 7 December 1944 and were housed in the *Ungarnlager*.

The archives contain several documents concerning Hungarian Jews, but the only personal document involving my family is a book of unofficial death certificates. Other documents describe the judicial system operated by the inmates within the camp, overseen by a group of functionaries and a committee elected by secret ballot. These people represented the inmates in dealings with the German administration and Jewish organizations. Specialized offices were established to deal with all aspects of life in the camp – health, education, religious affairs, food distribution, welfare and financial affairs, internal discipline and judiciary matters. This was a valiant attempt to maintain an element of normality in the face of increasing chaos. As the Wehrmacht withdrew both from the west and on the eastern front, Bergen-Belsen was flooded by new arrivals: more Hungarians from Austria and inmates evacuated from other concentration camps soon to be liberated by the advancing Red Army. It was then that all attempts at preserving the trappings of civilization were abandoned. There were no more codes of behaviour. There was only one rule: to survive.

Thomas Rahe and his staff were attentive and helpful. I was offered coffee: it was hot and strong, very different from the brew I had been obliged to drink in Bergen-Belsen nearly sixty years earlier.

14

The *Endtenfang* is one of three restaurants in the Fürstenhof Hotel in Celle. It boasts various accolades of culinary excellence, including one Michelin star. At the end of a numbingly cold, rainy October day, the *Endtenfang* proved irresistible. As the name suggests, duck is a specialty, and it features prominently both in the décor and in the menu. The *menu du jour* did not disappoint. An excellent terrine of foie gras with an exotic chutney-and-truffle punch was followed, somewhat surprisingly but utterly rewardingly, by two fish dishes. The first featured an angler fish with green tomatoes, almonds and sauce bourride. Fillet of turbot with brandade was garnished with purple artichokes and rocket in a light parsley sauce. The tenderest lamb was dressed with pimento olive sauce and served with fondant potatoes and rosemary-flavoured shallots. But the dessert was the real triumph: a bitter Valrhona soufflé was accompanied by a warm, smooth, slightly alcoholic chocolate sauce and white chocolate ice-cream. This excess of chocolate was complemented by an exquisite vanilla sauce, thin slices of bitter orange probably permeated by a drop or two of Grand Marnier providing an appropriate sensory contrast. Coffee arrived with a selection of petits fours. Each was in fact a mini-dessert in its own right: bite-sized fruit tarts, crisp almond tuiles, coffee bavarois. Each course was accompanied by a glass or two of wine selected specifically for the dish by the sommelier. It was a memorable meal, the staff as competent as they were charming, sufficiently friendly to lighten the solitude of a lonely diner.

After I rose from the table, I suddenly realized that it was not far from here that I had nearly died of starvation sixty years earlier.

15

I was searching on the internet for information on Hungarians who had been deported, like us, to Bergen-Belsen. I do not recall the precise keywords I typed in, but it was a complete surprise when I stumbled across a letter written by a young woman to her husband on 9 May 1945, the day after the war ended in Europe. It bore the title 'A Holocaust survivor's diary'.

The place where she had written it immediately attracted my attention: Hillersleben, the village in which we stayed after the Americans liberated us. And the name of another town stood out: Makó, my birthplace. Given the endearing terms in which she addressed her husband, it was apparent that they must have been separated shortly after their marriage, and the intimate tone of the first couple of lines confirmed this impression, making for uneasy reading, as if I was intruding on someone's privacy. But the letter must surely have been posted on the internet for the world to see. Overcome by curiosity, I continued to read, and my excitement increased as I scrolled down the screen, page after page. This woman, with a young daughter and her in-laws, had undertaken exactly the same journey as we had: transport from the ghetto in Makó to Szeged, then to Strasshof, finally arriving in Bergen-Belsen in December 1944. Here she witnessed the death of my father: she mentioned his name among those who had perished. If I needed further proof, it was there: from the concentration camp they embarked on the same train, which was liberated by Americans on 13 April 1945, and they had been recuperating in Hillersleben. The letter was signed Magdi (informal for Magda), addressed to Feri (for Ferenc). The daughter's name was Ági (Ágnes). I searched my memory, striving to recall a family with these names, but I could not put faces to them.

Had it been coincidence? Or luck? My cousin Mari knew that I was looking for people from Makó who had been in Bergen-Belsen. One day she asked: 'Do you remember the Hajdu family from Makó? They were also in Bergen-Belsen.' The name was familiar, but that was all; I had to confess ignorance. 'Why do not you give Magdi a ring? It could be an interesting encounter,' she persisted in the way of teachers trying to encourage reluctant pupils. I did telephone her, and a couple of months later I was standing, with a small bouquet of flowers, in the doorway of Magdi Hajdu's flat.

The heat of the August sun had not abated, even by late afternoon. A relentless heatwave had gripped Budapest since May. I had arrived in Budapest some ten days earlier, and the temperature had never sunk below 30 degrees during the day. I had been delighted that the address I sought was at the foot of the hills in Buda, an escape from the furnace of the city: a small private block in a fashionable part of town. As I pressed the bell, the door was opened and in a flash it dawned on me that the woman standing in front of me had been the author of the letter I had read several times. We had made the journey together.

She radiated poise and elegance: a quietly elegant woman in a quietly elegant flat, a simple dress, practically no make-up. Ungallantly I did some quick mental arithmetic to guess her age, but her appearance defied my calculations: she looked a good fifteen years younger.

The initial element of unease, meeting after so many years had soon melted away. With the eagerness of an apprentice journalist, I impatiently fired a salvo of questions. She answered with deliberation and style. Yes, she remembered us well. In Belsen we were not only in the same barrack, but our bunks were also quite close. Yes, she said, the latrine was outside, and that many people could not reach it in time. Yes, there was a large room with washbasins and taps spouting from a long duct. The water was ice cold, but those with will-power braved the temperature; it became natural for men and women to use this bathroom at the same time. And yes, there was electricity in the wire fence, and many inmates used this quick exit: when someone was found dead at the fence, no one could leave the barracks. She remembered my father's dying in the hospital barrack. Then I asked about my mother. 'She was self-contained,' she said. 'She looked after you very well.'

Ági, her daughter who was my age, contracted pneumonia in Bergen-Belsen and nearly died. Magdi volunteered to help by nursing patients; this was how she witnessed my father's death. Magdi's mother-in-law died after liberation: her grave is in the restored Jewish cemetery in Hillersleben. After liberation, in the calm of Hillersleben, on the first day of peace, Magdi poured out the memories of her journey in a letter as freely as if she were talking to her husband. The letter was later translated into English, more or less accurately, by her brother and posted on the internet. She gave me a copy of the typed version, and showed me the original letter. Written in pencil, the script is now slightly smudged and the paper gently frayed.

16

The back issues of the *British Medical Journal* and *The Lancet* are stored in the cavernous basement of the Royal Society of Medicine in Wimpole Street in central London. It is also here that the discontinued runs of journals of various medical schools gather dust: row upon row of shelves stretching from floor to ceiling. Closely stacked and heavy, they can be moved on their rail only by turning a wheel, and it requires considerable manpower to expose the required volumes. In the volumes from 1945 I found the information I was seeking. In its issue of 5 May 1945, *The Lancet* reported that in the preceding week ninety-seven senior medical students left London for Belsen, where, under the guidance of experts from the Ministry of Health and the Ministry of Food, they would be helping in the treatment of the starving.

The students had responded to a notice posted in the early spring in London medical schools requesting volunteers to join a party of one hundred for humanitarian work in Holland, attending to severe cases of starvation in the liberated Dutch cities. There was no shortage of response, and those selected were inoculated, instructed and equipped during the course of a twelve-week period. While waiting to be dispatched, they learned with interest and surprise that their original destination had changed from Holland to Belsen. The liberation of the concentration camp had created an acute medical emergency, which overrode the previous plan. After several false starts (departure had been frustrated by icy weather conditions) six

Dakotas finally took off from an airfield outside Cirencester, but only one arrived in Celle, the airfield nearest to the camp; another had been diverted to Brussels while the remaining four had to return to England. A couple of days later the operation was successfully completed with the last medical student disembarking in Celle.

Reading the accounts in the medical journals, one name sounded vaguely familiar: John Hankinson. His report, entitled simply 'Belsen', was published in the June issue of the *St Mary's Hospital Gazette*. It is compulsive reading, exuding compassion for the survivors and showing a sense of humour when describing the vicissitudes, improvisations and resourcefulness of the students and other medical personnel who had been confronted with a human tragedy on a scale previously unknown to them.

John Hankinson: the name suddenly came sharply into focus. The time: the 1970s. The place: Newcastle. The common ground: neuroscience. I had met Hankinson, professor of neurosurgery at Newcastle, some thirty years earlier. Of course, the author of the report could be an entirely different person, but the Medical Register dispelled my doubts. All I needed to know was there. He obtained his medical degree in 1946 in St Mary's Medical School in London to become consultant neurological surgeon in the Royal Victoria Infirmary and the Regional Neuroscience Centre in Newcastle, and professor of neurosurgery at the University of Newcastle upon Tyne. I wrote to him, explaining who I was and the reason for sending what by any standards must have seemed an unusual letter. By return of mail I received a warm reply, inviting me to visit him in Newcastle.

By this time, in 2004, I had not seen him for nearly thirty years. Yet I recognized him without any difficulty as soon as he entered the lobby. Time had been kind to him: his hair was thinner and his face more lined, but he had none of the frailty of an octogenarian. The glint of enquiring eyes behind his glasses had not been dimmed by age. We sat in the bar of a hotel just outside town, drinking gin and tonic before lunch, running over the more recent past, our encounter in Newcastle during the 1970s.

Over lunch we switched subjects and talked of Belsen. The medical students had worked in pairs; each pair had been allocated one barrack. Every morning they entered the barrack and tried to separate the living from those who had died during the night. The barracks were still overcrowded: in the hut in which Hankinson worked up to 300 people had been crammed into a space designed for 80. The corpses were removed by regular units of German and Hungarian soldiers: they were well treated and protected against infection, in striking contrast with their predecessors, the SS guards, who had been forced to carry the corpses with their bare hands.

In the circumstances they could do little actual medical work: even intravenous administration of plasma and serum preparation was impossible in the barracks. Those who needed medical help were gradually transferred to the hospital. The main function of the medical students was to supervise the proper distribution of suitable food to the survivors, and to improve, as far as possible, their living conditions. Many suffered from severe problems of digestion, and diarrhoea, with subsequent serious dehydration, was a major health hazard. The kindness and eagerness of British soldiers to help at the beginning misfired: the emaciated inmates, although they desperately needed nourishment after prolonged and severe starvation, could not digest food more suitable for healthy young men. Some of the patients were so thin that they lay or sat on their bones: the normal convex contours of the buttocks became, in the parlance of the medical students, the concave Belsen buttock. Stethoscopes failed to pick up the sounds of heartbeat or of respiration, since the protruding ribs prevented full contact with the chest. Infections, particularly typhus, were still rampant, with a high mortality rate: nearly all patients aged fifty or over died. In the hospital 20 per cent of patients had been diagnosed with tuberculosis.

After a stay of six weeks, their task having been completed and relieved by others who would continue the work of rehabilitating the survivors, the party of medical students was ready to travel back to England. Before his departure from Bergen-Belsen, Hankinson went back to Camp 1, the barracks of which had by then been burnt down. Yet the image of desolation, destruction and dirt, together with the lingering smell of burning, remained imprinted in his memory for a long time. Leaving, he was not the same man who had entered Bergen-Belsen a few weeks previously.

Over coffee, he suddenly said: 'I hope you don't mind, but I would like to give you something. A little present. Since both of us were in Belsen. And a little memento of our meeting today. I will understand if you do not want to accept it. But I hope you will.' And he produced a small, worn grey pouch from the pocket of his jacket, and pulled out a beautiful old silver pocket watch. I was moved, lost for words. Conflicting thoughts flashed through my mind. I cannot accept it; the watch belongs to him. It is his memento of Belsen; I should not take it. Nevertheless, it would be unkind to refuse it. I had no doubt that his offer was genuine: he wanted me to have the watch. Then I said hesitantly, still overcome by his generosity: 'I don't think I can accept it,' regretting this immediately.

'I was given it, just before my departure from Belsen, by a British soldier,' he explained. 'I do not remember exactly why, perhaps as a reward for the work we had done there. I would very much like you to have it.'

Embarrassed and confused, I accepted the watch and thanked him. I didn't know what else to say.

'It stopped a long time ago,' he said.

It was an Omega pocket watch with a white enamel face, crisp black Roman numerals and slender hands. At the bottom of the face there was a small second hand. The silver case was tarnished, but otherwise it was in perfect condition. On the hinged dust cover there was an ornamental relief of intertwining leaves. The back of the case opened easily to reveal the silent, motionless mechanism. The watch had stopped at twenty minutes to five, in a mirror image defying all those advertisements in which the hands are always fixed unfailingly at ten past ten, pointing exuberantly upward, as if trying to capture the passing minutes.

Perhaps the watch could be repaired. Back in London I took it to a well-known jeweller in Regent Street. 'No, we cannot repair it here,' one of the assistants said, 'but I can recommend someone whose services we frequently use.' And she gave me the name, address and telephone number of a watch repairer in Mayfair.

His shop was on the first floor of a building in one of the fashionable streets in Mayfair. I showed the watch to him. And I was pleasantly surprised when, after a general examination, he gave his diagnosis: 'Yes, it can be repaired. It will be ready within three to four weeks.'

17

The Imperial War Museum, previously a psychiatric hospital in Lambeth, South London, in addition to housing permanent displays and temporary exhibitions, is the guardian of an archive: a unique collection of documents relating to the two world wars and other military campaigns in which the United Kingdom and countries of the Commonwealth fought from 1914 onwards. It is there that I found further information on Bergen-Belsen.

The museum's Reading Room is in the former chapel of the

hospital. It is an octagonal room flooded with light from eight large semicircular windows in the dome. From the floor, on either side, a spiral staircase leads to a gallery, which runs along five walls: it is supported by six slender columns. If the visitor's suspicions as to the original function of this room are not immediately aroused by these architectural hints, a quick glance at the wall beneath the dome where the altar once must have stood clearly confirms it: the Ten Commandments, written in large gold lettering on a black background.

> 'Thou shalt do no murder.'
> 'Thou shalt not steal.'
> 'Thou shalt not covet thy neighbour's house.'

It is an odd convergence: the Ten Commandments and the documents of Belsen. The encounter of God and evil in a lunatic asylum.

In one of the museum's folders I made an unexpected find: Hitler's writing paper. Good-quality white paper, not too thick, not too thin. With black engraving. Good-quality dye, too: it has not faded. The Germans were always clever with dyes. Berlin W8. *Kanzlei des Führers der NSDAP. Amt I.* From the Chancellery of the Führer of the National Socialist German Workers' Party. The First Office. *Aktenzeichen*, file number empty. The space for the date is also empty. The whole page is empty. And yet it radiates malice. Untold threats. What could have been written on it?

FARSLEBEN: THE TRAIN TO FREEDOM

1

The plane landed ahead of schedule at Los Angeles International Airport, and despite increased security the immigration procedure was surprisingly quick and efficient. My Latino cab driver, who not only knew his freeways but was also courteous in an old-fashioned way, reminiscent more of the ancient etiquette of Spain than streamlined American politeness, reassured me as to my impeccable choice of hotel. I checked in at the Beverly Hilton, on Wilshire Boulevard in Beverly Hills: a hotel that fortunately has escaped the minimalist rub-down and has remained stubbornly redolent of faded (and not so faded) glamour. The early February sunshine pushed temperatures into the mid-twenties Celsius, and from the landscape window of my room I could see distant hills in the blue haze and opulent homes with the obligatory swimming pools. Reality improved on imagination: it was a perfect day. Even the breeze from the nearby hills knew the ideal speed and frequency at which to stroke sun-saturated bodies lying by the pool.

In the evening, while I was waiting in the lobby for my friend Fay to pick me up for dinner, I was drawn into a reception of a charity gala that had just got under way. Most of the guests appeared to have originated in some successful eugenic experiment: tall, perfectly proportioned bodies well honed by exercise and nourished on diets tuned to the latest fads, unblemished skin just the right shade of bronze without the vulgarity of cheap package holidays in the sun, each pore singing

the praises of natural moisturizers, flawlessly coiffed hair sufficient to shame shampoo advertisements, dresses that spoke of
both good taste and an open chequebook. Fay and I escaped to
a genuine old hamburger joint to recover from the shock of
this visual nirvana.

But the real antidote to this conspicuous perfection came the
next morning at the Greyhound depot in downtown Los
Angeles. After the long transatlantic flight I decided against
flying to San Diego; hiring a car was out of question for one
day, considering the diabolical freeway system, and I turned
down Fay's generous offer to drive me down the coast, since I
wanted to make this journey on my own. The bus depot was a
Third World island adrift in California. Listless drug addicts,
aggressive drunks shouting obscenities, emaciated Aids victims, people obese beyond plausibility: a depressing tableau
half an hour's taxi drive and worlds away from Beverly Hills.

The journey was long but comfortable: after the bus had
meandered its way through the endless southern suburbs of
Los Angeles, with their ubiquitous shopping malls, neglected
tenements and cheerless petrol stations, the freeway yielded a
more agreeable vista of a prosperous stretch of the Sunshine
State. The ocean soon sparkled unrestrained between exclusive
housing estates, luxuriant gardens and sleek office buildings.

The Greyhound bus arrived at the depot half an hour early.
Although it was early February, San Diego had lived up to its
reputation as the town with the most pleasant climate in the
United States, producing the cliché of a perfect day: warm
gentle sunshine in an unbroken blue sky. I scanned the milling
crowd in the arrivals hall, but could not see George Gross, the
man I had come to meet. As the hall gradually emptied, not
knowing what else to do, I decided to wait. After stalking me
for a while, a grossly overweight security guard, with a pendu-
lous girdle of flab overhanging his crotch and free-falling towards his knees, approached me and asked politely what my

business was. Wearing a light linen suit with a silk tie, I must have looked suspicious, too well dressed for this place. My explanation and the return Greyhound ticket to Los Angeles must have completely satisfied him, since he scuttled away towards the exit without any further questions. By now an unnatural silence had descended on the deserted arrivals hall.

I knew I would recognize George Gross when he arrived: he had sent two photographs. One was taken in March 1945, one month before he found our train. The young George Gross stands in front of his tank, the turret positioned behind his head, and the cannon, with its protective sleeve, sticking out over his right shoulder, aiming at nowhere in particular. A handsome young man in uniform, with an engaging smile, stares directly into the camera. With straight dark hair forming a wavy line above his high forehead, he nonchalantly holds a pipe. The other picture is a recent snapshot: the same man fifty-six years later in a dignified posture, a face with a hint of a smile, grey hair that has retreated to the higher slopes of the skull, leaving behind an even more dominating forehead, and glasses.

This was not our first meeting. We had met once before, fifty-seven years earlier: I was not quite six years old then and he must have been in his early twenties. He was a tank commander in the 743rd Tank Battalion of the 30th Division of the American 9th Army, and I was travelling on a train from Bergen-Belsen to an unknown destination. Our encounter had taken place outside the village of Farsleben, not far from Magdeburg, in eastern Germany. The date was 13 April 1945.

And now, in my sixties, I am about to meet him again. Waiting for him, I grow increasingly nervous: was it such a good idea to travel here in search of the past? What was I going to say? I would have liked to coin a phrase, something profound and eternally quotable. After all, he saved my life. But eloquence deserted me.

2

This extraordinary encounter was the climax of strange mixture of coincidence, luck and research. Four years earlier I had participated in a medical workshop convened by one of the senior neurologists of the National Institutes of Health in Bethesda, Maryland, just outside Washington, D.C. Our task was to agree on a set of diagnostic criteria by which a rare neurological disease, corticobasal degeneration, manifesting as a movement disorder and frequently complicated by dementia, could be recognized. The workshop consisted of a panel of a dozen or so invited international experts, and after a couple of sessions we arrived at a definition acceptable to all participants. With some time on my hands before flying back to London, I decided to visit the Holocaust Museum a few miles away.

My initial apprehension about visiting such a place was soon overcome by the unsettling beauty of the architecture, by the imaginative displays and the solemnity of the place, preserved even when hordes of tourists were milling around. On impulse I took a lift to the library. The abundance of books dealing with the Holocaust was overwhelming and came as a surprise: at the time I was unaware that the Final Solution had created a literary cottage industry. Room after room, shelf upon shelf of books and endless indices on the computer were available to satisfy every level of interest from historians to lay members of the public. Books on concentration camps were neatly arranged in alphabetical order: an obscene antithesis to the holiday destinations in a travel bookshop. Instead of the Algarve, Côte d'Azur, Florence, New York, Provence or Zanzibar, there was the spine-chilling list of Auschwitz, Bergen-Belsen, Dachau, Mathausen, Treblinka and many more: some of the names were hardly known to me. And under B, among the books on Bergen-Belsen, I came across a slim volume by Eberhard Kolb, with the title *Bergen-Belsen: from 1943 to 1945*, a much-condensed version of the original German work published in 1962 in Hanover. On page 40 of the second 1988 edition of the English version (pages 155–6 of the original German edition), I stumbled across a piece of information I had been searching for: the missing link between Bergen-Belsen and our liberation. This was the clue that led to the encounter in San Diego.

Kolb describes how, between 6 and 11 April 1945, three trains, carrying a total of some 7,000 inmates, left Bergen station. On 21 April one of these trains arrived in Theresienstadt, a camp not far from Prague. The other two trains, presumably also destined for Theresienstadt, travelled for days through northern Germany and were subjected to frequent air attacks. One train was halted on the open track near Magdeburg on 13 April and liberated by the Americans. The other was stopped on 23 April near the village of Tröbitz in the Niederlausitz region and liberated by the Russians. And suddenly seemingly disparate pieces of information, buried deep in the subconscious, emerged to fill a gap in the narrative of my journey. My mother and I had been on the train found by the Americans near Magdeburg.

3

The train was already at the station waiting for us: a few battered passenger carriages were greatly outnumbered by cattle wagons. The presence of the passenger carriages, however decrepit, was a novelty in our journey, since travelling in cattle wagons had become our accustomed means of transport. Scuffles broke out to get a place in one of the compartments rather than in the dreaded wagons. But order was soon restored, and those infirm or with children could claim the more comfortable accommodation. We were fortunate to get into one of the crowded compartments. To our surprise and relief some food, including bread, jam and cheese, was distributed.

For a long time nothing happened, and we waited with mounting impatience for the familiar whistle of the locomotive and for the train to pull out of the station. In the distance there was the sound of muffled explosions, and excitement ran through the train at the possibility that the Allies might arrive to capture the station before the train could depart. But the muffled noise was only the echoes of far-away raids, and after long hours of waiting through the night the train finally pulled out of Bergen station the next morning.

It was a long journey. The train travelled slowly, rarely gathering pace. Frequently it came to a halt, often on the open tracks, occasionally at small stations. Our food, however carefully rationed by my mother, did not last long: we were hungry and thirsty. The compartments were full, and there was not the remotest chance of stretching out. None the less, the train was more comfortable than those that had delivered us to Bergen-Belsen.

We were travelling with the aimlessness of a child's toy train, meandering round the same track again and again. The train changed directions several times, and we recognized places we had passed earlier. But if at first we were bored by the slow progress and monotonous rhythm of the train, we soon found excitement.

The guards accompanying us had anti-aircraft guns. These they fired at low-flying Allied aircrafts, which zoomed menacingly close to the train. We were terrified thinking that they were going to bomb us mistaking our train for a transport carrying German soldiers. Suddenly we heard explosions. Panic broke out. Everyone scrambled to leave and find safety under the trees, away from the track. We were no exception. Under the shelter of the trees, my mother again took me through a macabre but sensible procedure. She had already rehearsed me several times on what I should do and say in case I survived and she did not. I had to repeat my name and

my parents' name and our address at home as identification –
information I already knew. As a further safety measure she
introduced me to other women who would look after me
should she die: a reciprocal arrangement made by a couple of
mothers who agreed to become guardians of each other's
children.

But we survived the air raids, which ceased after a short
while: the pilots must have realized the nature of the train's
cargo. The journey continued, interminably: several days and
nights passed without any promise of arrival. We must have
been travelling for nearly a week. One day the train stopped on
the open track. There was nothing out of the ordinary to see; it
was just another stop, as had happened several times before.
This was the final halt, however. Apparently the driver lived in
a village nearby. He abandoned the train and went home.
Shortly afterwards, he died of typhus.

There was silence. Then, suddenly, we heard the noise of
heavy machine-guns firing and people shouting. We spotted a
couple of tanks without the Iron Cross, and soldiers in uniforms we had not seen before. Hesitantly, we disembarked.
There was no sign of the German guards. The soldiers smiled
and waved at us. They talked to us in a language we did not
understand. It was definitely not German. The soldiers were
Americans. It was 13 April 1945.

4

I was determined to find those who liberated our train. But the
only clue at my disposal was a single piece of information: our
train was found by American soldiers in the vicinity of
Magdeburg. To begin with, it was essential to identify the unit
of the US Army that had been operating near Magdeburg in
April 1945. In principle the quest seemed all too simple. On
closer scrutiny, however, identifying a small unit responsible

for the liberation of a train-load of Jews in the closing weeks of the war, given the rapid movement of the Allies through eastern Germany, appeared to be a more daunting task. But on this occasion luck was on my side. After some searching on the Internet, I found a lead in one of the military archives: the area in which our train was found was probably taken by elements of the 30th Infantry Division, part of XIX Corps of the Ninth US Army. Further search revealed that the 30th Division had a website, and my attention was drawn to a noticeboard designed for posting questions. And it was here that I posted my notice at the beginning of December 2000: 'April 1945 Hillersleben near Magdeburg. Anyone remembers a train load of Hungarian Jews being transported from Bergen-Belsen and liberated by one unit of your division, and then taken to Hillersleben. I was on the train as a child of five years of age. If anyone remembers or can help retrace any surviving members of that unit, I would be most grateful. Thank you.' And to my name I appended my e-mail address.

Within a few days I received a couple of responses, one from a young woman living in Connecticut whose father had served in the 30th Division. Although he was not a member of the unit that liberated our train, he had preserved a newspaper article reporting the rescue of 2,500 Jews from a German train outside the village of Farsleben. The brief article described how the prisoners were packed like cattle in wagons without sanitary facilities and without food.

A man who had been researching the history of the 30th Division, and whose father had also served in the division, sent relevant extracts from a couple of publications describing the finding of our transport.

But only in May 2001 did I receive the letter I was waiting for. It was from George Kennedy, editor of *30th Division News*. Having seen my note on their website, he decided to reproduce it in the winter edition of their newsletter. A few days later he received a letter from a Carroll S. Walsh, commander of one of the tanks (2nd Platoon, Company D, 743 Tank Battalion) that stopped our train. Walsh named another soldier, George C. Gross, who was with him when they found the train. On 30 May I received a letter from George Gross.

Greetings over a continent, an ocean, and fifty-six years! I am the George Gross who commanded one of the two tanks that came across your train and chased the few remaining SS guards away. (They were captured shortly after in a house nearby.) I stayed with your train through the night until relieved by people who could better care for you. My good comrade Carroll Walsh, who commanded the other tank, returned to our battalion headed for the battle of Magdeburg.

I remember setting up a guard perimeter with the ranking officer of a group of prisoners of war, who mustered his men promptly and set them on picket lines with great efficiency, armed with clubs and a few abandoned German weapons. That left me with time to greet all the people. I found myself facing a long line of men, women, and small children, all wanting to re-establish their identities as individual human beings. Each would introduce himself or herself personally or through an interpreter, a young woman on the train named GR. It seemed very important that they say their names, and I was proud and profoundly moved to shake their hands.

I have some pictures I shall send to you, along with a more extended description of the event as I remember it. One of the pictures was taken by Major Benjamin of our 743rd Tank Battalion just as a very few people are beginning to realize they have been liberated. It is very moving. I have another picture of a little boy who might be you, and others of the brave, emaciated people of the train, smiling despite their pain and weakness. Most of the pictures were taken by me with a little box Kodak, but my younger son, a professional photographer, can enlarge and clarify them pretty well. That may take a little time, but I'll send what I can right away.

Meanwhile, you may find it interesting that Carroll Walsh and I were commissioned a couple of weeks after the moving experience with the train. He went on to become a Superior Court Judge in the State of New

York, while I recently retired as a Professor of English at San Diego State University. With your academic medical career, it appears that all three of us have fared well over the years.

On Friday, 13 April 1945, George Gross was commanding a light tank in a column of the 743rd Tank Battalion moving south near the Elbe river towards Magdeburg. Suddenly he was ordered, together with his mate Sergeant Carroll Walsh, also in a light tank, to accompany Major Clarence Benjamin in a scouting foray to the east of the route the battalion had taken. Major Benjamin had earlier come across several emaciated Finnish soldiers: they recounted that they had escaped from a train full of starving prisoners a short distance away. The major led the two tanks, each carrying several infantrymen from the 30th Infantry Division on its deck, down a narrow road until they arrived at a valley with a small train station at its head. A train composed of an assortment of passenger carriages and goods wagons stood stationary in a siding, and there were masses of people sitting, lying or wandering aimlessly around, unaware at first of the arrival of the two tanks. George Gross pulled up his tank at the head of the train to indicate that it was under American protection. The other tank was sent back to join the battalion, and George Gross's tank, with its crew of infantrymen, was the only guard remaining for the rest of the day and the night of 13 April. In the mean time, George Gross was informed that the commander of the 823rd Tank Destroyer Battalion had ordered the burgomasters of nearby towns to prepare and deliver food to the train without delay. While waiting for the relief to arrive, George Gross met the passengers.

We stood in front of the tank as a long line of men, women and little children formed itself spontaneously, with great dignity and no confusion, to greet us. It is a time I cannot forget, for it was terribly moving to see the courtesy with which they treated each other, and the importance they seemed to place on reasserting their individuality in some seemingly official way. Each would stand at a position of rigid attention, held with some difficulty, and introduce himself or herself by what grew to be a sort of formula: the full name, followed by 'a Jew from Hungary' – or a similar phrase, giving both the origin and the home from which the person had been seized. Then each would shake hands in a solemn and dignified assertion of individual worth. Battle-hardened veterans learn to contain their emotion, but it was difficult then, and I cry now to think about it. What stamina and regenerative spirit those brave people showed.

Also tremendously moving were their smiles. I have one picture of several girls, spectre-thin, hollow-cheeked, with enormous eyes that had seen much evil and terror, and yet with smiles to break one's heart. Little children came around with shy smiles, and mothers with proud smiles happily pushed them forward to get their pictures taken. I walked up and down the train, seeing some lying in pain or lack of energy, and some sitting and making hopeful plans for a future that suddenly seemed possible again. Others followed everywhere I went, not intruding but just wanting to be close to a representative of the forces that had freed them. How sad it was that we had no food to give immediately, and no medical help, for during my short stay with the train sixteen or more bodies were carried up the hillside to await burial; brave hearts having lost the fight against starvation before we could help them.

The wagons were generally in very bad condition from having been the living quarters of far too many people, and the passenger compartments showed the same sign of overcrowding and unsanitary conditions. But people were not dirty. Their clothes were old and often ragged, but they were generally clean, and the people themselves had obviously taken great pains to look their best as they presented themselves to us. I was told that many had taken advantage of the cold stream that flowed through the lower part of the valley to wash themselves and their clothing. Once again I was impressed by the indomitable spirit of these courageous people.

We were relieved the next morning, started up the tank, waved goodbye to our new friends, and followed a guiding jeep down the road to rejoin our battalion.

So ends George Gross's story of finding our train, signed off on 3 June 2001 in Spring Valley, California.

5

On 16 April 1942, in Fort Lewis, Washington, nine officers and 108 enlisted men formed the core of the 743rd Tank Battalion. Exactly one month later it was officially incorporated in the US Army, and soon their equipment had been changed from light to medium tanks. After periods of training in California, and Arizona, the battalion embarked in New York on HMS *Aquitania* on 16 November 1943, and after crossing the Atlantic arrived in Gòurock, Scotland, one week later. On D-Day, 6 June 1944, they received their baptism of fire on Omaha Beach, and during subsequent months they fought their way through northern France, Belgium and Holland. Crossing the Siegfried Line at the beginning of October 1944, they pushed their way into Germany before returning to Belgium to participate in the Battle of the Bulge. They fought in the next major offensive, commencing on 23 February, crossed the River Roer, then the Rhine north of Düsseldorf, and advanced rapidly in a north-easterly direction towards Münster. Finally, traversing the Weser at Hameln, they were poised to take Magdeburg. And it was at this stage that members of the 743rd Tank Battalion came across our train.

A few miles northwest of Magdeburg there was a railroad siding in a wooded ravine not far from the Elbe River. Major Clarence Benjamin in a peep [jeep] was leading a small task force of two light tanks from Dog Company in a routine job of patrolling. The unit came upon some 200 shabby looking civilians by the side of the road. There was something immediately apparent about each one of these people, men and women, which arrested the attention. Each one of them was skeleton-thin with starvation, a sickness in their faces and the way in which they stood – and there was something else. At the sight of Americans they began laughing in joy – if it could be called laughing. It was an outpouring of pure, near-hysterical relief.

The tankers soon found out why. The reason was found at the railroad siding.

They came upon a long string of grimy, ancient boxcars standing silent on the tracks. On the banks by the tracks, as if to get some pitiful comfort from the thin April sun, a multitude of people in all shades of misery spread themselves in a sorry, despairing tableau. As the American uniforms were sighted, a great stir went through this strange camp. Many rushed towards the major's peep and the two light tanks.

Bit by bit, as the Major found some who spoke English, the story came out.

This had been – and was – a horror train. In those freight cars had been shipped 2,500 people, jam-packed in like sardines, and they were people who had two things in common, one with the other: they were prisoners of the German State and they were Jews.

These 2,500 wretched people, starved, beaten, ill, some dying, were political prisoners who had until a few days before been held at a concentration camp near Hannover. When the Allied armies smashed through beyond the Rhine and began slicing into central Germany, the tragic 2,500 had been loaded into old railroad cars – as many as 68 in one filthy boxcar – and brought in a tortuous journey to this railroad siding by the Elbe. They were to be taken still deeper into Germany beyond the Elbe when German trainmen got into an argument about the route and the cars had been shunted onto the siding. Here the tide of the Ninth Army's rush had found them.

They found it hard to believe that they were really in friendly hands once more: they were fearful that the Germans would return. They had been guarded by a large force of SS troopers, most of whom had disappeared into the night. Major Benjamin, knowing there were many German Army stragglers still in the area, left one of the light tanks there with its accompanying doughboys as a protective guard. The Major then returned to Division headquarters to report the plight of these people.

The above has been reproduced word for word from *Move Out, Verify: the Combat History of the 743rd Tank Battalion*, by Wayne Robinson. I have a copy of the book. George Gross dedicated it to me: the date is 3 February 2003.

6

I remember the first few hours of freedom. At the beginning no one knew what was happening: that the train had been stationary for such a long time was not surprising – endless stops on the open track were common. But this stop was different. More and more people were leaving the wagons, and the German guards, who had previously ordered us back to the trains, were nowhere to be seen. The train had come to a stop at a siding: there was a clearing with a few trees and bushes, and an embankment ran parallel with the track. We saw two tanks on the horizon, and those ahead of us started to shout: 'The Americans, the Americans.'

As the news spread, more and more left the train, still not believing that it was all over and that we were free. Soon it was all but deserted, although some were too weak to move, and a few had not survived the journey. We made our way towards the tanks, but we were so weak that the gentle slope of the embankment nearly defeated us. We managed to climb it slowly, and then we saw the first American soldiers. They were so different from us, and from anybody else we had seen during the last few months. They were very tall, or so it seemed to me, well-fed and clean. They displayed a facial expression that we had all but forgotten existed: they smiled at us. They explained (while someone translated from English into German and Hungarian) that they were going to get food and accommodation for us, but this might take some time.

While we were waiting, we found a stream nearby, and washed ourselves as best we could in the ice-cold water. I realized many years later, as we reconstructed the events of the day of our liberation, that this was more than an abortive attempt to clean ourselves of the grime of the journey, but a symbolic gesture: an eradication of the evil of the past months; an attempt to wash away Bergen-Belsen, Wiener Neustadt,

Strasshof, the ghetto in Szeged, the ghetto in Makó. To purify ourselves of the sins of others.

We joined the queue of those passing before the American soldiers and introducing themselves. A couple of the soldiers took photographs. Some of these snapshots are now in front of me. A number of pictures show a shallow valley with a pair of railway tracks and our train in a siding, with people in small groups or individually standing, walking around or lying on the ground. There are a few young trees and several bushes on the slopes, and the outline of a small forest in the distance; the trees are still leafless in the early spring. And then there are group photographs: one on the railway track, the other on the slope; adults and children wearing shabby clothes, some in overcoats, others just in jackets or sweaters, a couple waving at the photographer, most smiling. The snapshot taken on the slope shows the tracks, and a lonely figure sitting on the step of one of the carriages, too exhausted to join the group being photographed a couple of yards in front of him. In this group of nearly forty people half are children; the youngest cannot be more than four or five years of age. They are standing in the protective shadow of adults, or sitting on the ground.

Wedged between a girl and a young woman who must have been kneeling, since her head is level with the head of the girl, there is a young boy. And I experience a sudden recognition: this boy must be me. But I am uncertain, feel the nagging unease that follows an identity parade: did we pick the right person? The image is not very sharp; after all, the picture was taken fifty-seven years ago with a simple Kodak camera from a considerable distance, to frame as many people as possible with the train in the background. Is this little boy me? Or someone else? The face is at an angle, not directed towards the camera, and under the magnifying glass the features become blurred. I do not have my pictures taken soon after the war to aid positive identification: they were all lost after I left

Hungary. But the trousers the boy is wearing in the picture are very much like the trousers my mother favoured, and I recall wearing them at the time: the integral braces connected with a strip at the front.

The most dramatic photo has caught people in the moment when they realized they were free: two cattle wagons and naked trees form the background, and nearest to the camera is a mother with her daughter; close behind them two other women are climbing the slope towards the lens. The mother wears a skirt and a blouse with large white buttons; her thick stockings concertina down her legs and her hair is covered by a scarf tied at the back on her nape – she faces the camera and her expression hovers between a cry and a smile. I know this woman and recognize her face, but I cannot recover her name from the well of lost memories. She holds the hand of a little girl with a sad, angelic face. One of the two women further down the slope is crying; the other, wearing a thin overcoat and a black scarf, opens her arms widely in a declaration of welcome and smiles, but her smile is not a smile: it is the grin of a skeleton.

7

In San Diego, 2003 the quotidian necessities of life as usual came first: we had to find George Gross's son, who had parked his car nearby. And we started a brief guided tour, driving to the university campus where George had worked. His younger son John, a professional photographer who copied and enlarged the photographs his father took on 13 April 1945, drove the car. On the way to a restaurant we picked up the rest of the family: Marlo, George's wife of sixty-one years, Tim, his other son, who is an archaeologist, and Tim's wife Marcia. Both sons had inherited George's large frame, both sported beards and both radiated rotund joviality. After lunch we drove to Tim's house, a large, unpretentious, inviting home, for coffee and cake. Their daughter, Jennifer, joined us later. I knew that I had to tell my story: the days, months and years after 13 April 1945, life before and after liberation, that chronological milestone. By now I was feeling relaxed; I was in the company of good people. I also learned a little about their lives. After dusk they drove me back to the Greyhound depot. In the end I did not say anything profound or memorable. My visit was simply an occasion to express my gratitude for that momentous past event: the life I made is the expression of that gratitude, and George Gross knows it. During those few hours I recovered yet another missing fragment of my life on the journey from Bergen-Belsen. What happened on that railway siding in the cold spring of 1945 found its meaning fifty-six years later in the sunshine of San Diego.

HILLERSLEBEN:

ESCAPE FROM THE RUSSIANS

1

The excitement of liberation was gradually replaced by a sense of new uncertainty. The presence of the American tank at the head of the train was a visible guarantee of our freedom, but what would happen if the SS guards returned? My mother reassured me and kept repeating that we were free; the SS had gone for ever, and she promised, without much foundation, as it later turned out, that we could soon go home. But the comforting idea of home remained distant and unattainable: we were in the middle of nowhere in an enemy country. How long could it take to get home? And how would we travel? The war was still being waged but the rumours had now been confirmed: the Germans had been all but defeated. The Allies progressing rapidly from the west were soon going to meet up with the Russians attacking from the east. There was also news that the Russians had completed the liberation of Hungary at the beginning of April, a few days before our train was found.

We were hungry, and food was not immediately forthcoming. Someone who had talked to the Americans explained that they were trying to get food for us as soon as possible, and one of the commanders had ordered the inhabitants of nearby villages to prepare food and bake bread – even during the night if necessary.

The next day we heard that we were going to be transported to a village not very far from where the train had been found. On the way we learned the name of the village where the

Americans had found accommodation for us: Hillersleben. We were going to live there until we recovered and transport could be organized for our return home. First we all had to go through a process of disinfection. There was nothing new in this humiliation – we had been disinfected in Strasshof and Bergen-Belsen – but here it was far more thorough: there was no shortage of disinfectants, soap or water.

Hillersleben was a small place, and after Bergen-Belsen an oasis of tranquillity, freedom and abundance. Too small to attract Allied bombers, it seemed to have escaped most of the ravages of war. We made our temporary home in a large house that had previously accommodated officers of the retreating German army. My mother and I had our own room, and this new-found privacy further contributed to the general confusion of the first few days of freedom. Adjusting to this new environment after ten months of life as prisoners presented severe problems. For me the greatest challenge was food. Many months' chronic starvation had sapped our strength and reduced us to skeletons. The temptation to compensate for all the deprivation of the past was irresistible. It was my mother who firmly blocked all attempts fully to satisfy my hunger. She realized the danger inherent in sudden changes to physiological systems weakened by long deprivation. Without remorse and impervious to all pleading, for the first few days she insisted on a draconian diet: we ate very little but frequently, sometimes no more than a soldier of bread with cheese or jam, and this amount was then gradually increased. I rebelled against her regime, but she was fully vindicated. Many people who overate died from gastrointestinal complications.

During one of our first evenings in Hillersleben we received an unexpected visitor. After answering a knock on the door, a black man in American uniform stood on our doorstep. He was a giant, or at least this is how he seemed to me; he must have been well over six feet tall. As he entered the room he had to bow his head slightly to avoid a collision with the door frame. I had not seen a black man before, and we could not hide our surprise. He smiled to reveal a brilliantly white set of teeth: the contrast between the black face and the white teeth was dazzling. My eyes were glued to him, and I stood there mesmerized, not able to move. He kept smiling while saying something in English which we did not understand. The purpose of his visit became obvious as he quietly moved towards the windows and closed the shutters. The war was in its final days but blackout regulations were still operational: he had come to check that the light from our window would not invite an unlikely assault from a stray German plane. After he had closed the shutters he said goodbye and left the room.

He returned the next evening, at the same time. By now we had realized why he was visiting our room: it was his duty to check all the windows in the building every evening. On his second visit, after he had checked the shutters, he fished a piece of chocolate from his pocket and handed it to me. I just stood there without saying a word, not hesitating to accept the offering. At my mother's prompting I thanked him in Hungarian and then in German. With another gleaming flash of teeth, he said encouragingly: 'Thank you.' I repeated this after him, and the phrase entered my English vocabulary straight away to join two other words I had already picked up: 'hello' and 'goodbye'.

This was how our short-lived friendship started. Although there was no common language between us we seemed able to communicate and to understand each other. During his third visit he sat down and pulled a photograph of a woman and two small boys from his wallet. 'My wife and sons,' he said. My mother wanted to reciprocate and produced a dog-eared snapshot which she had kept throughout our journey. '*Er war mein Mann,*' she said in German, pointing at my father. '*Er ist leider in Bergen-Belsen gestorben. Ich habe auch einen älterer Sohn; er ist*

20 *Jahre alt*.' She performed a little pantomime to render the translation: 'This is my husband. He died in Bergen-Belsen. I also have an elder son who is twenty years old.'

And so his visits became the highlight of the day, his knock on the door at the regular hour eagerly awaited. He unfailingly brought some chocolate for me, and I developed Pavlovian reflexes: the thought of his visits invariably initiated profuse salivation. His visits became less frequent as the war ended: there was no longer any need to observe the blackout regulations. The last time we saw him, soon after the Americans departed from Hillersleben, I was rewarded with a larger than usual portion of chocolate. And before he left he picked me up from the floor, laughing. I could smell his breath: a mixture of nicotine and the menthol of chewing gum.

Daily life in Hillersleben must have been extraordinary at this time: a small German village at the end of a cataclysmic war had been caught up in unforeseen events. Its inhabitants must have been expecting a relatively peaceful conclusion to the hostilities when suddenly 2,500 lice-infested, disease-ridden skeletal phantoms appeared from nowhere in their midst. How awful must have been the realization that they were going to stay for a while. Not only were they going to stay, they were taking over the whole village, supported by foreign soldiers. But there was nothing the burgers of Hillersleben could do about it, and an uneasy cohabitation was accomplished. But not without problems. The mayor of Hillersleben brought a complaint to the attention of the special envoy of the rural district who had been dispatched to assess developments in the aftermath of the occupation of the village. The new residents, it was reported, were entering the gardens of the German estate and causing upheaval there. The nature of the disturbance was not specified, but the commander of the Allied Military Administration had also been informed. The peace of German gardens must not be disturbed.

With regular eating our strength began to return, and we explored the quiet leafy streets of Hillersleben. There were many Hungarians in the village, including children of my age. During this period of uncertainty we reclaimed the lost world of childhood and made the streets our playground. We formed little groups to play hide-and-seek, sometimes in houses vacated by the Germans and unoccupied by the passengers from the train, and soon acquired a couple of balls with which to play soccer. It was during such a game that I had an accident. Too preoccupied with the ball in my possession, I did not see a car turning the corner. Then I heard simultaneously the shouts of the other boys, the crescendo of the horn and the screeching of brakes: I looked up, saw the car and tried to run from its path, but it was too late. I remember a sudden pain and being thrown in the air. I regained consciousness in my mother's arms: she was rushing with me to the hospital to get first aid.

My playmates alerted my mother who recalled the events of that terrifying day several years after the accident. Since it happened in the street where we lived, it took only a couple of minutes for her to reach the scene. In her panic she did not have time to change: she rushed out into the street wearing a dressing-gown. With increasing shock she saw her son lying on the road, in a pool of blood, attended by American soldiers kneeling next to him. A jeep, its doors open, was parked at an odd angle at the side of the road. As she lifted me, a trickle of blood stained the front of her light-coloured dressing-gown. The American soldiers drove us to the hospital. Although it was only a short journey, by the time we arrived the front of my mother's dressing-gown was drenched in blood. Despite these gruesome details the accident was minor: the mudguard had torn the skin on my back, ploughing a long but superficial wound. I did not have any internal injuries.

For many years I preserved a souvenir of that afternoon game in Hillersleben: a neat scar on my back next to the protruding vertebrae. With the passing years it shrank and finally disappeared among the other ravages of ageing skin. An old memento, like so many others, lost in time.

Our stay in Hillersleben was transitory, but for the first week the future did not stretch further than the next day. At the end of the war in Europe on 8 May it was unclear whether we would remain under American protection until sufficiently recovered for transport to be organized for those who wanted to return to their home country. As usual, the rumours circulated first. There was to be a change in our administration: the Americans would be handing us over to the Russians. These rumours were soon confirmed: Hillersleben would become part of the Russian zone. But first the Americans were replaced for a short while by the British. It was a time when large American, British and Russian army units were manoeuvring in this region, lining up behind the agreed borders of the occupational zones. The area around Magdeburg, including Hillersleben, would become part of the Russian zone of occupation, and both the Americans and the British would soon withdraw towards the west, according to the official division of Germany into four zones of occupation.

By now, after the defeat of the common enemy, the unavoidable antagonism between the Western powers and the Soviet Union was coming to the fore: the final break-up of the alliance and the new enmity were sealed by Churchill's speech in Fulton one year later. Unfortunately, we ended up on the wrong side of the Iron Curtain. Before Hillersleben was finally handed over to the Russian military administration at the beginning of July, we were offered the opportunity of a new life in the United States, a chance only a few people took up, and those who didn't probably regretted their decision for the rest of their lives. Most of the former inmates of Bergen-Belsen were determined to return to their homes, from which they had been brutally expelled only a year earlier. They expected to find them as they had left them. They longed to be reunited with their families. They planned to restart their lives among those who not so long ago had so openly and decidedly rejected them. And my mother was no exception. For her, travelling to the United States and applying for American citizenship, however favourable our impression of Americans, were not even options; emigration was dismissed out of hand. After more than a year's absence she was desperate to get home, to be reunited with my elder brother and the rest of her family, and to pick up the shattered pieces of her life. How could she have known what was awaiting us at home?

2

Although it was not unexpected, the arrival of the Russians seemed as sudden as it was irreversible. We had ample time to prepare for the change. With the departure of the Americans, who were always friendly with their loud 'hellos' and big smiles, followed briefly by the British, suddenly the mood became sombre and the future seemed more uncertain than ever before. I particularly missed my black friend: with his departure my chocolate supply had dried up. Under the Russians the standard of food deteriorated. The only hope was that they would soon organize our transport back to Hungary, as the Russian officers assured us would be the case.

Days and weeks passed and nothing happened. We were given various dates for the journey home but each promised departure was postponed. There was a general sense of despair, since the Russians did not seem to be in control of the situation. They were disorganized, and their inefficiency was in striking contrast with the organizational skills of the Americans. No one doubted that they genuinely wanted to help, since getting rid of us would in any event have eased the burden of their responsibility for an unwanted and precarious cargo. Yet our trains did not materialize. Organizing our transport was simply not a priority for them. When a confrontational meeting with the Russian commander yielded only the promise of yet another deadline, my mother decided to act alone. I had not failed to observe that, even before this meeting, we had paid a couple of visits to the railway station. She was enquiring about trains home, she told me, swearing me to secrecy. But the news was depressing: there were no trains to Hungary. Then one day everything changed. 'We leave this evening,' she said.

We packed only the most essential clothing. We did not need much for the journey since it was late August and the weather was still warm. At dusk we left surreptitiously without saying goodbye to anybody. The Russians may have witnessed our departure but did nothing to prevent us leaving: our luggage was too small to arouse suspicions of escape. Nobody in their right minds would set out with a meagre amount of food and barely a change of clothing to travel halfway across Europe. This was an epic adventure, and I was bowled over by the daring of our plan: it was far more exciting than anything that happened in adventure stories. My enthusiasm quickly turned to dejection when I could not spot any passenger train at the station. There was only a decrepit goods train that was ready to depart, its locomotive already coughing out clouds of steam. 'This is our train,' my mother said and, foreseeing the coming protest, added: 'Give me your hand and shut up.'

We crossed the tracks, circumnavigated the train and ended up on the side that could not be seen from the station. Once we were out of sight, we climbed up into one of the open wagons. After a few seconds I realized that I was standing on a mountain of coal. There was coal everywhere I looked: the wagon was about two-thirds full. This was a goods train carrying coal, a scenario my mother had not allowed for in her escape plan. Nor was it going to Budapest, but to Prague; this fact my mother had found out during one of her earlier visits to the station. It mattered little that this was not a direct train to Budapest: Prague was nearer home, and it would be easier to catch a train from there.

Despite my original disappointment at the unglamorous nature of our transport, we soon settled in: we did not have much choice. Other wagons may have carried less dirty cargo, but to find this out we would have needed to climb from wagon to wagon, and once established we did not dare move for fear of being detected and hauled down from the train. Returning to the Russians with their endless, unfulfilled promises was judged by my mother the worse alternative.

The locomotive issued a final whistle and the train reluctantly pulled out of the station. We made our beds in one of the corners, laying our spare clothes out to lie on. It was not a comfortable night, but a sense of adventure more than compensated for any inconvenience I felt. At daybreak we ate our bread and cheese and an apple. We passed through mountain passages, small towns and villages and crossed rivers. When the train occasionally came to a halt or stopped at a station we quickly ducked to avoid prying eyes. By now we were covered with coal dust. To complete the camouflage I smeared more dust all over my face. 'Now no one can recognize me,' I explained to my mother, waiting for her approval, looking every bit like a kid from a black-and-white minstrel show, made up by someone who had had a very bad day. I felt an excitement I had never felt before: a mixture of danger and fun. Our escape was, or seemed to be, a fabulous game, and one which we were going to win for a change.

I do not remember whether there was any control at the border; if there was, only the driver and his assistant could have been involved, and no one bothered to search the train. This was only a couple of months after the war in Europe had ended, and the continent was witnessing the largest movement of people in recent history: refugees of the old order forcefully evicted from their homes trying to make their way back; migrants of the newly established order who had to leave their homes since they found themselves on the wrong side of a border on the freshly redrawn map of Europe; displaced persons from concentration and labour camps scattered all over the extended dominions of the collapsed Third Reich; armies securing the conquered territories; liberated prisoners of war; disorganized stragglers from defeated armies; civilians in search of their families. We were only two small drops in this ocean of people on the move. It was during this journey that for the first time I began to miss my father. Without him we were more vulnerable: on the journey home there were only the two of us.

3

Events in Hillersleben following our liberation have been poorly documented in the official archives. The Nazis must have destroyed some of the material, and the Russians subsequently removed most of the documentation spared by the Germans. Attempting to retrieve any documents from Magdeburg proved initially futile. My letter to the Country Archives (Landesarchiv) in Magdeburg, requesting any information about our stay, was politely answered. No, they did not have any documents concerning my family, or for that matter any individuals, and the documents of the former occupation powers were not available to them. Later, several documents relating to Hillersleben had been traced in one particular file, however.

At the end of the war, the President of the Rural District appointed one of its employees, RW, to determine the number of 'inmates' in the Hillersleben 'camp' and of Germans working there, to carry out an audit, to make suggestions for reducing expenses, and to establish the accuracy of the reported delivery of rations. While this commission was humanitarian without doubt, the language is indicative of the mentality inherited from the immediate past: we were still inmates in a camp. Reports were produced regularly and with meticulous detail. The exact numbers of Germans working in the hospitals, kitchens and on transport duties were carefully recorded; even the gravediggers and road sweepers did not escape the attention of this audit. The efficiency of the bureaucracy during the first few days of peace, amid the destruction of a defeated country, was nothing short of breathtaking; the same efficiency that so successfully organized the transport of millions to the concentration camps. Only the aim was different. As estimated by the Jewish Committee, there were about 1,800 Jews and 1,900 Poles and other foreign nationals living in Hillersleben at the end of May 1945. A more accurate head count carried out a few days later revised these figures to 1,987 Jews and 940 others, reflecting the fact that in the mean time many people had probably left the village and started their journey home. Clothing, underwear and shoes were in short supply, and on the orders of the commander of the Allied Military Administration arrangements were made to open a tailor's and a dressmaker's shop, as well as a cobbler's repair shop. For quick results, skilled hands altered the military uniforms found locally in abundance. Making new garments proved more difficult: although material was discovered in local shops, none of the essential accessories was available.

By the end of July, the Russian presence had grown more obvious and authoritarian. The Russian military commanding officer in Hillersleben had declared that the testing ground and the former firing range were strictly out of bounds to all civilians. Those without permits seen on the firing range would immediately be arrested and brought before a Russian military court.

4

Today Hillersleben is dominated by the twin towers of the church of the Benedictine monastery: simple, graceful and confident. While the Main Street channels the flow of traffic through the village, a narrow street lined by substantial houses, some behind cast-iron gates and fences, calmly meanders its way towards the church. There are old houses with sloping roofs, a couple of squat modern concrete blocks of two modest storeys, half-timbered houses of traditional design, a small children's playground, flowerbeds with zinnias and geraniums, French marigolds and dahlias, fir trees and chestnut trees. A small restaurant was firmly closed for a few days' holiday, the owners probably escaping the gloomy autumn rains to steal a brief summer interlude elsewhere; a pub sported outdoor murals depicting drunkards with overflowing beer mugs falling over each other; a large Skoda showroom, an unexpected find in such a small village, offered the instant gratification of cars, the most coveted and most potent symbol of Western society, to compensate for the lost certainties of dictatorship.

But there are also other bonuses for the previously deprived citizens of the German Democratic Republic: lurid posters advertise Sexy Oktober Fest, free strip shows for men on men's nights, speed dating and much else. And then there were the ill-tempered dogs, mercifully behind fences. Their enthusiasm for alien flesh seemed boundless, and given the chance they could strip the calf musculature of the unwary in record time. A search for a shop to buy a postcard to send to a friend who shared our journey to Hillersleben proved vain.

Not far from this pretty village, across a busy road lies a large compound, surrounded by walls and guarded by a sentry. It was in this the place, sometimes rather unromantically referred to as Hillersleben Two, where the Americans installed us in April 1945. Hillersleben Two has a chequered history, a mirror in which fast-changing fortunes of large armies are reflected. Our appearance was a mere glimpse in this frantic cavalcade of activity, much distorted by subsequent events.

In preparation for the war, an immense artillery ground was constructed between 1935 and 1938 immediately north of Hillersleben. The main firing range stretched for some 18 miles. Everything had been demolished to clear this vast space and farmers had to be resettled in other regions. Becoming a showcase and particularly excelling in ammunition development, after the war it drew unqualified praise from US Ordnance for the range and the magnitude of its facilities.

For the living quarters of the officers and the administration of the Wehrmacht, a large well-designed compound was built nearby. As an example of instant town planning of the 1930s, neat houses of one and two storeys were erected to line the landscaped streets and squares, adoringly named Adolf Hitler or Horst Wessel. It was this bucolic haven former prisoners of Bergen-Belsen had gate-crashed.

The Russians arrived in July 1945 and stayed for nearly fifty years. During this time they transformed the place into their own image with their own war memorial, busts of Lenin and other icons of Communism, a cultural forum and shopping centre. After the Russians' departure in 1994, the place became deserted. Plans to refurbish the whole compound never materialized in the turbulent post-unification years of Germany. And now the place is still deserted, a silent witness to changing destinies. Within ten years, units of the four largest armies the world had known at the time marched through its streets, housing the conquerors and the defeated, and caught between them an assembly of refugees in transit between the trauma of a concentration camp and the uncertainty of their homes.

I revisited the settlement on a perfect spring day in 2005. The trees had already unfurled their new leaves and wild flowers spread along the deserted streets. In the warm April sunshine decay was everywhere: the pockmarked and peeling yellow paint of the houses, the broken staircases, the shattered windowpanes, the unhinged doors like dislocated joints, the wrecked signposts, the faded welcome to the Russian shopping centre in Cyrillic; between the crushed paving stones weeds, nature's occupation force, were sprouting everywhere. The beauty of the place was as overwhelming as it was unexpected: it is a mistake to underestimate the allure and seduction of decay. I would have loved to identify the house in which we found shelter and to locate the street where I had my accident. But of course, it was only a wish.

But our past has been erased and Hillersleben now is only a memory of survival and freedom: the end of a nightmare; the memory of the first proper meal after a year of starvation and the first comfortable bed after a year of deprivation. Yet there is nothing tangible to connect the past with the present, only fading images. As if we had never been there; as if Hillersleben had been nothing but an acute hallucinatory episode after the shock of Bergen-Belsen. But of course we were there, and I have a document to prove it.

The list was compiled on 16 June 1945 in Hillersleben: it is a roll-call of Hungarian Jews who had been originally in Bergen-Belsen and were subsequently liberated on the train outside Farsleben transporting them to Theresienstadt. In fact I have three copies, from three different sources: two from Hungary, and one from Bergen-Belsen. Both my mother and I feature on this list. But it is incomplete, since some people died in Hillersleben.

Those who perished in Hillersleben were buried in an unrecorded plot near the hospital. After the fall of the Communist regime in East Germany, the local government agreed, under pressure from American Holocaust survivors, to restore the site as a cemetery. The precise boundaries of the original plot were difficult to establish, and archival material, together with original aerial reconnaissance photos, were used to agree on the perimeter. The cemetery was rebuilt in 1996–7, and is the resting place of 136 known and five unidentified former inmates of Bergen-Belsen. In recent years, more than once, it has been vandalized and tombstones have been overturned. Suspicion has fallen on extreme right-wing circles, but despite intense police investigations no culprits have been apprehended.

Prague:

THE KINDNESS OF STRANGERS

1

When our train arrived in Prague, nobody seemed to notice or care about the two figures covered in coal dust who climbed down from the wagon. We regained the use of our limbs with some difficulty: the night spent on the train had had paralysing effects. We looked for a place to wash and soon found a lavatory with running water. We refreshed ourselves as best we could and tidied up our makeshift luggage. In addition to our minimal wardrobe, my mother also carried a cardboard shoebox full of fudge. Prepared in Hillersleben, this was her homecoming present for my brother. When it had still been warm she had offered me a sample: its soft, velvety taste was easily recalled now as I longingly looked at the box. 'Can I have one?' I asked, but I knew that the answer was going to be no. Had she untied the string securing the lid of the box, no fudge would have been left for my brother.

While we were exploring the station and making enquiries about trains to Budapest, I became aware of a stall with a flag: a white flag with a red cross on it. Behind the stall two women were giving out pieces of bread and glasses of milk to people who were patiently waiting their turn. We joined the queue and received our allocated portion. But I was still hungry and decided to go back for more. My mother patiently explained that everybody could have only one portion, otherwise some people would not get any.

'They would recognize you as one of those who already had

received their portion and wouldn't give you a second helping anyway,' she said.

Herein lay a challenge. 'But if I put my jacket on over my shirt they wouldn't recognize me,' I suggested, as if a slight change of attire would provide a full disguise. It must have been the least convincing argument she had heard recently, and perhaps for that very reason she allowed me to join the queue for a second try. I waited nervously for my turn, and as I held out my hand the woman behind the stall handed me the bread and milk. No searching looks. No questions asked. As I walked triumphantly towards my mother, who was surveying my progress from a nearby platform, I did not notice that the woman's gaze was following me. Before I could reach my mother she was waving at us. We walked to the stall, which by now was deserted, with increasing apprehension. My little ploy had obviously failed. Still holding the bread and milk, I contemplated all the possible forms of punishment, and promptly concluded that the worst she could do was reclaim the food I had obtained with deception. To prevent such a humiliating retribution I quickly gulped down the milk and started to devour the bread. The woman was smiling as we stopped in front of her stall.

'You have an enterprising little son,' she told my mother in German. Then she looked at me, smiling broadly, and gave me yet another slice of bread.

We did not have to wait long at the station, since we were lucky enough to find a passenger train that was leaving later that day for Budapest.

2

The kindness of our anonymous benefactors at the railway station in Prague intrigued me for a long time, and I set out to discover who they were. I contacted the National Archives in

Prague, and they searched through the files of the Ministry of Labour and Social Welfare, the Czechoslovak Red Cross and the Ministry of Interior. They did not find any record of a transport going from Magdeburg to Hungary; not surprisingly since records of individual transports of displaced persons going through Prague were rarely preserved. Goods trains, as far as the cargo was delivered, went unrecorded.

The Ministry of Labour and Social Welfare ran reception centres at all of the railway stations in Prague, and various organizations, including the Union of Catholic Charity, the Czechoslovak Red Cross and Bohemian Heart provided humanitarian aid to displaced persons. A letter from the Ministry of Labour and Social Welfare sent to the United Nations Relief and Rehabilitation Administration (UNRRA) at the beginning of September, a couple of weeks after our short stay in Prague, paints an accurate picture of the magnitude of the problem. Although precise statistics were not available, it was estimated that about 1,350,000 persons were repatriated to, from and through Czechoslovakia. The reception centres at the three main railway termini in Prague assisted 359,427 displaced persons. My mother and I were two of them.

BUDAPEST: A BROTHER'S DEATH

1

The train from Prague was packed. Yet it was more comfortable than all the other trains of our previous journeys. We were lucky to be able to sit in a compartment with hard seats; many passengers were standing, and several were even sitting on the steps outside the carriage. They were later ordered inside by the ticket collector to find a seat wherever they could. All the corridors became blocked, and the passage to the lavatory had to be carefully negotiated.

The journey was long, and the train made several unscheduled stops, sometimes on the open tracks. Eventually it crossed the border with Hungary, and as we approached our destination we became progressively more impatient to arrive. When the locomotive pulled into the station in Budapest, releasing an exhausted plume of steam and screeching to a halt at the buffer, we clambered down the steps as if in a daze, clutching our luggage. We had arrived home.

There was bedlam in the station: a large milling crowd of Russian soldiers, many with machine guns; elderly peasant women from the country carrying wicker baskets loaded with goods for market; worn denizens of the capital, still unable to believe that the war was over.

We walked down the steps in front of the station and headed for the flat of Aunt Márta and Uncle Lajos. The streets were unrecognizable: there were ruins everywhere. Although the roads and most of the pavements had been cleared, whole houses had disappeared, leaving gaping craters filled with rubble where they had been standing. As a curtain rises in the theatre to reveal the set to an expectant audience, whole façades had crumbled away to expose cross-sections of timber joists. Private lives had been unmasked for strangers. Casual passers-by had become unwitting voyeurs of the misfortunes of others.

2

Uncle Lajos and Aunt Márta lived in the Seventh District, an area in which many Jews had lived before the war. Their short street ran between one of the major axial roads leading from the Eastern railway station to the heart of downtown and crossed a much narrower street, which followed a less confident route in the same direction towards a ring of boulevards; these neatly encircled the inner city. The street was lined by an odd assortment of buildings, mainly apartment blocks, but the monotonous rows of housing were enlivened by some more unusual edifices. On the south-western corner stood a fashion house, which at some stage during its chequered history aspired to be a classy department store. Its main door opened on to the wide boulevard, but several shop windows looked out on to our street. The displays reflected the rollercoaster ups and downs of the Hungarian economy during those years. On the same side of the street, several houses to the north, there was a low one-storey building with crumbling masonry. The purpose of this house was ostentatiously displayed day and night: it was a brothel. The lace curtains in the windows were often drawn back to afford a full view of one of the girls available at the time, while in good weather others lounged on chairs placed on the pavement and blatantly solicited business from men passing their door. This house of pleasure was one of the victims in the first frost of the Communist takeover: it was closed down during a city-wide clean-up in preparation for the World

Congress of Youth in 1949. Further along, a hospital occupied a long stretch on the other side of the street, its main entrance opposite my relatives' block.

My aunt's apartment block was a modern building of four unadorned floors; the curved lines of its balconies suggested a restrained modernist style. The main spiral staircase was marble with burgundy tiling halfway up the wall and with a cast-iron lift shaft housing a small cage of a lift with narrow double glass doors and a mirrored interior. Only one flat on each floor had its main entrance giving on to this staircase; the owners of all the others entered their flats from an open walkway which ran along three sides of the building. A second open staircase in happier times was used by domestics and for deliveries.

My aunt's flat was probably the best in the whole block: not only could it be entered from the main staircase, it was also on the top floor, with extensive views from the balcony. The entrance hall had doors leading to two large rooms, a kitchen, a bathroom and a separate lavatory. Beyond the kitchen, which gave on to the walkway, there was a further, small room for the maid. To avoid accusations of bourgeois indulgence, my aunt had made fundamental changes to downgrade this comfortable but far from ostentatious flat. She blocked the main entrance on the false pretext that the flat was vulnerable to burglars who could break in unobserved from the staircase after having sneaked up to the fourth floor. The ugliest piece of furniture, an ice chest, was pushed against the entrance door, and from then on everybody had to enter through the kitchen from the walkway. A block of ice, delivered regularly twice a week in the summer and less frequently in the winter, was fed into the chest's central container, which was flanked by two compartments on either side. Its incontinent tap dribbled water and ruined the parquet floor. The ice chest remained in place until the early 1960s, when it was replaced by a proper refrigerator.

Soon after our return the apartment had other occupants.

My aunt became worried about the fact that only two people were occupying such a large flat when so many did not have anywhere to live, and to prevent them from being forced to share with another family she invited, against her husband's wishes, her younger brother and his wife to move in with them. They occupied the larger of the two front rooms, while Aunt Márta and Uncle Lajos retreated to the smaller room with the balcony, that, with its window boxes planted with geraniums and petunias in the summer, was a pleasant space from which to observe the bustle of the street below: ambulances screeching to a halt in the courtyard of the hospital as patients were hurriedly carried on stretchers to the emergency department; occasional cars venturing away from the main boulevard to avoid traffic – endless sources of fascination for a small boy from the country. From here one could see the thrusting spires of a neo-Gothic church in the nearby square, our playground, to which we escaped whenever we could from the restricting dark well of the courtyard. And from the balcony we blew our soap bubbles and watched mesmerized as they billowed down and away, a private rainbow trapped in each.

The maid's room had been standing empty, since employing a live-in maid immediately after the war was unthinkable, and discouraged later under the Communists. This room had been let to male tenants.

3

Aunt Márta was in her early forties: a small woman with a prominent bust. Although she was well proportioned with short but attractive legs, this was the feature that drew immediate attention: her frontal protuberances were not counterbalanced by an equally large bottom, giving the impression that her centre of gravity was somewhat out of place, and that she might at any moment fall on her face. But in fact she moved with agility and grace. She had dark brown hair, which soon after the war turned grey: this was remedied for several years by dyeing it an aggressive red. She had mischievous eyes and a sparkling laugh. Her temper flared easily and spread uncontrollably like bushfire, but the rage subsided as quickly and unexpectedly as it had ignited, leaving green shoots of goodwill in its wake: an offer of a favourite dish, an unscheduled visit to the cinema or an increased allowance of pocket money. She suffered from high blood pressure, and malicious tongues in the family suggested that Uncle Lajos's chronic underperformance in bed may have been a contributory factor to my aunt's tantrums. These were frequently directed against my uncle.

The temperament of Uncle Lajos could not have been more different from that of my aunt: he was a quiet and placid man, readily given to long periods of silence, and not overflowing with a sense of humour. He was a short man, and when he sat back in an armchair his feet dangled freely in the air: a sight I found amusing as a child. He had straight anthracite-black hair, which to my aunt's annoyance and envy got thinner with the passing years but never turned grey. He took great pride in keeping his hair well groomed by combing it several times a day and neatly covering it with a hairnet at night, as if afraid that a couple of unruly hairs might escape while he was sleeping. A beaky nose, deep-set dark eyes and a light olive-coloured skin lent him an exotic aura. His chain-smoking earned my aunt's disapproval and was a frequent trigger of her outbursts. Despite ashtrays strategically placed throughout the flat, Uncle Lajos was often seen carrying one with him, as if frightened that his wife might suddenly confiscate all the foul-smelling receptacles. And this of course she did as part of her strategy in what I later called the cigarette wars.

Aunt Márta had waged several campaigns to convince my uncle to give up smoking, without any success: however placid my uncle was generally, on this particular issue he refused to budge. An ebony cigarette holder was a permanent feature and not just a temporary addition to his physiognomy: an inseparable lifeline that he kept in his mouth even in the short interval between two cigarettes. This ebony holder became an instrument emitting a range of sounds from which one could guess my uncle's state of mind more easily than from his words. Slow, drawn-out gurgling sounds were the sign of full satisfaction, indicating a happy unison between nicotine molecules and their receptors in the brain. As the cigarette was coming to an end, quieter sucking sounds accelerated in tempo in a vain effort to extract the same amount of nicotine from the diminishing stub. Short, dry, staccato whistles from the empty holder heralded the lighting of the next cigarette: these grew faster as the craving for the next fix increased.

Unlike my aunt, Uncle Lajos did not seem to have strong opinions; indeed, it is quite possible that he did not have opinions at all about many issues. More likely, he preferred to withhold his views to avoid clashes with my aunt. A familiar gesture after one of my aunt's outbursts said it all: a shrug of the shoulders, hands outspread, palms up, indicated that it would have been hopeless to argue. Yet despite the fundamental discrepancy in their temperaments, they learned to share each other's lives and to work as a team.

When young, my aunt was desperate to have children, but her wish was frustrated: who was infertile was never established, but in my aunt's mind there was not a shadow of doubt that it was not her fault. From their misfortune the nephews and nieces benefited, since they generously showered their unspent love on us. I was a particular favourite, and from an early age I spent my summer vacations with them. They took their guardianship seriously, yet they allowed me an element of independence. Since they trusted me, I could set out on little trips of discovery in the capital.

I never breached this trust, not until 1969, when I chose to

stay in England and not return to Hungary. My decision was a
serious blow to them. On the morning of my flight to London,
they came with me to the city air terminal in downtown
Budapest. And this was our last encounter.

4

Coming from the railway station, we could still enter from the
main staircase. We were out of breath as we pressed the bell:
the lift was not working.

Uncle Lajos answered the bell: after a cautious peep through
the open glass panel in the door, he removed the chain, and we
entered the coolness of the hall. Soon my aunt appeared; with
the sun behind her we could see only her silhouette. They
kissed my mother and then me. We followed them into the
large living-room: an almost empty space containing only a
table, a sofa and two ill-matched armchairs. Although we were
exhausted, my mother did not sit down. Standing in the middle
of the room, she could not restrain her eagerness to ask about
my brother. 'Gyuri?'

Silence. Aunt Márta looked at my uncle, as if asking for
help; then she walked towards my mother with open arms to
embrace her, but my mother, as if anticipating bad news, stepped back.

'He died last month. On 6 August,' said my aunt.

It is the cry I remember, a cry I have heard neither before
nor since, the howl of a wounded animal, alien and of elementary force. All the suppressed, condensed suffering of the last
fifteen months exploded in this single irreproducible cry. I
could not understand it then but I know now that this signalled
a fundamental change in her. At that moment all the suffering
of the past was transformed into strength to face the future.

I was too tired and confused to cry. Suddenly I remembered
the box of fudge my mother had made in Hillersleben as a

homecoming present for my brother. 'Can I have the fudge?' I asked. She looked at me uncomprehendingly, and then said without hesitation: 'Yes.'

And the four of us stood in the near-empty room: my mother by now having accepted the embracing arms of my aunt, my uncle nervously drawing on his cigarette, and I holding the box of fudge but unable to open it.

Homecoming

1

Our journey was now nearly over. We had been travelling for months, our lives an endless train journey through the heart of Europe, a journey of uncertain arrivals and non-existent time-tables. We embarked on the last stage in early September – on the train from Szeged that carried us home to Makó.

It was the end of a long hot summer. The train was full and airless. The passengers opened the windows on both sides of the carriage to encourage some breeze, only to receive clouds of soot spewed out by the ailing engine. We stopped at every village, however small, and at every stop there was a hubbub of departing passengers as new ones embarked to take their places, jostling for each empty seat. The early afternoon heat increased, and the short journey of 20 miles seemed never-ending. Suddenly the train slowed down further and chugged on to the bridge over the river. The locomotive emitted a tired shriek, more of terminal fatigue than to herald a triumphant arrival at its destination. I knew that our station could not be far off.

I could see the water only through the rusting iron lattice-work. In the distance I spotted the small beach that was to become, in later years, the source of much pleasure during the long summer vacations.

Finally the train pulled in to the station. We picked up our luggage and waited patiently to get off. Makó, the largest town on this now run-down line, was a popular stop, and quite a few

passengers, collecting their wicker baskets and makeshift belongings, were shuffling towards the door. The smell and the
heat in the now stationary train were overpowering, and I
pushed my way towards the carriage's steep wooden steps. My
mother lifted me off the last step, although I wanted to jump. I
remember even now feeling a sudden urge to get home.

We took the road leading towards the centre. As we walked
towards our house in the stale air of late summer, it appeared
possible that we could recover our home, that we could be within reach of regaining the life we had left behind.

2

As the passengers dispersed, we were suddenly alone in the
broad, empty street leading towards the town centre, and our
home. The street was lined by chestnut trees, their leaves
parched and heavy with dust, but not yet quite ready to fall.
Despite the dappled shade the mid-afternoon sun was merci-
less, and our walk seemed interminable.

'Mother, I need to pee,' I said. This declaration was a ploy to
break up the monotony of the walk rather than the expression
of a real need.

'No, you can't in the street. Wait until we get home,' was her
disappointing answer.

'But I must. I must,' I insisted.

My mother gave in. 'All right, go behind the newspaper
kiosk.'

Her giving in to my request reflected our changed relationship since we had left home. During our journey we had been
through so much together that I was not only her charge, a
son of six, but also her travelling companion. Our escape from
the Russians in Magdeburg in particular was an event which
sealed this change. My adventure in Prague, when I succeeded
in obtaining more than one portion of bread and milk from

the Red Cross, must, I felt, have increased my stock in her eyes.

The newspaper kiosk was a squat concrete building showing no signs of life: the newsagent must have decided to extend his lunch break to avoid the worst of the heat. The corrugated iron blind, firmly closed, was covered with layers of undisturbed dust: only the lower few slats bore the fingerprints of the hands that raised and lowered it. I disappeared behind the kiosk, and as my urine hit the dust with a thud a small cloud rose to dance in the light. I recognized where I was: the kiosk stood at the beginning of a side street in which, barely a hundred yards away, my grandfather's yard was located.

This recognition gave me further confidence, and soon we were in my grandparents' street. Although it was in the town centre, and home to the police station, it was completely empty. The house appeared to be deserted. Some of the blinds were lowered; other windows were naked, unprotected by curtains. The bell did not work, but the gate yielded at my mother's first attempt to enter. We had arrived home.

The house was silent: there was no one around. The hall was empty. We entered the large garden room. It was dark: the blind was lowered to exclude the sun, but its horizontal slats allowed shafts of light to penetrate the gloom. We noticed a slim figure reclining on the sofa. It was my mother's youngest brother, Jenő. He was smoking, and a couple of perfectly formed smoke rings were drifting through the air. His skill with cigarettes never ceased to amaze me. In later years he seriously attempted to smoke an entire cigarette without disposing of the ash, trying to maintain its shape. He never achieved this feat, but he could delicately balance impressive lengths of ash, to the annoyance of the cleaners, who had to mop up little pools of the stuff in the most unexpected places.

In the light of the open door Jenő recognized us and stood up. He was in his mid-thirties, a tall, lanky figure with a premature stoop, which became more pronounced with the passing years, and long, thin limbs. He started to lose his hair early and a large forehead dominated his hooked nose, warm brown eyes and generous lips.

'Ili, Peter,' he said, walking towards us. He embraced my mother, and planted a kiss on my head, then went to the window and raised the blind, allowing the late afternoon sunshine to pour in with unexpected ferocity. Suddenly we realized that the room was practically empty: a well-worn sofa, a small coffee table with an overflowing ashtray and a wooden stool were the only furnishings. The walls were bare: all the pictures had disappeared.

'Sit down,' Uncle said, gently tugging on my mother's arm. She sat down to share the sofa with him, leaving the stool to me. Then she asked the question that had been hanging in the air since we had first entered. 'Who has returned?' There was a long pause. No answer was forthcoming. The surreal, staccato nature of the questioning that followed has remained with me indelibly: it displayed the emotionless efficiency of a police interrogation as my mother went through the list of her brothers and sisters by age rather than according to any personal preference, as a schoolmistress might enquire about members of a class. 'Szerén,' she asked, 'and her husband and daughter?'

'She survived, as did her husband. They were not deported from Romania. The last I heard they were back in Arad,' Uncle answered. 'Dusi and Erika' – he was referring to their daughter and granddaughter – 'were in Strasshof but have returned.'

'Manó?'

'He is at home, here in Makó, with his wife and their two children.'

'Margit?'

'She and Mihály and István all died in Auschwitz.' Mihály was Margit's husband and István their son, my cousin, a few years my senior.

'Sándor?

'He died on the eastern front; Anna and Zsuzsi did not return from Auschwitz.'

This' news upset me. Since we had lived very near to Anna and Zsuzsi I had seen them every day, and I was very fond of Zsuzsi. Her father was a good amateur photographer who had taken several pictures of us. One snapshot I remember particularly well. Zsuzsi and I are standing holding hands in their large living-room, which is suffused with light: she is elegant in a tartan skirt and a white blouse, while I am wearing black velvet trousers with a matching waistcoat over a white shirt. We are both looking, unsmiling, into the camera. Behind us, our mothers are sitting on a large sofa. They are both wearing a yellow star.

'Izsó?' my mother continued relentlessly.

'He died in a labour camp, somewhere in Russia; we do not know where.' Uncle Izsó was a lawyer who had decided not to follow in his brothers' footsteps by entering the family business.

'László?'

'He did not return from the eastern front. He died in the Ukraine, but Panni and Mari have survived.' Panni, my aunt, and Mari, my cousin had been liberated in Theresienstadt.

My mother shifted on the sofa. For a moment I thought she wanted to stand up, but then she sank back. László had been her favourite brother, who, unusually for a Jewish family, became my godfather and whose name I had inherited as my middle name.

'And of course you know that Mother died in Strasshof,' Uncle volunteered. My mother nodded.

After each name the silence deepened. I expected my mother to cry: her tears would have relieved the tension. But she just sat there motionless and silent. She had been drained of all emotion. Only later did I understand, as I replayed the events of our first day at home over again in my mind, that grief has bounds and is deeply personal. One can mourn only for one person, not for many. Death had lost its novelty value, and one could become immune to sorrow.

And yet it could have been worse. After all, of eight brothers and sisters four died, four survived. Fifty-fifty: a certain balance. We did not know then that the loss was greater in my father's family: of eight children, five died and only three survived. In addition to my father, three of his sisters and one of his brothers had perished.

The fecundity of my grandparents, on both my paternal and my maternal side, had apparently paid off; it was as if they had taken out insurance against an as yet unknown catastrophe. And years later, when the names of those who perished were inscribed on enormous marble plaques screwed into the wall of the entrance hall of the synagogue, I could claim to other children that my family had lost more than anybody else's. In the synagogue this carried as much weight with other children as academic excellence and certainly more than prowess at games.

3

Uncle reached for his packet of cigarettes and lit another. Even at that young age he had a slight tremor which made his magical handling of the cigarette even more impressive. He asked in a faltering voice: 'You know what happened to Gyuri?'

The question was an introduction to an account of how my elder brother had died at the age of twenty. Of course my mother did know; we had heard a detailed account less than a week ago, in Budapest. But it had happened here; my uncle had been an eyewitness. It was a simple story. Its horror lay in the fact that it was such an unnecessary death. Uncle's account confirmed what we had already heard, but it was richer in detail and personal observation.

My brother had come back from the labour camp in Russia thin, covered in lice and depressed. We heard how he gradually recovered, put on weight and waited for us to return. He had been preparing for his university studies when he developed typhoid fever. Doctors at the local hospital misdiagnosed it first as a lung infection, and when the correct diagnosis was made it was already too late. He died there, less than a month before we arrived home. As Uncle neared the end of his story, his voice became more strained and he drew on his cigarette so deeply that I feared his lungs would burst.

My mother listened in silence and to my surprise did not express any emotion. Her composure was so different from her reaction when she had first learned of my brother's death. Over the next couple of months she conducted her own investigation into what had happened, from the moment my brother returned from labour camp to his last breath on the hospital bed. She found out that he had visited my uncle in hospital; at the time Jenő had typhoid fever, although the diagnosis had not yet been made. The implication was that Gyuri picked up the infection from my uncle, a terrible suspicion that, although it remained unspoken, settled between them.

According to the official death certificate, my brother died at 3 p.m. on 6 August 1945 at the age of twenty in the hospital in Makó. The cause of death was given as abdominal fever. On a recent visit to Hungary I attempted to gain access to my brother's clinical notes to resolve the uncertainties surrounding his death. But I was not successful. The chief archivist of Szeged, where the relevant documents are, could trace only some rudimentary information: he was admitted on 18 July 1945 and stayed in Room 29 of the St Stephen County Hospital. According to the archivist, one explanation for the lack of information could be that he was not insured, since his name did not appear on the list sent to the insurance company. The documents relating to uninsured patients from Makó had been lost.

Suddenly my mother stood up. 'I just want to look around the house,' she said, and walked into the next room. I stood up too and followed her, while my uncle remained seated, reclaiming the entire sofa. Our surprise increased as we walked from room to room. All were empty, completely empty, without any recognizable sign of life, as if no one had ever lived there. The emptiness was frightening, the complete loss of familiarity disorientating. No furniture, no carpets, no lights. Where pictures had once hung darker areas blotched the walls. Our footsteps on the bare wooden floor echoed from the high ceilings.

In this warren of empty spaces I suddenly spotted a sole landmark in the dining-room – the portraits of my grandparents. They were an unexpected find. Those who had removed everything from our house had shied away from taking these pictures which, being immediately identifiable, would have betrayed them. Although painted by the same hand a couple of years apart, they were strikingly different. Reflecting the domestic balance of power, my grandmother's portrait was larger, with the result that the two pictures were never hung side by side. My grandfather's portrait was artistically undoubtedly the better: the painter had captured the expression of a serene and benevolent man, who had been wise enough to run the family business quietly and efficiently but keep out of the domestic arena, allowing his wife free rein. He had been painted wearing a starched white wing-collar and black tie, although the satin finish of the dinner-jacket had been degraded by years of sunshine.

There could be no doubt that of the two pictures my grandmother's portrait attracted more attention. There was an inexplicable discrepancy between the informality of her dress and the power she radiated. For the sittings she was wearing an elegantly tailored but plain dress of green-grey material, her white hair unfussily rolled back at the back and sides. She had regular, handsome features. Only several years later, as an adolescent, did I realize that it was her eyes that gave the picture its mesmerizing power.

My mother must have turned back to talk to my uncle, since I suddenly found myself alone in the hall. Here I had three choices: to go back to the empty dining-room with my grandparents' portraits, to join my mother and uncle in one of the rooms facing the street, or to go to the kitchen, from which a few steps led down to the garden. I opted for the latter route. The kitchen had clearly seen no culinary activity for a considerable time: it was deserted, in sharp contrast to the bustling activity of the past. The large larder adjoining it was empty: all the shelves were bare. My uncle, we learned later, took his meals in a nearby small family restaurant.

The garden was neglected. Weeds had overrun the flower-beds; only a few zinnias had miraculously escaped, their harsh colours tempered only by rusty sunshine burns. The large box trees, usually trimmed to perfect spheres, were untidy, with branches poking out here and there, like overgrown hair needing ruthless cutting. In the shadow of these trees the earth had been disturbed: from a distance there appeared to be mole hills, but on closer inspection I could see that holes had been freshly dug and the earth piled up to one side. These were the result of my uncle's first search for the jewellery and money buried during the night in the last minutes before the family was forced to leave. His search was fruitless, and no jewellery was ever recovered. A couple of years later one of the gardeners dug up a jam jar stuffed with partly disintegrated banknotes. But by then there was a different currency, and the old banknotes lost their value in a period of inflation far worse than that which hit the Weimar Republic. The fate of the stashed-away jewellery remains unresolved to this day. Probably someone had witnessed its burial and had removed it while we were away. I was never tempted to turn amateur gold-digger to recover it.

I retraced my steps back to the house to join my mother and uncle. After a while there was a knock on the door, and one of our neighbours, Mrs Sz–, entered the room. She had obviously dressed for the occasion, and the contrast between her immaculate appearance and my mother's dishevelled state could not be greater; a complete reversal of their past roles.

'You are back,' she said, stating the obvious. 'Welcome home. Good to see you again. We were concerned that you might not come back. And I am so sorry for your family. What a terrible disaster!' She must have learned the fate of many family members from my uncle.

'Yes, it is good to be home again,' my mother said, without much conviction. 'And how is your family?' Since Mrs Sz– was a widow, my mother must have had her only son in mind.

'My son is well, and so am I, but you just cannot imagine: the Russians have taken all my preserves and cleared out our larder.' She shook her head in disbelief at such uncivilized behaviour.

Her son was indeed well, although a couple of years later I was given cause to wonder when, during my usual reconnaissance of the garden, I spotted him through a hole in the wooden fence wearing his mother's bra and pants. He was in his late thirties, overweight and already balding. He was dancing to some tune I could not hear. It was a hot summer day and perspiration flowed freely down his fat arms and thighs.

4

Surveying the succession of empty rooms, I could not foresee the transformation that would take place within the next couple of months. The first few nights we spent sleeping on the floor: there were no beds or even mattresses. Uncle Jenő produced a blanket, a sheet and a pillow, and we made our bed in one corner of an empty room: the parquet floor was uncomfortable, but for the first time for fifteen months we were finally sleeping under our own roof.

The decision was made quickly and without fuss the next day: my mother and I would join Uncle Jenő and live in the family house. My mother wasted no time in trying to recover some of our furniture, carpets, pictures and household goods, but she usually returned frustrated and empty-handed from her sorties to those places, including the synagogue, where deported Jews' belongings had apparently been stored.

Soon after our return something unexpected happened. The largely empty, substantial house in the centre of town, so near to police headquarters, proved a temptation that one of the officers of the local Russian garrison could not resist. He decided to move temporarily into the large corner room facing the street. Our life was never the same again. Sacha had a large frame, straw-coloured hair and pale blue eyes. He made sure that his room did not remain empty for long, and soon a truckload of furniture arrived at our house. To have enquired into its origins would have been undiplomatic, but my mother could guess anyway. A couple of pieces that could not be crammed into the officer's room found places elsewhere in the house. By that time my mother had also bought some second-hand furniture, and thus we ended up with the most extraordinary collection. There were ill-assorted dining chairs, rickety tables, beds with worn mattresses, a triple mirror surmounting a chest of drawers which in turn was flanked on either side by cupboards, a pair of oversize wardrobes with missing drawers, and several armchairs. The star attraction was undoubtedly a pair of empire-style armchairs covered in faded black velour. A bouquet of flowers in the centre of their backs, their colours mellowed by wear and sunshine, created a sense of elegance. But the piece I was most fond of, and insisted on keeping even after other pieces had been replaced by better furniture, was a simple table in the thirties modernist style. Its high-gloss, canary-yellow paint faded and developed a web of hairline cracks, but the burnt orange bands forming a square on its top surface somehow maintained their original vigour. It became a workbench and library desk during my years of studying medicine, since it fitted perfectly under the window and when I was preparing for major examinations in June the combined surface of the sill and the table provided all the space I needed for my books while affording a full view of the leafy street outside.

The presence of Russians transformed our everyday lives. The house became noisier, and there was a constant stream of visitors whose arrival was announced by the loud banging of the heavy wooden gate. Most of the visitors were men, but occasionally women arrived, sometimes accompanied by other men. We had never seen these women before: they were garishly dressed and loudly made up. On these occasions I was firmly told not to go anywhere near the officer's room. Frequently there were parties and the house reverberated with Russian songs. To my untrained ears these songs were either heart-breakingly sad, in which the last flicker of hope had long since been extinguished, or boisterous with repetitive rhythms and roof-raising crescendos. The partying guests drank large quantities of a colourless liquid, which I learned was vodka: a drink I became quite familiar with as a medical student many years later.

My mother and I did not learn much Russian from our lodger and his guests, save for a few obligatory words of everyday greeting and a phrase or two to do with eating and drinking, although I managed to pick up a few swear words. Uncle Jenő, however, was a far more diligent pupil, and was soon able to speak to his newly acquired friends. A couple of soldiers became regular guests at the house: they originally came to visit the officer but they could not help meeting us, and our many fleeting encounters gradually bred familiarity and trust, and as time passed these intruders eventually became friends.

Sacha occasionally joined us at mealtimes, and suddenly our gastronomic standards rose overnight: scarce foodstuffs, which my mother would not have been able to purchase, were miraculously delivered to the kitchen. Their source was never questioned: it was safer to assume they had been paid for.

My mother finally accepted the Russians during my short stay in the local hospital. I had developed tonsillitis, and the consultant decided on immediate removal of the offending lymphoid organ. I was admitted the next day and operated on without delay. My legs and arms were tied down with leather straps, and anaesthesia was delivered by means of a disc lined with gauze steeped in ether: even now I can smell the ether and recall the nauseating feeling of suffocation. I wanted to scream as I succumbed to the darkness, but I could not. As I resurfaced, the first thing I saw was the smiling face of my mother, flanked by two Russian soldiers who had brought a large tub of ice-cream for me. I returned home a couple of days later, after my mother had paid the consultant's fee in wheat – an unlikely method of payment if ever there was one, but by then inflation was raging on an unprecedented scale. The devaluation of the currency was so precipitous that no one accepted money any longer: fiscal activity had regressed to bartering, and services were paid for by goods. Two eggs, for example, ensured entry to the local cinema.

But one day something happened which changed our relationship with the Russians for ever. We were alone in the house when one of the Russian soldiers arrived looking for Sacha. Since he was not at home, the soldier left, but he returned a few minutes later. There was nothing unusual in this – we had become accustomed to the Russians' comings and goings, and by then we trusted them. The first I knew of the incident was when I heard my mother's voice from the large dining-room facing the street: '*Niet*.' It was an emphatic refusal but it did not cause me any sense of alarm until she repeated the same word increasingly loudly until eventually it became a cry for help.

I rushed to the dining-room. As I opened the door, I first noticed the overturned chairs, then my mother and the soldier, who were standing at opposite ends of the dining-table, each frozen for a split second, as if waiting for the director to resume filming, and each out of breath. My mother's hair was tousled and the arm of her blouse was torn. I realized she was in danger: the soldier must have been chasing her around the table, overturning the chairs one by one to get nearer to her. Suddenly the other door of the dining-room opened and Sacha entered. He looked first at my mother, then at the soldier, and finally lowered his gaze to me. I watched the unfolding drama with a mixture of fear and satisfaction waiting for the offender to be punished.

There was a moment's silence as Sacha assessed the situation. The soldier mumbled a few words, no doubt trying to find an explanation. As he spoke, he released a waft of alcohol into the air: he must have been drinking heavily. Sacha slowly walked towards him and, as he did so, he drew his gun. For a moment we froze, terrified at the thought that he was going to shoot the soldier in the middle of the dining-room. I could hear my mother shouting 'Niet' again, now in defence of her attacker. She was covering her eyes with her hands. Sacha was now standing in front of the offender, and he hit him with the butt of his gun with great force. I heard the sound of breaking bone and a jet of blood splashed on to the white tablecloth. The officer apologized to my mother then barked an order at the soldier, who limped away, blood still dripping from his face. We never saw him again.

Uncle Jenő enjoyed a close relationship with a couple of Russians who came to visit him frequently. He was particularly fond of a boisterous young officer who visited more often and usually stayed longer than the others.

During a recent visit to Makó I received a folder of old photographs from the son of the family with whom Uncle spent the last couple of decades of his life. He sold his share of the family house and drew up a contract with this family, who undertook to look after him in exchange for the proceeds of the sale. One of the photographs shows Uncle Jenő sitting at a small table, flanked by two young Russian officers: all three are formally dressed, wearing suits and ties, and there is a nearly empty carafe of red wine with three wine glasses and an old-fashioned bottle of soda water on the table. On the back of the photograph, in Uncle's spidery handwriting, is a dedication in Cyrillic to the memory of a friendship.

5

Of my mother's family only Aunt Szerén and Uncles Manó and Jenő had survived. Szerén and her husband were fortunate: having lived in Arad, in Romania, they had escaped deportation altogether. After the Trianon peace treaty, Arad, an agricultural centre in Transylvania, had been annexed by Romania; a country that was less inclined than Hungary to surrender its Jews to the Nazis. The uncles were spared since by the time they were called up for forced labour the Russian front all but collapsed, and instead of being transported to near-certain death on the eastern front, they served nearer to home. Why they survived and why their brothers and sister died was never discussed. Only my mother kept asking, as if anybody could give an answer: Why should her eldest son die at the age of twenty, so long after the war had ended? Such a pointless death.

Szerén was the most beautiful of the three Schwarcz girls and also the luckiest. Having suffered an overpowering mother, she was determined to escape from the suffocating atmosphere of the family house at the earliest opportunity. At a charity ball she met her future husband, and after a short courtship they married in 1914 and moved to Arad, where her husband owned an elegant shoe shop. In 1915, immediately after the birth of their daughter, their first and only child, Uncle Menyhért was called up for active military service to fight on the eastern front. He was captured by the Russians and for seven years remained their prisoner of war. This did not deter Aunt Szerén from enjoying life, and in order to gain more freedom she had dispatched her young daughter Magda to Makó into the care of my mother. After Uncle Menyhért returned from captivity she continued her charmed life, with a devoted husband by whose side she took part in all the events that the hectic society calendar of a provincial town between the two world wars could offer. Although their freedom was curtailed, they lived through the Second World War in their own home. After the war, when the Communists took power, visits to Romania became difficult and then impossible, despite the fact that by then both Hungary and Romania were firmly anchored in the socialist camp. We were not able to cross the border to visit my aunt and uncle, although they lived so near. My aunt's timing remained impeccable throughout her life, and she grabbed the first opportunity to emigrate with her husband to Israel as the Communist regime strengthened its hold on Romania.

I saw her there only once: in 1975, with my freshly-acquired British passport, I attended an international medical conference in Jerusalem, and from there I took a local bus to visit her in Petah Tiqwa, near Tel Aviv. By then she had buried her first husband but, needing a companion, had remarried. At the time of my visit she was nearly eighty and lived in a home for the elderly. She could move only with difficulty, yet she had preserved her beauty which, burnished with age, lent her an aura of timelessness: an image most old people aspire to, but very few attain. Once or twice a year she sent me a crate of oranges: their oily perfume lingered for a long time in my flat in Bedford Square.

6

Uncle Manó was the eldest son, and the natural inheritor of the family enterprise. Soon after my grandfather died in 1933, however, Manó decided to establish his own firm, buying and selling grain, leaving the timber yard to his two younger brothers. He married Anna, a self-effacing blond woman, whose placidity and ready submission were an ideal buffer to my uncle's strong, often dictatorial views and self-asserting temperament. He inherited not only the penetrating gaze of my grandmother but also her autocratic manners, and contradicting him was always a perilous option, as his wife and two children, a daughter and a son, had often discovered.

Andris was only one year my senior, and although we did not attend the same class we often did our homework together. He was the proud owner of a seemingly inexhaustible supply of colour stencils, which he unselfishly shared with me, allowing me to liven up that notebook of my conversation class. Quite a few years later, as a teenager, he lodged for a short time in what had been the maid's room in my Aunt Márta's flat in Budapest. He replaced the previous tenant, a tailor's apprentice whose cinema-idol good looks had attracted far too many female admirers for my aunt's liking. His departure was precipitated by the sight of a lady visitor climbing out of the window of his room to escape a head-on confrontation with my aunt in the kitchen.

It was Andris who showed me his first, recently acquired condom, blushingly giving a half-hearted demonstration. Without boasting, he did not leave me in any doubt that it was not going to remain in its pristine state for long. I restrained myself from deflating his pride by admitting that I had had a previous encounter with a rubber object of this nature in the bedside drawer of the parents of one of my friends, together with far more interesting drawings of male and female genitalia.

His sister, Vera, was a few years older, and this difference created a tension between the two siblings: Vera occasionally dismissed Andris as a child with the disdain of a precocious adult. She was pretty in a gamine way: her face was more pleasing than an analysis of its individual features would have allowed. Her smile and charm weakened the defences of adversaries, and in their sibling quarrels I frequently defected to her side, betraying Andris.

Later, as a teenager, when I became a devotee of French films, which had managed to stray into the Hungarian cultural desert of the 1950s, I identified her with Françoise Arnoult, my film goddess of the moment. And while we slaved over our homework, in the next room Vera engaged in heavy petting with her boyfriend, who later became her fiancé and then her husband. Interrupting them constituted an immediate *casus belli*, and the ensuing mêlée would be conducted with verbal and occasionally physical violence.

Since the boyfriend was a Gentile there had been some wagging of tongues in certain quarters: marrying a goy had a high novelty value in the depleted households of the local Jewry. This was not the first and definitely not the last occasion when a member of the family married outside the religion. One thing is certain, however: had my grandmother known, she would have been turning in her unmarked grave somewhere in Austria.

Uncle Manó's sharp mind coupled with an interest in social and political issues landed him in public office soon after the war. And he did not easily bend with the prevailing wind or lightly accept defeat when the tide went against him. By the time he returned from hard labour in the autumn of 1944, the Russians had liberated Makó. It was the first town in the territory of post-Trianon Hungary to be occupied by the Red Army, on 26 September 1944: a little over three months after our last train departed into the unknown. On 14 October 1944 the

commandant of the town issued a decree proclaiming the
equal rights of Jews who had already returned, or were on the
way home from their ordeal. As the returned Jews' spokesman,
however, Uncle Manó protested that the spirit of this decree
had been flouted in practice, and on 4 November 1944 he submitted a handwritten memorandum to the commandant.

In six ruthlessly logical paragraphs he set out the case for
helping rather than hindering the re-establishment of Jewish
businesses, for the cessation of further expropriation of Jewish
homes, for returning all property and belongings to their right-
ful owners, for the restoration and protection of damaged property, and for providing care for all those in need. He demanded
complete official revocation of all anti-Jewish legislation, as had
already happened in other cities, to enable a new start for the
Jewish community and to ensure human rights and equality
for all citizens. He advocated the establishment of a committee
dealing with Jewish affairs. The commandant of the town
agreed to his demands and appointed him chairman of this
new advisory body in his decree of 12 November 1944. Uncle
Manó served in this capacity until the committee was dissolved.
As an acknowledgement of his successful advocacy, he was
later elected to be the leader of the Jewish (Reform) community
of his home town.

From the beginning he was a prominent member of the
Social Democratic Party, a left-of-centre organization and one
of the many parties that mushroomed in the short-lived period
of democracy after the war. On a hot afternoon in July 1946,
while Uncle and his family enjoyed an excursion to the river, a
local man, a former member of the Arrow Cross (the
Hungarian Fascist Party) broke into his house and with a knife
threatened the mother of one of the storemen who at the time
was lodged in the courtyard flat attached to the house. He
alleged that a 'Hungarian' (that is a non-Jewish) man had been
abducted, murdered and then hidden in Uncle's house. The

terrified woman escaped to the main house and there she found a guest who had elected not to join the excursion party. The guest decided to telephone the police. A constable soon arrived and removed the offender from the house, but they hardly turned the corner when he released him. Not wasting a minute, the man promptly returned, now hurling a modified accusation: a small child had been murdered and hidden in my uncle's house.

By now a large crowd had gathered: one of the town's cinemas was around the corner and the early evening performance had just finished. As the audience shuffled out from the stifling interior of the movie house into the evening breeze they were mesmerized by the unfolding drama they stumbled across: one of the leaders of the Jewish community being accused of murder must have proved irresistible entertainment, far more exciting than the film they had just enjoyed.

The house guest and the elderly woman who had originally been threatened managed to escape from the house, unnoticed in the general upheaval. Suddenly the focus of attention shifted to the phalanx of four policemen who appeared and purposefully marched the offender off for a second time.

It was at this point that the drama veered towards the farcical: the accuser was released yet again and, knife still in hand, he returned for a third time to the house, repeating the charge of ritual murder. One of the resummoned policemen telephoned headquarters, and as a result three other policemen hurried to the scene, now on bicycles. They came not to arrest the offender, who had finally been led away at the request of his wife, but to carry out a search in my uncle's house. Apparently, they had reasonable suspicion that he was hiding large quantities of leather material and textiles. Of course, they did not find a hoard of leather goods and textile materials. Nor did they find a murdered Christian child under the floorboards.

Uncle Manó took issue with the local police chief, the lord

lieutenant of the county and the Ministry for the Interior. He dispatched a letter, dated 30 July 1946, to the deputy prime minister, who was the chairman of the Social Democrats, the party in which my uncle was a leading local figure.

As the Communists strengthened their influence with the outside support of the Soviet Union, the Red Army gradually turned from liberators to oppressors. The political parties disappeared one by one, leaving only the Communists and the Social Democrats. Then, in 1948, the Hungarian Workers' Party was formed from a forced merger between the Hungarian Communist Party and the Hungarian Social Democratic Party, effectively abolishing the Social Democrats as an independent moderating voice.

The last obstacle to a one-party system having thus been removed, Hungary entered the dark age of Stalinism. Uncle Manó immediately became the enemy of the people, not on one count but on at least two: he was both a capitalist and a Social Democrat. He lost his livelihood but not his will to remain independent. He and Aunt Anci came up with the idea of making carpets, and they purchased a loom, which was soon installed in the large entrance hall on the first floor. The machine occupied most of the free space, and it became impossible to arrive (and, more importantly, to disappear) without being seen by whoever was operating the loom. The carpets were made not from fine wool, since by then no one could afford expensive furnishings and decorative items, but from the cheapest possible material: cut-offs, end-of-bale remnants, old rags and tatters – cheap materials of all sorts and colours. These were acquired in large quantities, and shredded into narrow strips. The metamorphosis from rags to carpet was miraculous: I adored the random riot of colours and patterns.

The revolution of 1956 found Uncle Manó in good spirits. For a couple of febrile weeks, from 23 October 1956, the beginning of the uprising, to 4 November, when the Russian tanks reappeared, everything seemed possible, even the resurrection of his Social Democratic Party. In the revolutionary fervour, national committees were organized to represent the widest possible spectrum of the population. At a meeting to elect members for the local committee, when Uncle Manó, as a leading Social Democrat, was nominated, he was shouted down: 'We do not want Jews! We do not want Communist Jews!'

None the less, when it was all was over, and the retribution started, the so-called Workers' Militia (a new organization called into being by the Communist government to deal with 'counter-revolutionaries') came for him one night in January 1957 and took him to the local police station. He was accused of distributing guns to the 'counter-revolutionaries' from a courtyard near his home. At the interrogations he was severely beaten and suffered a stroke while in police custody. At the request of one of the attending doctors he was transferred to the neurological clinic in Szeged: the main reason was to save him from further interrogation. He never recovered and died soon afterwards. We never learned the full story of what had happened. Uncle Manó was a Communist to the mob, a capitalist and a counter-revolutionary to the police, but a Jew to all.

7

As food gradually disappeared from the shops at the beginning of the 1950s, becoming scarce even at the market, my mother and her youngest brother, who lived with us, were forced to embark on a programme of self-sufficiency. At first my mother decided to turn one of the rooms of the outbuilding into a chicken coop, and part of the flower garden in front of the outbuilding was separated by a wire fence from the rest to allow the chickens to roam without damaging the remainder of the garden, which by then, without the expertise of a gardener, had begun its gradual decline. This development heralded the end of our secret society: we found it decidedly undignified to negotiate our way through chicken droppings and climb the ladder while frightened birds fluttered their wings in protest at our intrusion. Finding freshly laid, still-warm eggs with their moist shells in unexpected places was the only consolation for this loss of territory. At the same time, while these alterations progressed, as a bribe to silence my protests, a swing was erected.

But more unpleasant events were soon to unfold: keeping chickens was just the first stage in the project. My uncle had more ambitious ideas: with the help of one of the butchers he had befriended, he drew up a plan to keep pigs. One day builders appeared and began to construct pigsties in the furthermost corner of the fruit garden: the material came from the timber yard, which by then was closed for trading but still had some unsold stock. They were meticulously built: there were three adjoining sties each with a roofed and an open area. The first sows were delivered soon after the building work finished and their presence transformed the tranquillity of the house. Although the sties were regularly swept clean, they attracted flies and their stench wafted towards the house, particularly on hot summer days. Encouraged by the initial success of his enterprise, my uncle embarked on a further, logical extension of his plan: not only to keep but also to breed pigs. For this purpose he hired a boar to impregnate the sows, and his investment was handsomely repaid. The beast performed with considerable zeal, and the noisy copulations were admired by any of my friends who happened to be around. Being in our early teens, feeling the first surges of testosterone, we were amazed how long these performances lasted, and drew entirely wrong conclusions about the length of the equivalent human activity based on hasty inter-species comparisons. Rosy-skinned and fluffy-haired litters were later delivered in excrement and blood.

This amateur but none the less quite successful pig farming came to a climax in the middle of each winter. The largest sow was selected to be killed. The date was carefully chosen weeks earlier, and the details discussed with the butcher. I dreaded this day, and part of me wanted to find an excuse to stay with a friend in order to escape, and yet I could not resist the morbid fascination of this well-choreographed act of violence.

As it was midwinter, often with snow on the ground, the day started early in unbroken darkness. The banging of doors, heavy-booted footsteps and shouts heralded the arrival of the butcher and his assistant. I could faintly hear the ritual of laying the set of knives on the kitchen table. From the arrival of the butcher to killing the animal took less than an hour, but the waiting seemed endless. I knew that the actual moment was approaching by the muffled noises surging in a crescendo as the animal was dragged out from the sty. More piercing noises were heard as increasing violence was used to force the animal to a convenient spot. Then silence: the animal, being overwhelmed, surrendered to its fate. A sudden, terrible, pro-tracted squeal shattered the silence as the pig was stuck. I tried to escape this horrible sound by digging deeply into the bed under the pillows and the eiderdown, but all in vain: it pene-trated through all my defences. I could not pretend that I had not heard this squeal; I can hear it now.

The butcher, a man in his late twenties with straight dark hair, deeply set black eyes and ungenerous lips beneath a crooked nose broken in a fight. Fortunately he was skilled and always managed to kill the animal with one well-aimed stab, severing the jugular vein; the resulting spray of blood was care-fully captured in a container to be used later in blood sausages. It was only then that I dared to leave my bedroom, to be con-fronted by a scene of disturbing beauty in the garden. He was holding a blowtorch to scorch off the animal's wiry hair. The snow was splattered with blood. As the butcher moved the blowtorch up and down over the hairy skin, the snow quickly surrendered to the heat, melting into a muddy, bloody pool around the animal. The air was filled with the thick smell of burning hair. After the hair was burnt off, the film of black keratin ash was scrubbed off to reveal shimmering white, and the corpse was hosed down with ice-cold water.

With the help of the assistant, the animal was carried to the kitchen, and lifted on to the table. Here the glistening knives suddenly sprang to life: the skinning, evisceration and disjointing had begun. The internal organs were removed one by one – heart, kidneys, liver, lungs and finally intestines. A systematic dissection then began: parts were carved and prepared for bacon, ham, chops and cutlets, muscles separated from bones and sinews discarded, thick layers of fat scooped out from under the skin to be melted down. Meanwhile the assistant washed the excrement from the intestines, boiled the rice for the sausages, and prepared the pepper, salt and paprika for seasoning. For me it was time to take refuge again in the sanctuary of my bedroom.

When I resurfaced mid-morning, the kitchen was still in a mess: the floor was covered in a slippery mixture of blood and excrement, while the intestines had been carefully rinsed out to be set aside in slithery coils in large shallow enamel pots, to be used later in the day to encase sausages. Some of the internal organs, including the bladder and the reproductive system, had been discarded, but in a tightly observed economy little else was wasted. The liver was put through a large mincer to end up as liver sausage in a piece of intestine. Some of the minced meat was generously flavoured with finely ground, mildly hot red paprika; the remainder was mixed with rice to produce a different type of sausage. The legs were carved in curvaceous shapes, and the fat, masses of runny fat, was collected in large enamel containers in which it froze into viscous white emulsion in the cold of the larder. Golden crackling was stored in large glass jars. In the absence of refrigeration, chops and cut-lets were fried and then covered in fat in airtight containers and put aside to be eaten at a later date.

By late afternoon the filth had receded, and order was gradu-ally restored. As we sat down to dinner, only tiny fragments of flesh and smears of fat that had escaped the assistant's system-atic scrubbing betrayed the earlier drama of the day.

After being smoked, the various sausages and the bacon ended up hanging from wooden poles in the larder, and as the year progressed they disappeared one by one; by the end of the year only a little lard remained, but by then, with winter ap-proaching, there was the promise of a fresh supply.

I was too young then to realize the subtle irony of amateur pig farming in my grandparents' house. Under my grand-mother's iron rule there were strictly observed religious laws, and having pigs in her house must have been one of the cardi-nal sins, even at times of severe food shortage. Had she been alive she would rather have starved, and I could occasionally feel her disapproving spirit hovering over the sacrilege we were committing in her house.

8

The Jewish cemetery in Makó lies well outside the boundaries of the town, in the middle of fields. Why the once-influential Jewish community decided to bury their dead in a remote, inaccessible spot remains a mystery: all the other denomina-tions were better advised and built their cemeteries well within the borders of the town, even if not in the centre. The argu-ment advanced later to justify what turned out to be the wrong decision was that this piece of land was the highest point around town, a fact not immediately obvious in the pancake flatness of the surrounding fields. Leaders of the community must have envisaged that one day the fast-growing town would engulf the land they had purchased, or perhaps, more probably, that the town would build a road leading to the cemetery. If this was their assumption, however, then they badly miscalculated: the cemetery was never connected to any artery of transport, and development of the town, stunted after the First World War, did not proceed quickly enough to reach the cemetery. It remained a strange and alien island in the middle of the surrounding arable land, accessible only by a dirt road, rendering every visit dependent on the hazards of the weather. During the rainy season the road was transformed into a sea of mud, and passage was impossible. In the long winter months heavy snowfall impeded any traffic, although the frozen ground, unless it was too bumpy, was not an obstacle. None the less, a visit to the Jewish cemetery always required planning well ahead of time. I do not recall visiting before the war, perhaps because we did not have anybody to grieve for, but after the war all that changed.

As a child I always had an uneasy feeling about these visits. While we had the timber yard, my mother arranged for a horse-drawn open carriage to arrive at our house to take us to the cemetery. Since we had to drive through the centre of town, I felt uncomfortable and self-conscious sitting in an open carriage with my mother: I imagined that every clank of the horseshoes on the road would attract unwanted attention. I fixed my eyes on the driver's back, looking neither left nor right, apprehensive that someone would recognize me and ask where we were going. I was not ashamed of our destination, but by being isolated from other people walking in the street, I felt exposed and vulnerable.

Once we had left the last houses of the town behind us, however, the journey became less stressful and more exciting: the horses changed from a stately pace to a leisurely gallop, encouraged by occasional lashes from the whip. The ride was occasionally bumpy as after heavy rains the mud was baked into solid ridges by the sun. Between the town and the cemetery there were a couple of farms partly hidden behind a copse of trees, but otherwise the horizon was open and wide.

As we arrived, the horses slowed down, the carriage braked to a gentle halt and the caretaker of the cemetery, having heard our approach, was already waiting to welcome us. My mother adjusted her hat, or in the summer her silk scarf, while I removed my skullcap from my pocket and reluctantly placed it on my head. I had masses of dark brown, slightly unruly hair, and when it was long my mother had to secure the skullcap with a hairpin; this I disliked immensely, but I learned to swallow my pride and not to protest.

We walked through the gate and into a plain building, whitewashed on the outside but dark inside: it was here that the mystery of death was laid bare and funeral services held. From the gloom of this building we walked out into the cemetery, a place of astonishing beauty. Its isolation, and the fact that it was so utterly and uncompromisingly different from everything else around it, endowed it with an air of serenity and peace, unmatched anywhere else. As a child I naïvely contemplated that as it was so far from man it must be near to God. Over the years, as I grew up, its attraction never faded: on the contrary, as the standard of its maintenance slipped with the gradual disappearance of the local Jewish community, its decay made it even more captivating. A wide central paved path, lined by an assortment of deciduous trees and conifers, led from the large wooden gate to the fence at the end. From this central alleyway narrow irregular paths ran to separate rows of graves.

I quickly said my prayer, and while my mother prayed I wandered around, always eager to make new discoveries. I was never disappointed. On finishing her prayer, my mother called me back from my wanderings: the visit was over. We placed a small stone on the grave as our visiting card, retraced our steps through the building, washed our hands and dried them with the towel prepared for us by the caretaker, left a few small coins, took our seat on the carriage, and drove back to town.

In later years, after the timber yard had closed down and a carriage was not at our disposal any more, our visits became greatly simplified: my mother negotiated a reasonable fare with one of the more enterprising taxi drivers, who came to pick us up from our house. But even then the visit remained an excursion that had to be planned rather than a spontaneous trip. Since these visits depended on good weather, in my memory the cemetery is always bathed in sunshine: thin and vulnerable in spring, pounding and scorching hot in summer, golden and tired in autumn, and sharp blue in winter.

The last time I visited the cemetery before leaving for England was in the summer of 1968. My aunt from Budapest and my uncle joined me. I carried my mother's ashes in an urn for an informal burial. The rabbi from Szeged refused to conduct a formal ceremony. When my mother died I had her cremated – it was clear to me that she would not want to be buried in a new grave but should finally be reunited with my brother. Unfortunately, an Orthodox Jew such as this rabbi did not approve of cremation, and for him strict observance of the law was more important than an act of compassion.

9

The Maros River is romantic, wild and unruly. From its source in the Transylvanian mountains it hurries through the plains to empty its fast muddy waters into the much bigger Tisza, skirting Makó to the south some 20 miles upstream. Traditionally the Maros was an artery of the region's vibrant economy, being used to transport salt and, in more recent times, building materials on large rafts.

Its banks had not been disciplined by any sophisticated engineering work at the time and were densely populated by a forest of oaks, willows and poplars. In the early spring, when the snow melted in the mountains, and at times of sustained rain, floods were common. The river would breach its banks and storm the dyke that had been built to protect the town, not always successfully.

In a large clearing of trees by the river there was the beach called 'the strand' by the locals. 'Going to the strand' was a popular pastime in the summer, particularly at weekends, although it was not easy to reach. The distance between the town centre, where we lived, and the beach was barely 4 kilometres, but it was too far to walk in the heat and too difficult to negotiate by car. The easiest way was to cycle there: a short journey full of fun. As the houses in the main street leading towards the river thinned out, the road crossed the dyke, which in places reached a vertiginous height of 4 or 5 metres. Its sides were seeded with grass and colonized by weeds; small bushes grew unplanned from seeds dropped by birds. The surface of the dyke was relatively smooth, flattened by the lazy flow of agricultural traffic: peasants' carts and horse-drawn carriages greatly outnumbered trucks and the occasional private car.

Having left the town behind, cycling on the dyke was exhilarating. The crowns of trees were below us, and we could see the town to the north, its church spires standing out like arrows piercing the sky, while to the south dense growths of trees and bushes hid the river. After a mile or two, one had to descend towards the river and an important decision had to be made. Either one took the cowardly option of dismounting from one's bike and, with the brake on, gingerly navigating a descent down the deep side of the dyke, or, having taken a deep breath and hoping for the best, one continued down the slope with increasing speed. Pedalling down the dyke involved an element of danger, since the last 100 metres before the beach were on a narrow, winding dirt path cut into the dense copse of trees. Applying the brake was optional but frowned upon – for a glamorous arrival one had to whiz down, sounding the bell continuously and slowing down only at the last second, at the entrance to the beach.

There were rows of wooden cabins on the beach, and it cost next to nothing to rent one for the whole season. A small restaurant had a limited menu of simple hot dishes, and dispensed beer and soft drinks. The clearing on the river bank had a carpet of grass, which, being rather erratically mowed, often grew long and silky. At the height of a rainless summer the river retreated more and more into its bed, leaving behind a muddy surface baked solid by the sun. Normally, however, the current was fast and treacherous, and two barriers constructed of wooden poles chained together clearly indicated how far one could go: children and non-swimmers were allowed only up to the first barrier, and only good swimmers could proceed to the second. It was a rule that we often broke: we made our way among the trees up the river bank and swam down with the current. When we wanted to stop for a while it was easy to catch a tree branch conveniently arching over the water, then let it go to complete our journey. The whistle of the midday train, a noise impossible to miss, indicated time for lunch.

10

Restarting the family business proved to be even more difficult than restoring life in the family house. The timber yard had ceased to trade: the director nominated by the mayor of Makó was incompetent. He was a stooge, and problems emerged early under his management. On 25 July 1945, at the time when my mother and I were still in Germany, Uncle Manó, the elder of the two surviving sons, was called to police headquarters to appear as witnesses at the trial of the mayor, who by then had been indicted for crimes committed during the war. In his evidence my uncle stated that the appointment of the mayor's nominee was irregular, since according to the legislation the director of the firm should have been not only a Christian but also an employee with long-term experience of the affairs of the business. He did not hesitate to give the name of at least two employees who had been better qualified than the mayor's candidate. The appointment had been a clever plot for personal gain: through his chosen man the mayor could gain access to and influence the direction of a profitable business.

Soon after our return in September, the first tentative steps were taken to reorganize the business on borrowed money. Workers were recruited: many were old hands who had been employed before the war and were keen to earn a living in difficult times. The engine house was renovated and the office block reorganized. The picture of the Regent, Admiral Horthy, had been unceremonially removed from the wall, but, resisting an impulse to throw it out, my mother hid it behind one of the large filing cabinets. Perhaps she could foresee that one day, as has happened, the Admiral would be resurrected from the dustbin of history and his role in recent Hungarian history would be more favourably assessed. My mother and uncles Manó and Jenő were running the firm on a day-to-day basis, although Manó by then had also restarted his trade in wheat and corn. The timber yard enjoyed its second renaissance and flourished until 1949. Then suddenly everything changed.

Immediately after their ascension to power, the Communists commenced the systematic destruction of the country's economy on the template of the Soviet experience. All industrial concerns, factories, banks and private enterprises had been gradually nationalized and by the end of 1949 even small manufacturers and workshops with more than ten employees were taken away from their owners. They were branded class aliens:

a label that carried an indelible social stigma. And in the perverse social stratification of Communist society those classified as class aliens were also enemies of the people.

The precise number of workers employed in the timber yard could not be ascertained at the time: the books were not cooked, but there were a number of temporary workers who did not appear on the regular payroll. Soon after the Communist takeover the timber yard ceased trading. Although legally the family still enjoyed ownership, in practice we could not claim any right to what was still our property.

During the early 1950s one did not have the right to question the authorities or challenge their decisions. History, at least in terms of the family annals, seemed to be repeating itself, and within a short time. The family business was expropriated twice within five years: first by the Fascists in 1944 and now by the Communists. And in a macabre replay of the events of 1944, having been freshly stigmatized as class aliens, there was a real threat that we might be interned, as so many people had been at that time. Bank accounts were emptied before they could be seized, and most money was spent on goods that could be classified as personal belongings.

It was at this time that my mother paid several visits to a jeweller in Szeged to purchase gold and diamond jewellery: necklaces, rings and bracelets. These were carefully hidden at home, and during the ensuing years they were sold one by one to complement my mother's meagre earnings as a cashier. These transactions were conducted in great secrecy, since privately buying and selling gold and other precious metals were illegal. My mother wore a couple of the less ostentatious pieces: a gold necklace and matching bracelet of a classical design were favourites of mine. The last piece to go, a heavy bracelet made of large chunks of red, white and yellow gold, was sold much later to finance my university studies. From the remnants of this sale I acquired a double-breasted dinner-jacket for my graduation. This travelled with me to London, and when I wore it here for the first and last time at a concert at the Royal Festival Hall at the end of 1968 I looked truly ridiculous in its uncompromising starched formality in a sea of flowery casual wear.

While my mother was buying jewellery, Uncle Jenő had invested his money in a powerful motorcycle. This remained unridden until the day he sold it in virgin condition. For reasons I never understood he decided to park it permanently in the dining-room next to the large table rather than in one of the outbuildings. And there it stood, all gleaming metal and glossy paint, a much-discussed and coveted object of desire, leaking petrol on to the parquet floor. A statue rather than a vehicle, it became an obstacle when we wanted to ride our bicycles around the dining-table, a pastime much disapproved of by my mother. The arrival of the motorcycle was the final acknowledgement that, despite her heroic efforts, the house would never be properly furnished again to restore it to its pre-war dignity.

By then the family house was owned by four inheritors: my mother, Uncle Jenő, and the children of two of my other uncles. In 1959 Uncle Jenő joined forces with other owners to sell three-quarters of the house. This changed our everyday lives: instead of enjoying the comfort of a large house we were restricted to the use of one large room and the kitchen. Most painful was the loss of the bathroom; a makeshift facility was created in the space leading to the loft. I left home in September 1958 to begin my first semester at medical school, but my return visits every weekend were a sad reminder of the disappearance of our home. My mother finally sold her share in 1965, and with the proceeds of the sale we paid the deposit on the flat in Szeged.

In September 1960, as the political repression eased and a new, more liberal economic policy was introduced, Uncle Jenő, representing the family, sold the timber firm to a state-owned building enterprise, which had in any case been using the yard for many years: this transaction merely legalized the unlawful occupation that had taken place at the beginning of 1950 and represented the final chapter in the history of the family firm.

Uncle Jenő found employment as an accountant in one of the small industrial collectives, a poorly paid but not particularly demanding job which saw him through to his retirement. He visited me twice in London, and we rediscovered the warmth we had lost when he decided to sell his share of the family house. He still chain-smoked, and after his departure the heavy curtains retained the smell of his strong Hungarian cigarettes. In 1986, on my return to London from Portugal where I lectured at a medical training course, a telegram was waiting for me with news of his death. By then he had already been buried. He had suffered a massive heart attack during lunch at the Crown Hotel in Makó, and had been laid out on the table at which he had been eating. By the time the ambulance arrived he could not be resuscitated, and he was transported to the mortuary of the local hospital. Between the hotel and the mortuary his wristwatch disappeared.

11

Finding a job proved more difficult for my mother. For a short time she worked in one of the nationalized local banks, but as a class alien she was soon hounded out. She became a cashier in one of the grocery stores: a large barn of a place in the centre of town. In better times its counter might have displayed a variety of local produce, but in the early 1950s, under the Communist regime, choice was limited, and unbelievably there were food shortages at times. The displays were frequently composed of pyramids of tins, and not much else. Her till, located near the entrance; was exposed to cold draughts in the winter, while it was stiflingly hot in the summer. She regarded her move to one of the small clothes shops as a promotion, and undoubtedly it was a more agreeable place to work. These were jobs she would never have considered doing normally yet she accepted them with dignity and without complaint.

Facing north, the new shop was a rather dark, dingy place, devoid of elegance, and the drab, poorly made merchandise did not inject any colour into the grey surroundings. Who wanted to buy any of these garments remained a mystery. With the beginning of the 1960s there was an explosion of colour; not only did local merchandise improve but Western goods also began appearing on the shelves.

Our own generally rather drab garments had already begun to be livened up by clothing sent from America. One of my mother's cousins, an engineer who emigrated to the United States in the early 1920s, had traced us after the war, and his offer of help was accepted without fuss. The parcels were a real cornucopia of surprises, particularly for a teenage boy. Poplin shirts, plain and striped, flannel trousers and jeans, a leather anorak with a zip, ties with jazzy designs, soft cotton T-shirts – these were articles of clothing unheard of, let alone seen, in the early 1950s in a small provincial town in Hungary. Even more enticing were items of stationery: soft crayons, colour pencils, erasers disguised as pencils and picture books of New York with breathtaking scenes of skyscrapers. The dispatch of the parcels was announced in a letter giving itemized details of the contents: this was scrupulously scrutinized on arrival, and each item individually ticked off to ensure that nothing had been removed in transit.

12

I was enrolled in primary school in September 1946, one month before my seventh birthday. I was unable to start the year before since, being born in October, I was not quite six at the beginning of the school year. We had also just arrived back in Makó, and it would have been difficult to go to school without a chance to adapt to normal life. My mother had also felt that I was not ready physically: my weight was still considerably below normal for a child of my age. She instituted a high-calorie diet and I was encouraged to replenish my still-depleted subcutaneous fat. At this time there was not yet any shortage of food: the local peasants produced a cornucopia of meat, poultry, vegetables and fruit which they displayed at market, and with these my mother produced the most sustaining dishes. Every evening before I went to bed she prepared a cup of hot chocolate: drinking this became a ritual until I went to secondary school. Yet I remained thin. As a gesture of further encouragement she promised to buy me a grown-up watch when I hit the 30-kilogram mark on the scale.

But there were other consequences of our journey, less obvious than that of being undernourished. I was different from other children: I was Jewish. One of my best friends at school was Tibor. He was a perfect little boy, bright and boisterous with a winning smile. He was prone to minor truancy, but these disciplinary trespasses were easily forgiven by the teachers because of the good results he achieved in class. During one of our school excursions, we had agreed to deviate from the path in a small forest, and were meandering among the trees. Suddenly, without any warning or relevant prior conversation, he declared: 'I do not like Jews.' This was an irrevocable statement: firm and dogmatic, but without the slightest touch of malice. It was a pre-formed opinion, picked up from adults. I was overwhelmed by surprise: I did not know what to do or say. After I recovered, I could articulate only one question, which, with hindsight, was the right one: 'Why not?'

His answer was unexpected: 'Because,' he said with a grin, 'they spit in the street.'

I plucked up my courage to tell him what I was sure he already knew: 'Tibor, I am Jewish, and I do not spit in the street, or anywhere.'

'But I like you,' he answered with a liberal dose of his winning smile. And we retraced our steps to join the others.

Tibor and I remained the very best of friends until our paths separated: with the reorganization of educational boundaries I was assigned to a different school.

Some fifty years later, I came across a small collection of photographs of Hungarian synagoguges, taken in black and white. The artist, as I discovered with a pleasant surprise, was none other than Tibor.

One evening in March 1957, on the eve of the anniversary of 15 March 1848, the Hungarian uprising against Austria, the town was tense. The Communist regime, only just re-established after the uprising in October 1956, was still insecure and apprehensive about demonstrations for which the anniversary provided the ideal opportunity. And students were an easy target for the Workers' Militia and policemen.

It was already dark and I was going to visit Mari, my cousin. She was a couple of years younger than me and, having inherited both her mother's and her father's good looks, she had grown into a real beauty. As children we had spent some of the summer vacation together, and at high school, where she had no shortage of potential boyfriends, I was proud of her. I was eager to show her a new guidebook on Israel which had arrived the preceding day from my aunt, now living in Petah Tiqwa. I was wearing my school cap. The street was deserted: people were still reluctant to go out after dark.

Suddenly a policeman loomed large in front of me and asked me to stop. He looked me up and down, and his gaze lingered for a second or two on my school cap. I sensed trouble and his opening gambit confirmed my suspicion. 'Did they not teach you to say good evening?' He was obviously preparing the ground for an argument, but I did not yet know how our confrontation would develop.

'Sorry, I did not know that I should wish good evening to someone I do not know.' As soon as I uttered the sentence I regretted it; I thought he would find it insolent.

Surprisingly, he changed tactics. 'What are you carrying? Show it to me!' he demanded.

Without a word I offered him the slim guidebook on Israel I was clutching in my hand.

'I did not know you were Jewish,' he said. 'I thought Jews were nice people.' He was still in the middle of the sentence when he hit me across the face with the back of his hand. The blow was so hard that it sent my school cap and the guidebook, which he had handed back a second earlier, flying. He then continued his walk without another word.

I retrieved my school cap and guidebook from the pavement. I gave up the idea of visiting my cousin and turned in the direction of home, as if nothing had happened. Yet my humiliation was complete: a sense of rage and impotence; the realization that I was powerless. My upper lip was bleeding. This did not escape my mother's attention when I arrived home, and she immediately wanted to know what had happened. I was reluctant to tell her the truth, and to reveal the ugliness of my humiliation. My impulse was to invent a story of a fight with other boys, but instinctively I knew that my mother would not give it much credit. Reluctantly I recounted the events of the evening. Her response was swift and unexpected: she went straight to the police station, asked for the officer in charge and lodged an official complaint. Surprisingly, an apology was received in due course. I could later savour the irony of someone declaring Jews to be nice people and at the same time beating one up just for fun.

13

The incident with the policeman was part of the retribution the Communist authorities, regaining power and confidence after the shock of the Revolution in October 1956, waged against students whom they perceived, with some justification, to be enemies of the restored system of oppression. At the age of fourteen I entered the local secondary school or gymnasium. Named after the Hungarian poet Attila József, who was a former pupil, the gymnasium maintained a high standard despite heavy-handed political influence and economic restrictions. The director of the school, a brilliant pedagogue with a razor-sharp mind, had a theological background and was trained by the Jesuits: later he joined the Communist Party and became a member of their inner cabinet in town. He was admired and feared in equal measure. In the heady days of the Revolution, the unsavoury fact emerged that the loudspeakers in the schoolrooms were wired in such a way that he could eavesdrop on the classes. After my baccalaureate he summoned me to warn me in the gentlest possible way to be circumspect about my political views and to watch what I was saying and to whom. Whether his advice was based on his own spying in the past or on a report from one of his informants I will never know.

My class was oriented towards the humanities, with an extensive curriculum embracing world history and literature, grammar, Latin and modern languages (of which Russian by then had become compulsory), but also mathematics, algebra, geometry, biology, physics, chemistry, geography, music (in the first year only), physical education and history of art (optional in the fourth year). Having contracted rheumatic fever with myocardial complications at the end of summer, I could not start with my classmates at the beginning of September, but when I joined them a couple of months later I delved into these subjects with unbridled enthusiasm.

Our form mistress was strict, fair, upright and practical. She taught Russian and German, and it is to her credit that I overcame my emotional resistance to the Russian language, the tongue of the oppressors, when I realized its beauty and the immense literature it had produced. But above all she created a disciplined and competitive yet relaxed atmosphere in which she endeavoured to bring out the best in everybody. She organized excursions into the mountains in the north of the country and to Lake Balaton: in the mid-1950s these were great occasions. Her class was the best in the school, admired and envied by others.

Our literature teacher, an oddly beautiful woman in her early thirties, injected such passion into her lectures that even the most insensitive students were inspired to join her in the world of a Shakespeare drama, a Hungarian family saga, a Molière comedy or a Heine poem. She had deeply set dark eyes, which spoke of an inner drama: this she never unburdened to us.

I also enjoyed the mathematics classes: our teacher was a large, heavy-set man with freely sprouting eyebrows and hair which, despite his frequently sweeping it back with his hand, always landed on his forehead. Under his guidance I entered a national competition in mathematics in which I did well, and he encouraged me to pursue a career in his subject. He was also an amateur musician, and the rendering of Mozart's *Eine kleine Nachtmusik* by the school orchestra, conducted by him, was a red-letter event in the school's diary. But it was the performance of the Hebrew slaves' chorus from Verdi's *Nabucco* which brought the house down. We all sang our hearts and lungs out, for we could easily identify with the oppressed.

Although history of art was an optional subject, I shall be grateful for the rest of my life that I subscribed to this course. Our teacher was a young man who took us on a leisurely tour of discovery. Paintings and statues sprang to life; two-dimensional pictures of great architectural monuments regained their lost dimensions and perspectives in his descriptions. Sitting in his class, I could not know that many years later I would be standing in front of these pictures and statues, visiting the buildings he had described, and I would still remember his classes.

In front of the school was the memorial to the Red Army. And in October 1956 this memorial, like so many others throughout Hungary, was torn down in a manifestation of national independence, with far-reaching consequences for our school.

The demonstration on 26 October started peacefully. We lined up in the courtyard of the school, senior students at the head of the march followed by the junior classes. National flags, horizontal stripes of red, white and green without the more recent embellishment of the Communist coat of arms, were carried at the head of the march, together with a hurriedly produced example of the country's old coat of arms, illegal under the Communist regime. The demonstration was allowed to go ahead by the local chief of police, whose elder son was one of the senior students organizing the march, on condition that strict discipline was enforced. And this was indeed maintained throughout the demonstration.

Returning to school, however, we realized that other forces were at work: the aim of some of the crowd who gathered in front of our school was to destroy the Soviet memorial. Their determination was not matched by reasoned calculation of the power they needed to topple the monument, and the demolition succeeded only after several setbacks. First, the rope tied around the obelisk was fastened too low, and neither manpower nor a hastily recruited tractor could accomplish the task. Only when the noose was attached further up did the upper third come tumbling down, crashing on to the ladder below. The rest was removed piecemeal after an unseemly and long struggle. We were strictly forbidden to participate, and the main gate of the school facing the square where the monument stood was firmly locked. In spite of this, a few students escaped to witness the unfolding drama at close quarters.

Retribution came in the winter of 1956/7, the penultimate year before the final examinations, the baccalaureate. Our curriculum had already been severely disrupted by the revolution and ensuing events. Teaching had been suspended soon after the Russian intervention and a protracted miners' strike caused further delays. It was well into 1957 before the normal curriculum was resumed. The dissipated tension came to a head on 23 February, the anniversary of the creation of the Red Army. A celebration to commemorate this event was organized in the morning and involved laying wreaths at the recently restored Russian memorial. For several years 4 April, the day of the liberation of Hungary by the Red Army, had been a national holiday, as had been 7 November, the anniversary of the revolution in Russia, but celebrating the birth of the Red Army was an excuse to demonstrate the consolidation of the power of the dictatorship.

The precise sequence of events that unfolded in front of our school has been disputed ever since, but there is no doubt that the behaviour of some of the students disturbed the solemnity of the occasion: catcalls, whistles, rude remarks and even small projectiles were aimed at the assembled crowd. The reaction of the authorities was swift and brutal. Members of the Workers' Guard occupied the school: no one could leave or enter. They broke into our class, which was on the second floor in the middle of the corridor, affording a vantage point over the ceremony below. The guards wore special padded anoraks and carried machine guns. 'Stand up,' they shouted. 'Put your satchels on top of your benches! Hands up! Line up against the wall!'

They proceeded to search us meticulously. Then they searched our satchels. They spilled books, little wooden boxes containing pens and pencils and loose sheets of paper on top of the benches. They even unwrapped our elevenses. They were looking for anti-Communist or anti-Soviet leaflets. The search revealed, in one girl's Latin grammar book, a patriotic poem, written by another student: this was deemed to be inflammatory and seditious in exhorting the uprising of 1956, which by then had officially been labelled counter-revolutionary. The girl was ordered to leave the class with them. We were humiliated and shocked.

After the departure of the Workers' Guard and accompanying plainclothes policemen, the school was in chaos. Several students were taken from other classes and temporarily detained. They were later interrogated, threatened with expulsion and pressurized to spy on other students in return for not facing charges. The teachers were equally shattered. They felt powerless: their students had been humiliated in front of them and they could do nothing about it. Two days later the local chief of police issued an ultimatum demanding severe punishment for the offending students: within nine days four students had been expelled from the school and five other students, including our classmate, had been reprimanded by the school director. Life at school changed for ever; although the old camaraderie survived, we had lost our innocence. The raid was more than an invasion: it was a violation of our youth.

Despite the interruptions to our third year, we all completed our studies. The final examinations took place at the end of the fourth year, in June 1958. I had prepared with enthusiasm – by then I had decided to study medicine. I knew that it was difficult to get into medical school: the number of applicants greatly exceeded the number of available places. In my baccalaureate I passed the four compulsory subjects: literature, history, mathematics and physics, and an optional subject, German, with good results. I submitted my application to the Medical University in Szeged. Although the summer offered many diversions, I immediately turned my attention single-mindedly to the two subjects that would feature in the entry

examination: biology and physics. On the date specified I travelled to Szeged and was grilled by a formal but friendly admission committee. I thought I had done well: later I learned
unofficially that I had scored 19 out of 20 possible points.

In an optimistic mood I waited for a letter from the university's admissions office. But nothing came. The first semester
was due to start at the beginning of September, and as I idled
away the long summer days in mounting uncertainty, my
mother decided to make enquiries. The dean of the Medical
University was an old acquaintance of the family, and one evening my mother reluctantly decided to visit him. She was not
away for long. It was the end of a hot day: the windows of our
house were open and I heard her brisk returning footsteps.
The news was not good. 'You are not going to be admitted.'
She looked upset and her smudged make-up betrayed the fact
that she had been crying.

'But why on earth not? I finished school with distinction and
did well in the entrance examination,' I said despondently.

'I know, and so do they. But in the official documents processed by the admissions office you are apparently designated
as a class alien. You also talked too much in 1956.'

This was very bad news indeed. In 1958 to be branded a
class alien was a death sentence to my aspiration to study medicine. For my mother this was a replay of the not too distant
past: her elder son, however brilliant he had been at school,
could not even dream of going to university in 1943 because he
was Jewish. And now the same fate was facing her younger
son on account of the long-lost family fortune. At the time
there were strict regulations that 50 per cent of all university
admissions should come from working-class and peasant families. The rest of the available places could be taken up by children of professional people and of those in other occupations,
but not those from families branded as class aliens. The social
class known as 'other occupations' was not well defined and

remained a grey area where an element of flexibility and good-will could be exercised: it had been known to include small shopkeepers, independent artisans, administrators and the like. 'Well, I can try again next year,' I said feebly. I was determined to study medicine, and in the face of this rejection I had no alternative plan.

But my mother was not to be easily defeated. 'I am going to see the secretary of the committee of the local party.' And before I could say anything she was off.

Her case was straightforward. She argued that there was no reason why her son should be labelled a class alien since her husband had been an accountant and, after the introduction of anti-Jewish legislation, had earned his living as a labourer. She conceded a fact known to everybody in town, that her parents had owned an industrial enterprise, but reasoned that the third generation should not be punished for the 'crime of the grand-parents being capitalist'. Her plea was granted, and I was promoted to the social class of 'others'. A letter followed at the end of August from the admissions office informing me that I had been admitted to the Medical University of Szeged. I obtained one of the few places reserved for late applicants and pending cases, and enrolled, ready for the first semester, in September. This was my first step on the path that led me, exactly ten years later, to board a flight to London.

LONDON: A NEW START

1

The last time nightmares haunted me was soon after I refused to return to Hungary. After the completion of my research fellowship in London, I decided to stay in England. And those nightmares were always the same.

On an autumn morning I am boarding a Malév flight from Budapest to London. A steward politely ushers me to my seat. By a surprising coincidence I am sitting next to an old friend, who could not be a more pleasant travelling companion. She is one of the librarians at the Faculty of Humanities, a beautiful woman in her twenties with the most amazing blue-grey eyes.

This is my first journey by air to a Western country and I am looking forward to the flight. We fasten our seat belts and are ready for take-off. Suddenly a stewardess, in her early forties, with an erect, schoolmistressy posture, walks down the aisle towards me and stops not far from my seat. Her face is a bland landscape in which even an oft-returning visitor would fail to discover any memorable features. Suddenly an acute sense of foreboding envelops me: something appalling and irreversible is going to happen.

'Dr Lantos,' she says in a clipped voice. The intonation hovers between question and statement, as if giving me a chance to deny my identity, to claim that I am someone else. And indeed this is what I would like to do: to erase my name from the passenger list, or to transform myself into one of the other passengers. But there is no escape; I am trapped – I cannot disappear or disguise myself, since she, of course, knows exactly who I am. And at this moment I realize in an unexpectedly painful flash of illumination what will happen: she will ask me to disembark. I will never reach my destination.

'I am Dr Lantos,' I answer, amazed that I can articulate anything, since all the muscles in my face and tongue feel completely paralysed, my mouth utterly parched. Yet I hear myself, barely audible, confirming my identity.

I unfasten my safety belt and stand up; we are presently the only people standing in the whole plane, the stewardess and I. All the other passengers have stopped talking, and in the deepening silence everybody is staring at us.

'Would you like to follow me?' the stewardess asks, but this is clearly an order rather than a request; disobeying is out of question. I rehearse potential escape routes: fleeing the plane, disappearing into thin air, metamorphosing into a hitherto unknown form of non-existence. But there is no possible escape: the trap is closing around me, the image of London fading away, and the future is suddenly full of unfathomable horror. There is not even a precipice, the usual convenient exit from all nightmares, into which I can fall. The interior of the plane has become hermetically sealed.

And at this point, terror-struck, I woke up in the depths of the night. It must have taken only a second or two to resurface to consciousness and recover my senses, although time seemed infinite on that threshold. Then I realized with relief and elation that I was, after all, in London.

My bed was soaked in sweat. This was not one of those polite little perspirations that characterize an uncomfortable night after a heavy meal, with too much drink or coffee, but the flood that marks the resolution of a serious infectious disease. If I had screamed, my scream would have been muffled or completely mute, since my landlord, who slept on the floor below, never complained; if he did hear anything, he was too polite to raise the question of strange noises emanating from my room at night.

The nightmare persisted, and returned again and again with small variations: little changes in the sequence of events or in the characters, as if a film director was not satisfied with the takes he had and was reshooting the scene with minor alterations. A couple of months later they ceased, as unexpectedly as they had started, never to return.

Not until recently, when I tried, in vain, to find my birthplace.

2

Fortunately, the journey from Budapest to London did not follow the pattern of the nightmares: it all happened differently in life. I did embark on the plane, I did sit next to the librarian, I did fasten my seat belt, and the stewardess came only to ask about the comfort of my seat. The plane took off without delay and I landed at Heathrow two hours later on a crisp, late October afternoon in 1968. My plan was to stay for one year on a research fellowship in medicine I had received two years earlier from the Wellcome Trust.

These days the arrival of a young postgraduate doctor from an eastern European country to work on a research project is commonplace, but in the 1960s it was nothing short of miraculous. The trip was, in fact, my second visit to London: the result of three years of planning and equal measures of luck and disappointment. Three years earlier, in September 1965, I had arrived at Victoria Station on the Golden Arrow from Paris as a tourist, ready to discover a city I knew only from books and films. Although my English was limited, I felt immediately at home for reasons I do not understand even now. But London then was a different place from the world city of today.

That time, as my vacation ended, my meagre resources

rapidly exhausted, I returned to Hungary determined to come back one day. I had recently graduated in medicine, and taken up my first appointment as an assistant lecturer in the Department of Histopathology, or, as it was then known, Morbid Anatomy, at the Medical University, Szeged. I was eager to be engaged in research, but my routine workload, coupled with a busy training schedule, was far too exhausting for a structured research career to develop. My salary was appallingly low, and in addition to my full-time job I also worked for the emergency service in the city. Being on call at night two or three times a week was gruelling: after the initial excitement it became a treadmill to work around the clock for thirty-six hours. I also gave lectures to nurses – only with all this supplementary income was it possible for me to pay my bills. The future looked bleak, and the prospect of working abroad for a year seemed, even if only as a temporary escape, increasingly attractive.

These were the years when the political oppression following the 1956 revolution had begun to ease – for the first time travel to Western countries had become possible for the general public. Despite the fact that several of my professors had visited Western Europe or the United States on research fellowships, it was most unusual for a newly qualified doctor with little research training to obtain such a coveted prize. My chances of returning to England on a fellowship seemed remote.

Nothing seemed impossible, however, to my English teacher Kátya, who, over the years, had also become a close friend and confidante. I met her at the beginning of my studies as a medical student: her younger daughter was in the same year at the university. Kátya taught foreign languages, Russian and English, at the university, and I became one of her private students. My English tuition took place in her flat in a leafy street near the university campus. The once-large flat had been divided up between her and her husband after they divorced, and she ended up with a comfortable but much smaller establishment. The room in which she gave her English lessons was full of mementoes of her travels, including visits to Britain. I soon realized that we shared at least one obsession: our enthusiasm for travel was boundless.

My lesson was usually the last on her schedule, sometimes starting as late as ten o'clock in the evening. This nocturnal scheduling was intentional. Kátya was not a person who readily accepted compromise or second best, and she expected each student to perform to the best of his ability. Use of the wrong tense provoked an immediate and terse 'No', accentuated by several exclamation marks and a cool glint of blue eyes behind her thick glasses. In more conciliatory mood, she would say: 'Now try again.' Making a second mistake was definitely inadvisable. Being a relatively docile and dutiful pupil, and determined to learn English, I needed little prodding. I usually did all the homework without much fuss, and was reasonably quick in picking up grammar, so for her my lesson was a relatively stress-free hour at the end of her day. More importantly, after the formal business of the tutorial was concluded, we could freely discuss our common passion for travel. She recounted her past trips, illustrating her descriptions with photographs, postcards, tickets to museums, exhibitions and theatres, tickets for trains, subways, buses and trams, maps of countries, regions and cities – all the paraphernalia of travel, now preserved so that she could experience them afresh.

In our fantasy we planned detailed itineraries, window-shopping for trips that would enable us to escape from the present. These plans were never fulfilled, but all these imaginary journeys gave us great pleasure. The small room was suddenly transformed from a language laboratory into a makeshift travel agency. Guidebooks in English had recently become available in one of the local bookshops, and together with maps and travel brochures, these were carefully laid out in Kátya's flat. With their help we enjoyed virtual journeys all over the world.

On those occasions time passed unbelievably quickly, and it was often after midnight when I walked back to my bedsit through the ill-lit, deserted streets of the town.

3

It was during one of these late-night sessions after returning from my visit at the end of September 1965 that Kátya hatched a plan that three years later landed me in London. I was unhappy and lost, feeling as if the horizon were closing in on me. I saw my future as a blind alley. I craved the challenge of a new environment, in which I could test my ability without the social, political and professional restrictions of life in my country. I had made a compromise during the years of my clinical studies: I abandoned my original plan to become a paediatrician and decided to apply after qualifying for a junior lectureship in histopathology. Such a position, I hoped, would enable me to pursue a more active research programme than bedside training would have allowed.

The opportunities were far from ideal, however. Although we were encouraged to undertake research, the demands of diagnostic work and teaching left us little spare time to pursue this. To obtain scientific fellowship to a Western country, a solution to all my problems, was beyond any reasonable expectation.

Not for Kátya. For her the concept of impossibility was unthinkable except to lesser mortals. Her strategy was simple: she suggested that I write to the Cultural Attaché of the British embassy in Budapest to request an appointment. I found this idea naïve and refused, at first, to follow her advice. She was not easily discouraged, however, and during my next tutorial she produced the name of the Attaché and the full address of the British embassy. 'We are going to write a letter and you will ask for an appointment,' she said. 'What can you lose? Nothing.'

Her logic was impeccable, so I did as I was told. In the letter, which required frequent recourse to dictionaries to find the best possible idiomatic phrasing, I briefly introduced myself and explained why I was seeking an appointment. I awaited the reply with trepidation: I expected a polite refusal. My surprise could not have been greater when, by return of mail, a neat stiff envelope bearing the royal coat of arms arrived. I was stunned to read that an appointment had been granted. Suddenly I was excited. I was embarking on an adventure; where it was going to lead, I could not fathom.

On the given date, dressed in my best suit and more than a little nervous, I presented myself at the reception of the British embassy. Crossing its threshold, I became aware that I was entering a parallel universe in which efficiency and politeness ruled. I was seamlessly processed, with minimal fuss and maximum courtesy – from receptionist to secretary, and from secretary to the Cultural Attaché. I found this treatment unsettling: during my occasional dealings with officials in my native land I had become accustomed to an experience in which the applicant or client mattered little and the bureaucrats were not necessarily there to help.

I was ushered into a room which was rather grand yet welcoming. After formal introductions, this being mid-afternoon, I was offered tea. Clumsily clutching my teacup, and being more than a little nervous, I haltingly recounted to the Cultural Attaché that, as a young doctor with aspirations towards a career in academic medicine, I aimed, if at all possible, to spend a year in England to acquire training in research methodology. I also expressed my wish to improve my English, the importance of which had become increasingly obvious, well beyond the realms of scientific and medical literature. My mouth dried out and I could hear lame echoes of my faltering English sentences. He listened quietly and without interruption, occasionally nodding with approval.

Then, without wasting any time, the Attaché rolled off a list of the existing exchange programmes available between the United Kingdom and Hungary, including one run by the British Council, and then proceeded to produce a couple of thick volumes listing all the fellowships available in the United Kingdom in alphabetical order. By now I was beginning to relax and became more animated. He leafed through the books and read out the names of a couple of organizations he considered potential sources of support, pausing briefly at the British Postgraduate Medical Federation. This was an umbrella organization embracing all postgraduate medical specialities, hospitals and their attached academic institutes, which disappeared long ago in the revolution that permanently remodelled British academic medicine.

I left the embassy with mixed feelings. As the euphoria of my reception evaporated, doubts began to multiply: I could not believe that a fellowship was within my reach. Why should the British Postgraduate Medical Federation consider a freshly qualified, unknown doctor from Hungary? (Twenty years later, when I was sitting on the Academic Board of the Federation, and chairing one of their committees, which considered academic appointments, the same question would occur to me again.)

In spite of these doubts, I did write to the British Postgraduate Medical Federation. I promptly received a reply, acknowledging my letter and enclosing a form. I was amused that one of the questions enquired about my bank account in the United Kingdom. I did not even have a bank account in Hungary. Our monthly salary was paid in cash, the head of department's secretary counting out used banknotes. The Cultural Attaché volunteered to testify to my proficiency in English.

Six months later, in July 1966, the unexpected happened: I received a letter from the Wellcome Trust, a medical charity, offering me a fellowship for one year at a stipend of £1,200 per annum at the Middlesex Hospital Medical School. Thus Kátya was vindicated: everything is indeed possible; one simply has to try. Incredibly, it took only nine months to conjure up this opportunity from the inception of a most unlikely idea; yet in that moment of elation I was not to know that it would be some time before I could take up the fellowship in London.

4

A passport that enabled its bearer to travel anywhere in Europe was a veritable rarity in the early 1960s in Hungary. I remember the amazement I felt when, in 1963, I opened the official letter containing the light blue document, my first passport valid for Europe, with particulars in three languages: Hungarian, French and Russian. Although the passport was valid for ten years, its use was carefully controlled. One could use it for one trip only, and each proposed visit to a Western European country required a special exit visa.

A passport was more than a travel permit: its possession endowed the bearer with an illusion of personal freedom. Although I was still a medical student, I celebrated my new passport by organizing a long trip to Italy with two friends in the summer of 1963. Crossing the border on the train from Budapest to Vienna was an intoxicating experience – it was the first time we were able to leave behind, even for a short time, all the limitations that enclosed our lives. Two years later, sponsored by a cousin living in New York, I saved enough money for another trip. I did not experience any problems in acquiring another permit to leave, and thus it was that in September 1965, after a stormy Channel crossing, I arrived at Victoria Station on the Golden Arrow.

My luck ran out the third time, however. Soon after I received notification of the research fellowship from the Wellcome Trust, I applied for an exit visa. My request was flatly turned down: no explanation was offered, nor had I any right to expect one. Those who made the decision were accountable only to those above them in the hierarchy. One year later, in 1967, I applied again, and the response was the same. I was becoming increasingly frustrated, and terrified at the possibility of losing my fellowship; the only consolation was a letter from the Wellcome Trust in which they confirmed that the stipend would be reserved for me until such time as I could commence work in London. But I feared that such a time would never arrive.

5

In February 1968 my mother died. I had spent the weekend with a friend whose father was making some of the furniture for the dining-room of our newly acquired flat in Szeged, paid for by the last residue of family fortune: two rooms in a modern block built for employees of the university. It was a freezing cold Sunday evening when I arrived home, and the silence, undisturbed by any recent activity, had already congealed in the empty flat.

In the kitchen I found the Sunday roast waiting for me, ready to be carved for dinner. On the dining-table there were fresh flowers, as always. My mother had her priorities absolutely right; even in times of hardship she always started her shopping expedition to the local market by buying a bunch of whatever seasonal flowers were on display. I waited with growing anxiety: it was unusual for her to go out on her own late in the evening, particularly when she expected me home. By then it was well after ten o'clock, and I became increasingly anxious.

We did not yet have a telephone – there was a long waiting list, and no guarantee that one would get one – so I rushed to Kátya's place. From her flat I telephoned the emergency services. Their response calmed me down: they had not admitted anyone with my mother's name or anyone who corresponded to her description. Then I telephoned the police. Their response was shattering. During the afternoon my mother had had an accident involving a tram: she had been taken to one of the hospitals. The news was worse than I had feared. My mother was deeply unconscious and not reacting to any stimuli. I did not require any further explanation: I knew immediately that she must have suffered severe brain damage.

By then it was well after midnight, and the consultant discouraged me from going to the hospital immediately. There was nothing else he could say: they would have a clearer picture the next day, after carrying out a comprehensive neurological assessment. I was strangely relieved to have an excuse not to rush to the hospital, since I did not feel able to face my mother that night. Kátya, always practical, suggested that I should spend the night in her flat, and I was happy to accept her invitation. She gave me a couple of sleeping tablets to see me through the night.

I woke to a crisp, cold and bright morning. I walked to the hospital, barely a mile away, a most uneventful walk in the winter sunshine. I did not know it then, but I now realize that I finally grew up during the course of that walk: I had crossed an invisible line between youth and adulthood. I arrived at the hospital, went to my mother's ward and sat by her bedside.

After a neurological consultation, the neurosurgeons performed an explorative biopsy on both sides of her skull: to relieve pressure within the cranial cavity and to identify a potential source of haemorrhage inside the brain. In the latter aim they were unsuccessful. Her right leg also had to be amputated since it had suffered multiple fractures, as had bones in her face: both the lower and upper jaws were broken in several places. She was on a life support system.

I said goodbye to her. I went to work. The life support system was switched off forty-eight hours later. If I were granted the privilege of replaying a single episode of my life, this is the one I would choose: I would stay at her bedside until the final moment. I have regretted ever since that I escaped in such a cowardly fashion.

Her post-mortem examination by one of the forensic pathologists, whom I knew well since we worked in the same dilapidated building, was exemplary. He confirmed that in addition to the injuries to her face, as a result of severe head trauma, extensive bleeding had occurred both in the coverings and the substance of the brain. This was incompatible with life: there was no chance of recovery.

The police report later confirmed that my mother crossed the street contrary to regulations, ignoring the oncoming tram, which rang its bell and braked. It was too late. She was dragged under the carriage before she could reach the safety of the pavement.

There had been a couple of witnesses to the accident, and I tried to reconstruct the event. An elderly woman with a bundle of magazines under her arm crosses the road on a quiet Sunday afternoon, on her way to see friends. With bad peripheral vision she underestimates the distance of the oncoming tram, thinking that she can get to the safety of the pavement, but just misses the kerb and falls back, scattering old copies of *Paris Match*, which we received regularly from Paris, in the street. There is the sudden scream of the brake, iron grating against iron; passengers getting off the tram; passers-by stopping; an air of impotence until the ambulance arrives. An ordinary accident in a quiet street on a cold Sunday afternoon in winter.

6

In the spring of 1968 I applied for an exit visa, but by then I had abandoned hope. If I had not been granted a visa on the two previous occasions, when my mother was still alive, I told myself, my chances would be much lower now that I had become completely independent. As she was a pensioner, I supported her, however meagre my own income, and her existence was a sort of guarantee of my return; she was a hostage against my 'defection'. But the ways of officialdom are unfathomable: in the summer of 1968 I was notified that the exit visa had been granted. I was invited to collect my passport in person from the police. At the end of my interview, as a parting shot, the officer in charge, who worked for the special branch, asked me whether I had visited the British embassy. I said yes, and supplied the dates. I had no doubt that those interested already knew of my appointments, and had I denied them my passport might have been withheld at the last minute.

On the day I set out to visit the visa section of the British embassy in Budapest, Hungarian State Radio announced the invasion of Czechoslovakia – or, as it was described then in immaculate Orwellian newsspeak, the extension of 'brotherly help' to the people of that unfortunate country. This was the end of the Prague Spring and of our hope that Dubček's experiment with Communism with a human face might succeed. For us Hungarians, it was a replay on a much smaller scale, and without extensive bloodshed, of the events of 1956. International tension increased overnight; and there were rumours that our southern neighbour, Yugoslavia, might also benefit from 'brotherly help'. For a while I was concerned that I might not obtain a British visa, but this fear was fortunately unfounded.

Despite the deepening international conflict, I could proceed with preparations for my trip, and I purchased an air ticket to London for the end of October. The day before the flight I caught the train to Budapest. Events, even important ones, may fade from consciousness, but my departure remains sharply etched in my memory. Even after so many years I can still summon up the ambiance of our flat: the antique furniture in my mother's room under dust covers, the couple of good

Persian rugs on the parquet floor, her empty wardrobe and chest of drawers from which her personal belongings had been removed after her death; in my room the bookshelves groaning under their heavy load, the slick modern daybed, the coffee table with its made-to-measure handmade low bench, cushions covering the seat, the brand-new dove-grey wall-to-wall carpet, a prize acquisition through an old friend who was the director of a large department store in Budapest; the penetrating smell of strategically placed mothballs; the old pottery plates, all faded reds and greens, on the white walls of the dining-room, partly separated by a narrow partition from the kitchen in which, since my mother's death I had conducted a few not particularly encouraging culinary experiments; the empty larder shelves, from which all perishable items had been removed (not that they had been fully stocked hitherto); the narrow entrance hall with its cast-iron umbrella stand and matching clothes hooks. I can conjure up the moment of switching off the last light in the hall, leaving the flat enveloped in darkness.

As I locked the door behind me, I did not know that I would never return.

7

The plane landed on time. To my surprise, I was met at the airport by my new English boss, a well-known scientist from the Middlesex Hospital Medical School, and his female assistant. As we were walking towards the car park, and I was trying to piece together a couple of ungrammatical sentences of thanks, the woman asked rather abruptly, in slightly accented but perfect Hungarian, whether the weather was as chilly in Budapest as it was in London. She was Hungarian and settled in London after the Revolution of 1956.

I arrived with a small suitcase and five pounds in my pocket. I had left my previous life behind: my friends and relatives, my career and flat, all my belongings, including my books and all the family documents and mementoes that had survived the war or had accumulated since then. I was closing that chapter of my life and starting something new and untried, and I looked forward to the challenge.

The first few nights, until I found a temporary bedsit in Bayswater, I spent in Astor College, the hall of residence of the Middlesex Hospital Medical School. This was a 1960s brick building in the shadow of the Post Office Tower, one of the architectural symbols of the technological revolution. From there I set out over the following few days to discover the neighbourhood of the hospital, a part of central London that was to become my home: the rag-trade district around Mortimer Street, still displaying flair; the grandeur of the BBC headquarters, an ocean liner running aground in the grey stone sea of Upper Regent Street, within a few yards of John Nash's All Souls, one of the most delightful churches in London; the narrow Dickensian passages of Fitzrovia with their decaying houses; the elegance of the town houses in Percy Street; the Greek Cypriot greengrocer's in Goodge Street with its three sets of prices, none displayed: cheapest for compatriots, moderate for local residents and highest for gullible tourists; the gourmet's paradise in Charlotte Street; and, most eccentric of all, Schmidt's – on the ground floor a German delicatessen with a female cashier sporting a veritable moustache, and up above a restaurant with waiters whose rudeness was legendary and whose disdain for their employer marginally exceeded the spontaneous dislike of customers.

Crossing Tottenham Court Road and proceeding into leafy Bloomsbury I encountered the perfect Georgian harmony of Bedford Square. Further north, in Regent's Park, lined by grand neo-classical terraces, each of different design but all painted in glossy cream, the roses were still in bloom, refusing to die even at the beginning of November. There was the confident run of Harley Street, with the lovingly polished nameplates of fashionable consultants, and the beauty of Epstein's Madonna and Child, benignly overseeing the traffic in Cavendish Square from a stone arch linking two buildings at the entrance to a mews. Cars were tame and drivers courteous, and buses completed their journeys without breaking down en route. Taxis were black and unblemished by advertisements. Rampant commercialism had yet to be unleashed on the British public: as yet not every free surface was disfigured by garish advertisments. Black cabs and red buses, red telephone kiosks and red pillar boxes forged an immediately recognizable, self-confident yet dignified civic identity for London.

During my perambulations at the first weekend, not very far from the Middlesex Hospital, I came across Dillon's bookshop and spent half my available cash, on Anthony Sampson's *Anatomy of Britain* – 50 shillings, a small fortune then, but an investment I have never regretted. The book proved a valuable introduction to the institutions of the country.

By now I had a secure income, however: my stipend had been increased from the original award of £1,200 to £1,960 per annum, a not inconsiderable sum in 1968. For the weekends I would cash in five pounds in the small sub-office of the Cavendish Square branch of Coutts and Co., just off the main hall of the Middlesex Hospital. The cashier, wearing a morning coat, counted out crisp one-pound notes: these were exchanged for a couple of meals and a theatre, concert or cinema ticket, and there was enough left for modest shopping in the delicatessen and greengrocer. The Coutts office has long since gone, replaced by a NatWest cash dispenser.

The day after my arrival in London, I started work in the laboratory on the ground floor of the Courtauld Institute of Biochemistry, then part of the Middlesex Hospital Medical School. It was the beginning of a professional career in academic medicine, which spanned some thirty-four years. The

Department of Histochemistry was a small unit, but carefully planned down to the last detail and equipped with the latest technology. Although space was limited, the department provided a congenial atmosphere for budding scientists from several countries, including Brazil, Egypt and what was then still Rhodesia.

It would have been difficult to find a better place at which to learn than the Courtauld's Department of Histochemistry, since its head was one of the leading international authorities in the field. Every morning I woke full of excitement, raring to reap the promise of the coming day. Sources of new knowledge in the laboratory seemed boundless, and at the same time I was continuing to discover London. The city was still floating on its newly discovered cloud of self-importance and glamour; the gradual decline, which reached its nadir in the late 1970s, had not yet commenced, or if it had this was not immediately obvious to a newly-arrived Hungarian.

8

A couple months after my arrival, I found my first digs in a small Georgian house in Colville Place, a narrow passage that runs between Charlotte Street and Whitfield Street. Although it was undoubtedly a picturesque place, it did not have the calculated prettiness of a similar mews in Chelsea, Belgravia or South Kensington: there was an element of raffishness and bloody-minded individuality very much in accord with the overall atmosphere of Fitzrovia. Although only a few yards from the hurly-burly of Tottenham Court Road, which at the time was better known for its furniture emporia than for its later plague of electronics shops, only a few people ventured in to discover this oasis, since Colville Place did not offer anything more exciting than its own tranquillity. At one end there was a modern gallery where I bought my first picture: a numbered and signed Elizabeth Frink print from her horse and rider series; this picture, together with another pair acquired later, now hangs in the hall of the house in Regent's Park. The gallery faced a derelict space, probably a bomb site, a late reminder of the war: now it has been transformed into a little park. Although I rented only one room for £5 a week (which amazingly included heating, electricity and bed linen), the entire top floor was at my disposal. This allowed access to one other room at the back, affording a panoramic view over the rooftops. An electric heater with two bars passed for heating, but mercifully worked without a meter: an advantage of having an enlightened landlord who, although he worked in the advertising industry, could not have been less mercenary. The basement bathroom was a dank place in which face flannels froze into ragged sharp discs during the winter. But the greatest advantage of Colville Place was its central location, within easy walking distance of the theatres of Shaftsbury Avenue, the shops of Oxford Street and the restaurants of Soho; more importantly it was only a couple of minutes' walk from the Middlesex Hospital. And in London it was a great luxury to be able to walk to work.

9

In the summer of 1969 I began to contemplate my return to Hungary: in October my fellowship was coming to end. I was beginning to acknowledge, however, as the date of my departure drew nearer, that I wanted to stay in London. I had to make a decision that could be irreversible, with unforeseeable consequences; it could not be postponed any longer. After several months of living in London the city was not a foreign place any more: it had become home. I had made new friends. I had begun to enjoy the freedom of my professional life. My lifestyle had also become more liberated: for the first time I was able to give my aspirations free rein. I found the challenge of starting a new life exhilarating. And before the end of the summer I had made up my mind.

Often, before a difficult and far-reaching decision has to be made, a minor unexpected event renders the psychological pressure, the burden of decision-making, so much easier that suddenly all the carefully weighed arguments become instantaneously obsolete. Such an intermezzo unexpectedly unfolded in the summer of 1969 and dispelled any doubt, if I still had any, that my decision not to return to Hungary was the right one. My cousin, who had lived in New York since the end of the Second World War, invited me to visit him and his family for a couple of weeks in the summer. They had a large, comfortable house in Englewood Cliffs, a smart suburb in New Jersey, not far from where the George Washington Bridge disgorges its traffic from Manhattan. I had not yet been to the United States, so I was looking forward enormously to the vacation.

Since my passport was valid only for Europe, I had to pay a visit to the Hungarian embassy to arrange authorization for the trip. There they informed me that this minor bureaucratic procedure could not be effected in London; the decision would have to be made in Budapest. Several enquiries and a couple of months later I was notified of the decision: they were refusing my request to extend the validity of the passport to the United States, and consequently I could not travel.

The meanness, stupidity and malice of this decision took me by surprise. What difference did it make to these officials where I spent my holiday? Why should an apparatchik decide what I did in my free time? And how could my holidaying in America in any way damage or influence the Hungarian People's Republic?

In the end I did not visit the United States on that occasion. But I had decided that whatever happened I would try to continue to work in England. I asked for an interview with my boss. He was not surprised when I declared my intention to stay in England (or, in the tired jargon of the Cold War, to 'defect'). He sought to verify, however, that my decision not to return to my native country was definite, even if it turned out I could not stay in England. When I confirmed that this was indeed the case, he, in the best tradition of English pragmatism, began to explore avenues of help.

For a permit to stay in the United Kingdom I had to apply to the Home Office. I entered the interview room there with newly-gained confidence, strengthened by the support several people had extended to me. I stated that I did not wish to apply for political asylum, merely an extension to stay in the United Kingdom, since I was not preferentially discriminated against in Hungary, and my life was not any worse or more restricted than that of 10 million other Hungarians. This was more or less true, and I did not wish to colour my application with a political issue, chiefly out of consideration for the relatives and friends I had left behind.

Not long after the interview, and well before my permit expired, I was granted an extension to stay for one year; this was to be renewed on a yearly basis for four years, at the end of which time I became a Permanent Resident of the United Kingdom and another year later, a British citizen. Before the tenure of my grant expired, I was offered a position as a research associate in the Department of Neurological Studies at the Middlesex Hospital Medical School from 1 November 1969. This was to run for three years in the first instance, with a starting salary of £2,175.

10

At the end of October I had to write a formal letter of resignation to my workplace at the Medical University in Szeged. It was not an easy task. I justified my decision to stay in England with an array of personal and professional reasons: I wanted to tell the truth without offending anybody, and what I said was indeed true, albeit not the whole truth. This letter triggered a chain of events with far-reaching consequences. The response was not entirely unforeseen, but it did shock me in its brutality. First, the rector of the university ordered disciplinary action on account of my refusing to return to Hungary. I had fifteen days to present my case, and when I failed to comply I was summarily dismissed from employment. But this was not the end of the matter. As well as being accused of abusing my employer's trust and setting a bad example, I was also indicted with a criminal charge of refusing to return to Hungary. A date was set for the trial.

A defence lawyer, the wife of one of my colleagues at the university, was nominated to represent me. In mid-January 1970, even before I had been officially dismissed from my employment, she contacted me, asking for additional explanations for my decision to strengthen her defence. Although I was convinced that she was trying to do her best, I knew that there was very little she could hope to achieve – the outcome was not in doubt. My mood roller-coastered between the extremes of apathy and outrage, but most days I was unconcerned about the proceedings that were unfolding so far away. Undeniably there was an element of Kafkaesque unreality about the forthcoming trial: I was the centre of attention in a drama in which I was not participating. The only crime I had committed was making a decision to take responsibility for my life.

The trial took place on 9 February 1970 in the District Court in Szeged. In the name of the Hungarian People's Republic I was sentenced, *in absentia*, to one year and four months' imprisonment as principal punishment and complete confiscation of all my belongings as secondary punishment. I was ordered to pay all the costs of the legal proceedings incurred before, during and after the trial.

There was a particular justification for the secondary

sentence. The last but one paragraph of the sentence stated: 'Since similar behaviour has been noticed in recent years in professional circles, the total confiscation of belongings as a secondary sentence is warranted as a general preventive measure according to . . .' etcetera. The message, intended as a deterrent, was clear: to defect is a serious crime and retribution will be commensurately severe. The decision was made public by posting the sentence on the District Court noticeboard for fifteen days after the trial. My lawyer informed me of the result by letter, and in her last paragraph she added rather charmingly that the sentence could be considered rather mild. I did not beg to differ; I could only hope that among the more severe penalties that could have been inflicted on me she did not have capital punishment in mind. In 1975 I received a letter from her in which she informed me that the prison sentence meted out by the Szeged district court had been quashed.

Later I learned from friends that my flat was sealed by the police and its contents auctioned. The flat itself was put on the market. I did not mind the loss of the flat, the furniture, pictures, carpets and books; it was gratifying to know that others appreciated our taste – apparently everything was sold very quickly. But I lament the loss of family memorabilia: these I cannot replace.

At the time all my earthly possessions were confiscated I was only thirty years old. During those three decades of my life we had lost everything, or nearly everything, three times: first the Fascists looted and completely denuded our house in 1944; five years later, in 1949, the Communists closed down the timber yard that represented our livelihood; and finally officialdom confiscated all that remained. But then these were only possessions, inanimate objects, temporary accretions of life. Their loss did not diminish anybody and, as pruning stimulates new growth in a plant, it may have been an impetus to new beginnings.

11

By the time I was officially notified of the outcome of the trial I was fully engaged in my new job. My appointment was funded by what later became known as 'biscuit money': a major donation by the Weston family, owners of Fortnum and Mason in Piccadilly, to the Middlesex Hospital contributed to the creation of a new research institute, the Institute of Neurological Studies. I was the first research scientist to be employed out of this endowment.

My interview was a mere formality. After a few standard questions about my background, training and previous experience, my interviewer, one of the consultants suddenly stood up, walked straight over to the blackboard and chalked up a sentence which, at first sight, did not make much sense. Smiling, she asked me to read it out aloud.

'This rough cough ploughs me through, though.'

After my attempt she asked rhetorically, 'Isn't English funny? One spells these words exactly the same way, yet one pronounces them differently.'

Concerned that this was a hint about my not entirely satisfactory English, I volunteered to go to an elocution class.

'You should do nothing of the sort,' she responded. 'You just mingle with the English. Your accent is' – she paused for a second, as a butterfly collector who has found a somewhat unusual species hesitates before pinning it in the appropriate box – 'foreign, slight and quite pleasant. With a Hungarian singsong. Spit out your consonants,' she advised.

And I followed her advice. I did not go to an elocution class and I have practised spitting out the consonants ever since.

The first few months after my 'defection' were exhilarating. All my uncertainties about the future disappeared. I enjoyed absolute freedom: even at work I could come and go as I pleased, since I had not as yet been burdened with clinical duties. But research was so exciting that I spent long hours in the laboratory, staying late at night or turning up at weekends, since I lived within walking distance of the hospital. At the end of the 1960s research was still unencumbered by excessive bureaucracy and not yet plagued by chronic shortage of funds.

By then I had realized that the organ of the body which truly fascinated me was the brain. We considered two alternative research projects: one was multiple sclerosis, the other brain tumours. Since I had always been interested in tumours, and even as a medical student had been awarded a prize for a project involving carcinogenesis, I was delighted to embark on a project on brain tumours.

12

During my first few years in England I discovered the pleasures of travel, and eagerly ventured further and further afield, as if to compensate for the earlier restrictions I had experienced in Hungary. I travelled in North America from east to west coast, in South America from top to bottom, in many countries of Asia and Africa, and even purchased a round-the-world air ticket in 1976 to celebrate becoming a Member of the Royal College of Pathologists.

But as a result of the prison sentence I could not visit my native country. Although the sentence was quashed in 1975, I did not avail myself of the fresh opportunity to visit Hungary. My reluctance was fuelled by fear. The nightmares of earlier years were still vivid: what would happen if I was prevented from leaving, if the nightmares turned out to be reality, and if, instead of waking up in London as the nightmare abruptly ended, I found myself in a prison cell in Hungary? This deep-seated, irrational fear may seem far-fetched now, but it was real then. Not until 1989 did I embark on my first visit, twenty-one years after I flew from Budapest to London.

The date had a particular significance: it was the twenty-fifth anniversary of my graduating in medicine, an occasion for a reunion and a party organized by alumni of the Medical University in Szeged. Since I had not been able to attend such events, which were held every five years, in the past, I was eager not to miss this one. When I boarded the British Airways plane at Heathrow I did not know that my first trip back after such a long time would be memorable for an entirely different reason.

I landed at Budapest airport shortly before two o'clock in the afternoon. I walked through the claustrophobic immigration hall and exchanged a couple of pleasantries with the immigration officer in Hungarian. Returning to Hungary after an absence of twenty years was an unsettling experience. I had been born in this country, but my home was not here any more. Speaking Hungarian again was strange. Although I had a few Hungarian friends in London, those whom I saw regularly were also doctors, and our conversation easily slipped into English when discussing professional matters. And at social gatherings, in the presence of English friends, chatting in our native tongue would have been discourteous, if not downright rude. Having completed the formalities, I proceeded into the brightly-lit arrivals hall to be met by my cousin and her husband.

Some ten hours later, at midnight, the Hungarian government, still officially dominated by the old-guard socialists, ordered the opening of the border with Austria. Unforgettable television pictures showed Hungarian border guards cutting the barbed-wire fence and the subsequent flow of East German tourists to the West. It was the beginning of the end, the first sizeable gap in the Iron Curtain: two months later, in November, the Berlin Wall tumbled down and Communism in eastern Europe ended after forty years. Before long, while I was still in Hungary, Parliament passed a law that guaranteed citizens' inalienable right to freedom of travel. By sheer coincidence I could not have chosen a better, more fitting date for my visit.

The people set about removing as many symbols of Communist rule as possible. One of the wittiest examples of this instant eradication of the past was the fate of the large red star, a potent emblem of the regime, made up of red salvias, in the central traffic island of one of the busiest roundabouts in Budapest: the five points were shorn overnight to leave only a circle of red flowers. Other symbols and legacies, however, persisted for considerably longer.

I spent three hectic weeks in Hungary. Before my return flight there was a terrifying moment at the airport in Budapest. The morose, tight-lipped immigration officer took my passport and carefully looked me up and down without speaking a single word. Then he asked: 'Are you Hungarian?' The question was superfluous: my name is Hungarian and my British passport clearly specified a birthplace in Hungary.

'I am a British citizen, but born in Hungary,' was my reply. At that moment, the passport still in front of him, the officer lifted the telephone receiver and started a conversation, his gaze alternating between me and the passport. I did not fail to notice that the queues at other windows were moving much faster, and some of the passengers were already ogling me with that mixture of curiosity and pity that is usually reserved for someone who is in trouble. With a glass wall between us I could not hear anything the man was saying, nor could I lipread. I tried to hide my anxiety, which was growing exponentially with every passing second. This was the nightmare becoming reality: I would not be able to board the plane; I could never return to London. I do not know how long he was engaged in conversation, probably only a couple of minutes, but to me it seemed an eternity. Then he replaced the receiver, looked at me for the last time, said,

'Have a good journey,' and handed back my passport, without a smile.

I will never know what the conversation was about. He may have been checking out my credentials with his superiors. Equally, he may just have been having a chat with his girlfriend or fixing to meet one of his colleagues for a drink after work. But whatever the reason for my delayed departure, I was relieved eventually to enter the welcoming cocoon of the plane.

Epilogue

1

On my visit in 2004, summer had arrived with a vengeance in Makó, a premature heatwave expelling lingering spring as temperatures nudged 30 degrees Celsius. In the midst of the people going about their business as if heading for the beach, I felt distinctly uncomfortable in my dark suit and tie.

The ceremony to commemorate the sixtieth anniversary of the Holocaust was held in the newly rebuilt Orthodox synagogue. The day of remembrance was carefully chosen to coincide with the day when the Jews of the town were herded into the ghetto: the beginning of the journey. It was a solemn occasion. Speeches were made, poems recited. A young woman played the violin. Someone sang accompanied by a guitar. An old woman who saved several Jews by hiding them was honoured somewhat belatedly and given a large bouquet of flowers.

It was a secular event: no prayers were said. Not even the Kaddish, the prayer for the dead. Fewer than ten Jews currently live in Makó, not enough to make up the compulsory quota for prayers, but on this occasion the synagogue was full. People were standing at the back, craning their necks to catch the words without amplification. The sun poured in through the windows. In the gallery, where women used to pray, there was an exhibition of sculptures and paintings.

At the end, people walked out into the courtyard. Some, uncertain what to do next, quietly scuttled away. Others stood silently and bowed their heads in front of three large marble tablets bearing the names of those who perished. A few laid flowers. Pieces of stone or pebbles were placed at the foot of the memorial. After a while the small crowd dispersed in the warmth of the early evening.

<h2 style="text-align:center">2</h2>

Thinking back over our journey in the synagogue that day, I realized that for the first time in my life I had come to accept Bergen-Belsen. It had become part of my life without being any longer an emotional burden. The experience had finally been incorporated into my existence; it lives in my memory. Sitting in the synagogue and recalling the horrors of sixty years ago, I suddenly appreciated that I have arrived, towards the end of my life, at a perfect moment of peace. I feel no pain, no anger and no hate. I have never hated, and it is now too late to learn. And whom should I choose to hate? The Nazis who established the camp? The Hungarian Fascists who delivered us there? The gendarmes in Makó who helped them? The people who stole our belongings while we were away? The guards on the train who beat us? The supervisors in the camp who terrified us? Or those Jews who, in their desperation, tried to steal our bread rations?

There is one question one should not ask: why? There is no answer. Or if there is, I do not know it. Perhaps it lies in an understanding of evil. Understanding evil is more difficult than understanding God. Hannah Arendt, the German philosopher and writer, reporting from the Eichmann trial in Jerusalem in 1961, spoke of the banality of evil. Eichmann, a slender, middle-aged man with receding hair, heavy glasses and ill-fitting dentures, answering questions about train timetables, could have been a railway employee whose reckless behaviour had caused a minor accident – a little man of no importance giving monotonous details of railway lines and stations and timetables. So ordinary, so everyday. But the trains were transporting a human cargo towards death, organized by this man, flanked by two uniformed Israeli guards in the vacuum of a glass cage. The plan to erase the Jews from the face of the earth was brilliant in conception, majestic in scale, unwavering in its morbid obsession and faultless in its execution.

Bergen-Belsen was the ultimate test of survival, the worst and the best event in my life: the best because, like a survivor of an air crash, I seem to have walked away unscathed. I gathered strength from the belief that nothing in my subsequent life could match our experience there. Now, having revisited all the stages of our journey, I have found true compensation for the evil of the past in the help, kindness and understanding of many people along my way. But when all is said and done, it was only a journey from a small provincial town in Hungary to somewhere else and then back again.

3

The house in which I was born is still there. Its wooden gate, shaded by trees, was inviting, but I resisted the temptation to press the bell and declare to the current inhabitants that I was born there. The four large windows were covered by heavy wooden shutters against the pounding heat of the August sun. In the street there were flower-beds in front of several houses, and plum trees laden with fruit, not quite ready for picking but none the less tempting to passers-by.

Our family house has changed. The new owners, a school friend and his wife, decided to create a separate self-contained flat for the wife's mother with its own entrance from the street: the symmetry of the long frontage of the house has been broken by a modern door, an unsightly gash on a friendly face. But the spacious rooms have been freshly decorated, and my friend still remembers the time when, as children, we cycled around the dining-table in what was then the dining-room. The outbuildings have been restored, and the loft, headquarters of our secret society, is still there; the only access to it is, at it was in my childhood, by means of a vertiginous ladder. The artesian well has gone, but water seeping from the ground is a reminder of its previous existence. The box trees have grown out of all proportion and long ago lost their tidy shape. The back garden has been overgrown by weeds, but some of the fruit trees have survived. The street now appears wider: the lime trees have been uprooted to make way for streetlights, but the chestnut trees still spread their shade over the road. The nearby park has lost all its secrets: the eyes can scan its open features in one sweep. It has not become smaller, only the visitor has grown older. It harbours an unexpected surprise, such as one can occasionally find in a small provincial town with a penchant for quirky municipal gestures: an Esperanto tree, planted in 1967 by the Esperantists of Makó to commemorate the fiftieth anniversary of the death of Zamenhof, creator of the artificial language that somehow never took off.

The timber yard is operational no more. Today it is a sadly neglected place, a far cry from the bustling activity of my childhood. The building that housed the engines has survived, as has the office block: this latter has changed a great deal, more in function than in appearance. Now it is a bar, run by a young man with finely-chiselled features. He was oblivious to the building's history, and I did not feel that I could tell him more than that we once owned this place, and a lot more beyond.

*

I found the cemetery profoundly changed. Gone were the luxuriant wild undergrowth and the curtains of climbers. The combination of chemical warfare and physical weeding has resulted in a much tidier place, but has destroyed most of the beauty and the mystery that stems from neglect. Having emerged from their overgrown surroundings, the tombstones lean this way and that: an army of drunken soldiers waiting to be called to attention for the last judgement. The roof of the mortuary has finally caved in, and the outside walls have all but collapsed. The cemetery remains an island of memory in the middle of nowhere. If there is resurrection, it will start there.

The three marble tablets displaying the names of all those who perished during the war, originally in the entrance hall of the Reform synagogue until this was demolished in 1965, have found a home in the courtyard of the newly restored Orthodox synagogue. Twelve members of my family are on this list, not including those who did not live in Makó.

The house in the ghetto where we stayed has been beautifully restored, and easily stands out as the most attractive building in the street, painted a creamy white, with all its architectural details picked out in faded yellow. In front of it, in the dusty heat of late August, rose bushes bore the last flowers of summer. In the street nothing moved, except for a cobweb trembling in the breeze. It is a place of serenity and peace. The memory of that distant May in 1944, when we were forced to live in this house with people we hardly knew, fades. Was it really here that our journey started?

The railway station in Makó, where we were forced into wagons at the beginning of the journey, has been transformed beyond recognition, the old building replaced by a soulless concrete and brick edifice.

*

The athletic ground in the suburb of Szeged, scene of our first brief stopover, has gained a new lease of life after that untypical intermezzo: it now has a well-tended soccer field and several tennis courts. Stumps of concrete embedded in the ground are probably remnants of the old viewing terrace.

The brick factory on the outskirts of Szeged is closing. Its extensive grounds and haphazard collection of odd buildings – a large, partly open shed with a sloping roof, a small white-washed workshop with roof slates missing, a brick edifice with unhinged doors partly hidden behind trees, a flat-roofed garage containing piles of twisted, rusting metal, phalanxes of stored bricks and a large central space now covered in concrete with clumps of grass forcing their way between the slabs – are blatantly unsuitable for any purposeful industrial production. It was here that the lists were compiled in July 1944: 'you go on the first train and you on the second'.

On the sixtieth anniversary of deportation a small black marble obelisk was erected by the city of Szeged in memory of those who had never returned from the journey.

The Rókus railway station in Szeged, where our journey to the West started, now runs a limited service, chiefly on one line, connecting the city with a couple of provincial towns in the south-east. On a late summer afternoon it had an abandoned air: no trains were leaving or arriving. The only sign of life was in the station café: two people too drunk to speak peered vacantly into their empty beer mugs as the remaining froth slid down the sides.

*

In Strasshof the unfortunate events that brought thousands of Hungarian Jews into this small town towards the end of the Second World War are but a distant fading memory. It was, after all, only the vagaries of railway connections which created the camp, a convenient transit point from home to hard labour and death. A couple of weeks before the Russian Army arrived, the leadership of the camp escaped to Bavaria, taking all the documents. The occupying Russian forces did not need the camp and soon it fell into decay. All usable material soon disappeared and the land was later reclaimed for agriculture. Today only a few trees, planted in 1941, and the foundation of a couple of buildings overrun by weeds, are reminders of the camp. A modest memorial was dedicated in 1988 by the local municipality to the victims of National Socialism who were in the Strasshof *Lager* between 1939 and 1945.

*

And in Bergen-Belsen there is the memorial for all to see. Visitors and tourists, driven by curiosity or remorse, are delivered here in coaches and cars. Old inmates hanging to the past by thinning threads of memory conduct their last pilgrimage. Schoolchildren in groups, wide eyed and disbelieving, are escorted by solemn teachers, their mission to learn about what happened here several decades ago. There is a permanent exhibition. In a small cinema a documentary film is played and replayed at regular intervals. The memorial is a quiet place for reflection. Fortunately there are no shops or restaurants.

In April 2005 on the sixtieth anniversary of the liberation of the camp, the cornerstone of a new Exhibition Centre was laid, and a two-volume Book of Remembrance, containing some 50,000 names of former inmates published.

*

The pocket watch from Bergen-Belsen has now been repaired. It keeps good time. Not a minute too fast, not a minute too slow.

Sources of material

Braham Randolph L., *The Politics of Genocide: The Holocaust in Hungary*, Columbia University Press, New York, 1981.

Kolb, Eberhard, *Bergen-Belsen*, Verlag für Literatur und Zeitgeschehen, Hannover, 1962.

Kolb, Eberhard, *Bergen-Belsen from 1943 to 1945*, Vandenhoeck and Ruprecht, Göttingen, 2002.

Molnár Judit, *Zsidósors 1944-ben az V. (szegedi) Csendőrkerületben (The Fate of Jews in 1944 in the Vth (Szeged) Gendarmerie District)*, Scientia Hungariae Cserépfalvi Kiadása, 1995 (in Hungarian with English summary).

Neidhart Josef, *Strasshofer Heimatbuch*, Strasshof, 1989.

Pierrepoint, Albert, *Executioner: Pierrepoint*, Coronet: Hodder and Stoughton, London, 1977.

Phillips, R. (ed.), *The Belsen Trial. Trial of Josef Kramer and Forty-four Others*, William Hodge, London, Edinburgh, Glasgow, 1949.

Reilly, Joanne, *Belsen. The Liberation of a Concentration Camp*, Routledge, London and New York, 1998.

Szita, Szabolcs, *Utak a Pokolból (Roads from Hell)*, Metalon Manager Iroda, 1991 (in Hungarian with English and German summary).

Urbancsok, Zsolt (ed.), *Makói Holokauszt Emlékkönyv (The Holocaust Memorial Book of Makó)*, Szegedi Zsidó Hitközség, 2004 (in Hungarian with English summary).